Essentials of
Risk Management

Volume 2

Essentials of
Risk Management

Volume 2

George L. Head, Ph.D., CPCU, ARM, CSP, CLU
Vice President
Insurance Institute of America

Stephen Horn II, CPCU, ARM, AAI
Stephen Horn Insurance Services

Third Edition • 1997
Insurance Institute of America
720 Providence Road, Malvern, Pennsylvania 19355-0770

Contents

Chapter 8

Examining the Feasibility of Alternative Risk Management Techniques

Educational Objectives

1. Given a situation involving loss exposures facing one or more organizations or individuals, describe possible (or identify impossible) applications of risk management techniques for specific property, liability, personnel, net income, or business loss exposures.

   In support of the above education objective, you should be able to do the following:
   a. Enumerate the fourteen risk management techniques.
   b. Distinguish among applications of these risk management techniques in specific fact situations.
   c. Illustrate each of these risk management techniques.
   d. Differentiate risk control from risk financing.
   e. Analyze relationships among specific risk management techniques applied to the same loss exposure.

Outline

Risk Control Techniques
  Exposure Avoidance
  Loss Prevention
  Loss Reduction
  Segregation of Exposure Units
  Contractual Transfer for Risk Control

Risk Financing Techniques
  Risk Financing Through Retention
  Risk Financing Through Transfer

Review

Summary

2. Identify and explain the significance of factors (other than the loss exposures) that also influence the appropriate uses of specific risk management techniques.
3. Define or describe each of the Key Words and Phrases for this assignment.

Examining the Feasibility of Alternative Risk Management Techniques

Examining alternative risk management techniques—assessing the feasibility and the costs and benefits of various risk control and risk financing options—is the second step of the risk management decision process. In sequence, it lies between the first step of identifying and analyzing loss exposures (the subject of Chapters 3 through 7 of this text) and the third step of selecting what appear to be the best risk management techniques (which will be the focus of Chapters 9 through 12).

Systematically examining alternative risk management techniques is a crucial, yet often overlooked, step in the practice of sound risk management. It is crucial because an alternative cannot be chosen unless it is recognized. The overlooked alternative might turn out to have been the most cost-effective choice. Restricting risk management choices to just the traditional insurance or safety measures that senior management has accepted for years prevents many organizations' risk management programs from contributing fully to profits or operating efficiency. All too often, the rush to deal with a particular loss exposure leaves too little time for carefully exploring all risk management options. (Once an exposure has been identified, pressure often arises to deal with it immediately even though the immediately apparent option might not be the best choice.)

A risk management professional can minimize such oversights by doing the following:

- Using the catalog of fourteen risk management techniques presented in this chapter to examine all the major categories of risk management techniques.

- Determining which techniques are sufficiently feasible to merit at least more detailed examination.

- Identifying the broad types of costs and benefits that each technique is likely to entail. With practice, using this catalog of techniques will become automatic for the risk management professional. Every time he or she considers how to treat an exposure, all of the alternatives will come to mind.

This analysis enables the risk management professional to do the following:

- Describe and distinguish among each of the various risk control and risk financing techniques
- Imagine how, if at all, each technique could be applied to any specific property, liability, personnel, net income, or business loss exposure that an organization faces

Imagination is important in considering alternatives because, at this stage in the risk management process, free thinking (even brainstorming) should be encouraged. The objective is to identify as many feasible alternatives as possible. The less workable options can then be discarded in the third step of selecting which techniques to implement. In the second step, however, no reasonable alternative should be rejected—any option overlooked here could be lost forever. Further, failing to take the time for this second, creative step—going directly from exposure identification to the selection of risk management techniques—can rob a risk management program of much of its vitality and capacity for innovation.

This chapter outlines the fourteen alternative risk management techniques, first presented in Chapter 1 and listed here in Exhibit 8-1, for dealing with exposures to loss. Six of the fourteen alternatives are risk control techniques, and eight are risk financing techniques. Of these alternatives, all except the risk financing technique of hedging generally apply to both risks of accidental loss and risks of business loss. For each technique, the chapter first defines that technique and, if appropriate, differentiates it from other techniques. The chapter then illustrates how, if at all, that technique could apply to particular property, liability, personnel, and net income exposures to accidental loss, as well as to risks of business loss. This cataloging of risk management alternatives provides the foundation for the third step in the risk management decision process, selecting the apparently best (most cost-effective, profitable, or efficient) risk management techniques for the combination of exposures to accidental losses and to business losses that an organization faces at any particular time. In the review section near the end of the chapter, students can apply virtually all of the techniques to many loss exposures that faced Wheeler's Tire Disposal and Aunt Melinda's Cookie Company in the tire fire case.

This chapter makes some simplifying assumptions. It does not consider any legal restrictions that may limit an organization's choices among various risk management techniques. Thus, the following paragraphs ignore the possibility that a statute may require an organization to install a firefighting system even though such an installation might not be in an organization's best financial interest.

Likewise, this discussion assumes that no requirements imposed by bond holders, other creditors, or those with whom the organization has entered into business contracts require it to purchase insurance rather than choosing, for example, to retain the financial burden of those accidental losses that it might wish to absorb directly. Similarly, this discussion assumes that if an organization wants to establish a funded reserve or rely on any other recognized risk financing technique, then no statutes preclude it from doing so. These assumptions are generally valid for profit-seeking organizations, but some state statutes or local ordinances may restrict the options that some organizations—particularly public entities— might wish to exercise. In practice, every organization's risk management professional should check for such legal limitations on a particular organization's risk management choices. If such restrictions apply, the affected organization should comply with them or work to have them changed.

Finally, a particular measure may involve elements of two or more risk management techniques. For example, regarding damage to Sheltering Arms's ambulances in highway accidents, driving at reduced speeds can involve both loss prevention (reducing the frequency with which these accidents occur) and loss reduction (reducing the severity of accidents because of the reduced energy involved in any collisions). The fact that a given measure involves two or more risk management techniques does not make it any less valid as an example provided that both the loss prevention and loss reduction effects are separately distinguished.

Risk Control Techniques

> **What are the distinguishing characteristics of each risk control technique?**
>
> **How do risk control techniques apply to accident losses?**
>
> **How do risk control techniques apply to business losses?**

As discussed in Chapter 1, risk management techniques include both *risk control* and *risk financing* techniques. Exhibit 8-1 presents the fourteen alternative risk management techniques. Of these fourteen techniques, all six of the risk control techniques shown in Exhibit 8-1 generally apply to both exposures to accidental losses and to exposures to business losses. Of the eight risk financing techniques listed in this exhibit, all but one—hedging—also apply to most loss exposures, whether to accidental or to business losses. As explained in Chapter 1 and noted later in this chapter, hedging is germane to managing only those business risks that arise from changes in the prices of commodities that an organization buys or sells in its normal operations. Exhibit 8-1 both briefly reviews all the risk management techniques introduced in previous chapters and previews this chapter's survey of these techniques for a common loss exposure facing both individuals and organizations: physical damage to an owned automobile. The specific actions that Exhibit 8-1 indicates for applying each risk management technique (except hedging) to the automobile physical damage exposure should be clear from previous chapters or should become evident as this chapter explains how these techniques apply to some of Wheeler's and Aunt Melinda's significant property, liability, personnel, net income, and business loss exposures.

For the second step in the risk management decision process, having the objective to consider all alternatives in a systematic fashion, the thought process through the sequence of alternatives charted in Exhibit 8-1 is very efficient. However, this thought process does not consider the relative practical significance of various risk control and risk financing techniques. For example, exposure avoidance—treated first among the risk control techniques because, conceptually, it is the most complete form of risk control—is quite rare. Exposure avoidance requires sacrificing all the potential benefits from the asset or activity associated with the avoided exposure. The risk control techniques of loss prevention and reduction, discussed second and third, are used much more frequently. Segregation of exposure units and contractual transfer apply less frequently but can be very effective.

Exposure Avoidance

Exposure avoidance is a decision not to create a particular loss exposure or to eliminate completely any existing exposure. Such a decision reduces the probability of any loss to zero for any one person, firm, or society as a whole. For example, a person who chooses to "not go near the water" under any circumstances avoids the exposure to drowning in water—the person does not allow that exposure to exist. The swimming pool owner who fills in his or her pool with concrete avoids the exposure of being found liable to the heirs of someone who might drown in the pool. Properly practiced, exposure avoidance is a completely self-sufficient risk management technique. An exposure that has been completely avoided cannot produce a loss. Therefore, there is no further need to try to prevent, reduce, or pay to restore the impossible loss. This reasoning assumes that the probability of loss from the avoided exposure is absolutely zero and not merely some very small number (in which case, some other risk management techniques would be appropriate).

Although exposure avoidance is a self-sufficient risk management technique requiring no other risk control or risk financing action, it has only very limited application. To avoid the exposure of drowning in water, for example, a person must literally *never* go near *any* water in which he or she could drown. This

Exhibit 8-1
Alternative Risk Management Techniques

If you are considering buying a new car but are concerned about possible physical damage to it, you can do the following:

I. Apply Six Risk Control Techniques—making losses less frequent, less severe, or more predictable—through these general techniques and specific actions.

General Technique		Examples of Specific Actions
1. Exposure Avoidance (make loss impossible)	→	Do not buy or lease a car.
2. Loss Prevention (reduce frequency)	→	Drive carefully. Maintain the car well. Choose drivers cautiously.
3. Loss Reduction (make losses smaller)	→	Drive slowly (reduce collision impact). Get a smaller, cheaper car.
4. Segregation by Separation (use several units regularly)	→	Own and operate two cars routinely.
5. Segregation by Duplication (keep backups, spares)	→	Use a spare, temporary, substitute vehicle.
6. Contractual Transfer for Risk Control (shift exposure—possibility of loss—by contract)	→	Use a leased car.

II. Apply Eight Risk Financing Techniques—making payment to finance recovery from losses that occur despite risk control efforts—through these general techniques and specific actions.

General Technique		Examples of Specific Actions
7. Retention Through Current Expensing	→	Pay for damage directly from current income.
8. Retention Through Unfunded Reserving	→	Recognize the need to be ready to pay for car damage.
9. Retention Through Funded Reserving	→	Set aside funds to be ready to pay for car damage.
10. Retention Through Borrowing	→	Use a loan or credit card to pay for damage.
11. Retention Through an Affiliated ("Captive") Insurer	→	Form or join a "captive" for car damage.
12. Contractual Transfer for Risk Financing	→	Find a noninsurance indemnitor to pay for damage.
13. Commercial Insurance	→	Purchase automobile physical damage insurance.
14. Hedging—taking offsetting market positions to neutralize business risks	→	No application to exposure to accidental losses.

person cannot, for instance, wash in customary ways, drink or otherwise consume water in quantities that could cause drowning, or take airline flights over any bodies of water into which the airplane might crash. (In reality, a person cannot possibly avoid the exposure to drowning in water.)

In short, simply existing unavoidably subjects individuals and organizations to some exposures to loss. The only way to avoid all types of property loss is to possess no property whatever. Furthermore, only by never earning (and never hoping to earn) any net income can an individual or organization avoid all exposures to net income loss. Therefore, exposure avoidance is not a feasible alternative against the broad categories of loss exposure.

Certain narrower exposures can definitely be avoided. Suppose a manufacturing company, located on an island and concerned about the weakened condition of the one bridge over which trucks carry its output to market, wants to avoid the exposure of losing a shipment in a bridge collapse. The company can avoid this exposure by transporting its output to the mainland on boats (which do not pass under the bridge lest they be damaged in a possible bridge collapse). Using boats avoids the exposure to trucks being lost in a bridge collapse, but this action exposes shipments to boating accidents. Avoiding one loss exposure often creates another.

If this company's real concern is not with exposure to bridge collapse, but rather with the broader exposure to damage of the company's output while trucks are in transit to the mainland, boats may be no better than trucks. The only ways for the company to avoid the exposure to damage to its output in transit over water are not to transport to the mainland at all or to move its manufacturing plant to the mainland.

Exposure avoidance is often mistaken for either loss prevention or contractual transfer for risk control. The proper distinctions among them appear in the discussions of loss prevention and of contractual transfer for risk control.

Beyond exposures to accidental losses, the risk management technique of exposure avoidance applies equally well to business risks. For example, avoiding business risks associated with being in a particular industry or occupation requires never entering, or promptly leaving, that industry or occupation. As with possibilities of accidents, however, avoiding exposures to business losses requires adhering to some rather stringent conditions. Suppose, for instance that, for ethical, economic, or regulatory reasons, the management of a particular organization wants to avoid the risks of being in the tobacco business. At an elementary level, exposure avoidance here would mean only staying completely away from manufacturing, buying, or selling any products or services that relate to the tobacco industry—including, for example, any machinery, paper, lubricants, or other items used in making or marketing tobacco products.

At a more sophisticated level, the management of an organization that truly wants to avoid the ethical or economic dangers of doing business that in any way depend on tobacco would have to avoid buying or selling anything to another organization whose economic well-being depended on tobacco. Having a customer or supplier whose reliability could be endangered by financial adversities in the tobacco industry would indirectly expose the organization to "tobacco industry risks" that it originally sought to avoid. This organization's management should recognize that a customer or supplier whose prosperity depends on tobacco might someday be unable to pay its bills or fulfill its delivery contracts if the tobacco industry nose-dives for some reason. Given the complex interdependencies among organizations, exposure avoidance of many business risks is often very difficult. Loss prevention—reducing but not completely eliminating all chances of loss—is often a more realistic strategy for managing business risks.

Loss Prevention

Loss prevention is any measure that reduces the probability, or *frequency*, of a particular loss but does not completely eliminate all possibility of that loss, as does exposure avoidance. Loss prevention reduces loss frequency without completely eliminating all chance of loss and without necessarily having an effect on the likely severity of loss. Conceptually, loss prevention differs from exposure avoidance because loss prevention does not eliminate all chance of loss.

Loss prevention is also different from loss reduction because loss reduction focuses on reducing the *severity* of losses, not on their probability or frequency. In practice, a risk management action might combine elements of both loss prevention and loss reduction. For example, the reduction in the legal highway speed limit in the late 1970s cut both the number of automobile accidents (because drivers had more time to react to dangerous situations) and the seriousness of those accidents that did occur (because less kinetic energy was released when slow-moving vehicles collided with any other object).

The differences among exposure avoidance, loss prevention, and loss reduction are highly important. Because exposure avoidance eliminates all possibility of loss, it is the self-sufficient risk management technique in those rare situations when it can be successfully and thoroughly applied. When exposure avoidance completely eliminates a risk exposure, no other risk control or risk financing technique is needed. If, however, a safety measure only reduces the probability of loss, then sound risk management requires at least some risk financing plan and perhaps further risk control measures for coping with the remaining exposure.

Similarly, the distinction between loss prevention and loss reduction is critical to effective risk management. A safety measure that reduces the likely frequency of loss (but does nothing to reduce the probable severity of the losses that do occur—for example, "No Smoking" signs to reduce fire damage) might reduce the aggregate losses that an organization suffers over a period of time, but the size of individual losses probably will not be reduced. Loss prevention measures that have no loss reduction effects, therefore, cannot justify lowering an organization's top limits of financial protection against accidental losses.

Most loss prevention measures are related to how losses are caused. In general, a loss prevention measure is an action taken or a physical safeguard installed before a loss occurs to break the chain of circumstances or causes that are thought to lead to the loss. Breaking the chain is supposed to stop the loss from happening, or at least make it less likely.

Because of the close link between loss causation and loss prevention, developing effective loss prevention measures usually requires a careful study of how particular losses are caused. For example, following H. W. Heinrich's theory of accident causation, most work injuries have traditionally been thought to result from a chain of events that includes an unsafe act or an unsafe condition. Consequently, work safety efforts have focused on trying to eliminate specific, unsafe acts or unsafe conditions.[1] As another illustration, fire safety engineers speak of a "fire triangle," the three elements of fuel, oxygen, and an ignition source that must be present for fire to occur. Preventing fire requires removing at least one of the three legs of the fire triangle.[2]

Common law holds that a person can be liable for negligent conduct only if the following four conditions occur together:

1. A duty owed to another
2. A breach of that duty
3. Resulting harm to another
4. A sufficiently close or "proximate" causal connection between the breach and the harm

Therefore, efforts to prevent liability losses focus most frequently on removing at least one of these four necessary elements for liability, most often by trying to eliminate conduct that breaches duties owed to others.

However, another set of strategies for preventing liability losses seeks to remove a fifth condition that is necessary for a liability loss to occur. This condition is the bringing of a legal claim against an organization or other defendant alleged to have committed some legal wrong. (Remember from Chapter 4 that there can be no liability loss without a legal claim: the claim—not the legal wrong—is the peril that causes liability losses.) Therefore, even an organization or individual having committed a legal wrong can prevent resulting liability losses by dissuading potential claimants from suing or by raising procedural or economic barriers to such lawsuits.

Losses from business risks also can be prevented by controlling the conditions that make such losses likely. For example, a toy manufacturer planning to introduce a new style of doll for the coming Christmas shopping season could lower the probability that it would suffer business losses because of the following:

1. The marketing risk that customers will not be willing to pay the manufacturer's suggested retail price by surveying potential customers about how much they like this new doll

2. The manufacturing (technological) risk that producing the doll would be unexpectedly expensive by testing the efficiency of the production process at various levels of output

3. The price risk that the manufacturer's costs of raw materials will rise to unaffordable levels by purchasing in advance adequate supplies of the essential components of the doll

4. The cash-flow risk that the manufacturer will not have sufficient funds to continue producing dolls (if the initial sales of the doll are slower than expected, reducing revenues available to finance continuing production) by arranging in advance with banks and other potential lenders lines of credit on which the manufacturer can draw as needed

5. Other business risks by adhering to a generally conservative style of business

Note that none of these business risk prevention measures avoids, or completely eliminates, all exposures to various dangers of business losses from these risks. The measures only make business losses less likely. The only way to completely eliminate these and other business risks would be to refrain from manufacturing the new style of doll, which would be exposure avoidance, not loss prevention, with respect to these business risks. Note also that, for business (or speculative) risks that offer opportunities for gains as well as losses, loss prevention measures that reduce chances of business losses also reduce chances of business gains. As an illustration, the doll manufacturer that purchases in advance an ample supply of all components needed to make the dolls reduces its raw material prices risk. However, this manufacturer also reduces its potential profits by committing extra funds to inventories of components that it does not currently need (and may never need if the market demand for this new doll falls short of expectations). The manufacturer thereby foregoes any opportunity to buy these components at some lower price in the future.

Loss Reduction

Loss reduction measures reduce the severity of those losses that do occur. To analyze loss reduction opportunities, a risk management professional must assume that a loss has occurred and then ask what could have been done, either before or after the loss, to reduce its size or extent.

The two broad categories of loss reduction measures for any type of loss from any peril are (1) pre-loss measures, those applied before the loss occurs and (2) post-loss measures, those applied after the loss occurs. Pre-loss efforts to reduce loss severity might also reduce loss frequency—driving ambulances at lower speeds in nonemergency situations, for example. Pre-loss measures generally reduce the amount of property, the number of persons, or other things of value that might suffer loss from a single event. Post-loss measures typically focus on emergency procedures, salvage operations, rehabilitation activities, or legal defenses to halt the spread of loss or to counter its effects. Erecting firewalls to limit the amount of damage from any one fire is a pre-loss measure; an effective fire detection/suppression system is a post-loss measure.

Loss reduction is also a valid risk management strategy for business risks, applicable both before and after a business loss occurs. Reducing the size of business losses usually involves either reducing an organization's commitment to a particularly risky venture before any loss occurs or "cutting one's losses" after an uncertain venture has soured by salvaging what one can from a bad business situation. For example, the doll manufacturer seeking to introduce a new product for the Christmas season could reduce its potential business losses on the new doll by producing only a limited number while also producing its usual number of other, more traditional dolls. Testing the production and marketing success of this doll without fully committing the manufacturer's resources to it would limit the manufacturer's potential losses if the doll did not prove profitable. (On the other hand, this strategy also would limit the manufacturer's gains if the doll became popular.)

After the loss—perhaps after the doll fails to sell as expected—the manufacturer could perhaps reduce its loss by modifying its unsold dolls, by trying to market its remaining inventory abroad at a reduced price, or by donating the remaining dolls to a charity to obtain an income tax deduction for the manufacturer's cost of producing the unsold dolls. There might be other ways that such a manufacturer could recoup some revenue from the unsold dolls. If the manufacturer is a tax-paying organization, any of those options would limit the manufacturer's loss of net cash flows from a less-than-successful venture with this new doll.

Segregation of Exposure Units   *EXPENSIVE*

The blanket term **segregation of loss exposure units** encompasses two distinct but closely-related risk management techniques: **separation of loss exposure units** and **duplication of loss exposure units**. Both strive to reduce an organization's dependence on any single asset, activity, or person, thus tending to make individual losses smaller and more predictable. The logic of segregation of exposure units is exemplified in the maxim, "Don't put all your eggs in one basket." When losses become smaller and more predictable, they become easier to manage and less disruptive.

Separation involves dividing an organization's existing single asset or operation into two or more separate units. (Three examples are dividing an existing inventory between two warehouses, erecting fire walls to create separate fire divisions within a single building, and manufacturing in two plants a component part formerly produced in only one plant.) Separation is appropriate when an organization can meet its goals with only a portion of these separate units left intact. If total loss is suffered by any one unit, the portion of the assets or operations at the other location(s) is sufficient. With separation, all separated units are normally kept in daily use in the organization's operations.

Duplication involves complete reproduction of an organization's own standby asset or facility to be kept in reserve. This duplication is not used unless the primary asset or activity is damaged or destroyed. Duplication is appropriate when an entire asset or activity is so important that the consequence of its loss justifies the expense and time of maintaining a duplication. Two sets of accounting records or key items of equipment and backup employees are examples of duplication of exposure units.

Separation and duplication are distinct from one another, and both are distinct from other means of loss reduction. Four points need to be noted. First, unlike other means of loss reduction, neither separation nor duplication of exposure units makes any special attempt to reduce the severity of loss to any one single unit. Second, both separation and duplication reduce the severity of an individual loss, but they can have different effects on loss frequency. Using two distantly separated warehouses instead of one is likely to increase loss frequency because two units are now exposed to loss rather than just one. Duplication is not likely to increase loss frequency, presuming that the duplicated unit is kept in reserve and not used—is not as exposed to loss as is the primary unit put to daily use. (For example, a duplicate vehicle presumably is garaged and is not as vulnerable to highway accidents as is the primary vehicle.) Third, duplication is therefore likely to reduce the average, or expected, annual loss from a given exposure because duplication reduces loss severity without increasing loss frequency. Fourth, separation may or may not decrease the average expected loss. Much depends on whether the reduction in loss severity from separation is more important than, or is overshadowed by, the increased loss frequency that separation normally entails.

Both separation and duplication tend to be expensive, sometimes impractical, risk management techniques. Separation, in particular, is seldom undertaken for its own sake but, instead, is a byproduct of other management decisions. For example, few organizations build and use a second warehouse simply to reduce the severity of losses to the former warehouse. However, if an organization is considering the construction of a second warehouse, the purchase of another vehicle, the hiring of another key computer operator, or other expansion, the risk management implications of creating these new, ideally separate, exposure units may be an additional argument in favor of the expansion.

In contrast, duplication—keeping a spare unit on standby for emergency use—often is primarily prompted by risk management considerations. Senior management recognizes the crucial nature of the duplicated operation or asset and is willing to invest in the duplicate as a safeguard against being without this essential element of its operations. Duplicate records, spare machinery parts, and cross-training employees to do several jobs within their department are typical risk management safeguards and are recognized and justified as such.

For cost reasons, separation of exposure units (and keeping all units in daily use) typically has more practical applications than does duplication (in which standby units remain idle except during emergencies).

For business risks, segregation of exposure units once again involves "putting one's eggs in more than one basket" in the hope that at least one "basket" proves sufficiently profitable (or otherwise productive for nonprofit organizations). For example, the toy manufacturer cited in previous examples could, instead of introducing only one new style of doll, introduce both a doll and a set of toy soldiers. Even if one of these two failed to generate a profit, the other might be successful, and perhaps both would succeed (but ideally both would not fail). If the toy manufacturer introduced both the doll and the soldiers simultaneously, this would exemplify segregation by separation, relying on both new units (both new toys) simultaneously. If the manufacturer held in reserve its plans for the new set of soldiers until it found out how the new doll was succeeding, it would be practicing segregation by duplication—relying primarily on the new doll but being ready to fall back on the reserve of new soldiers if needed. In either case, segregation of exposures to business risks in various ventures implies management's willingness to accept the average profitability or productivity of all of the ventures (units) undertaken.

Contractual Transfer for Risk Control

Contracts are an integral element of several risk management techniques. For example, if an organization decides it would rather use leased automobiles than purchase those vehicles, the lease contract leaves with the lessor many of the property loss exposures that would otherwise be associated with owning the cars. This arrangement is a **contractual transfer for risk control**. Again, one organization may agree to reimburse another for certain types of losses that the other suffers. This agreement is essentially an insurance contract except that, in this particular case, neither of these organizations is an insurer. Such an arrangement, often called a "hold harmless agreement" or an "indemnity agreement," is a contractual transfer for risk financing.

The diverse contracts used in risk management have many names. The fundamental distinction is between the following:

- Contractual transfer for risk control—a contract that transfers to another entity the legal responsibility for performing a particular activity and for bearing specified types of losses that might arise from that activity.

- Contractual transfer for risk financing—a contract that transfers the financial burden of particular losses to another entity (not a commercial insurer) who acts as a transferee by agreeing to pay losses to or on behalf of the transferor. A contractual transfer for risk financing is conceptually equivalent to commercial insurance except that the transferee is not an insurer. Commercial insurance is a contract that transfers the financial burden of particular losses to a commercial insurer who acts as a transferee by agreeing to pay losses to or on behalf of the transferor [insured].

A contractual transfer for risk control is an agreement under which a transferor shifts to another (the transferee) the loss exposures associated with an asset or activity. The transferor requires the transferee to perform certain activities and, as an element of those activities, to assume certain exposures and to bear any losses that arise from those exposures. Under a contractual transfer for risk control, the transferor seeks no indemnity or other compensation from the transferee but, rather, expects the transferee to perform certain activities that the transferor deems unduly hazardous.

Under contractual transfers for risk financing, the transferee makes a financial promise to pay for particular losses but does not promise to perform any other activity (except perhaps safety inspections, accident investigations, or other activities tangential to that duty to pay). The transferor is entitled to financial payment for particular losses, making this transferor also an indemnitee. With contractual transfers for risk control, the transferor is entitled to the performance of a particular, risky activity by the transferee. Here, the transferor does not expect an indemnity payment for any resulting losses because, under the contract, the transferee performing the risky activity is responsible for any losses that might result.

Exhibit 8-2 presents a simplified hypothetical example of the distinctions between these types of contractual transfer. This example shows that these distinctions rest on all of the following:

- Which party is performing the "risky" activity,
- Whether the transferee's commitment is to perform an activity or to pay money, and
- On whom any loss falls if the transferee fails to perform as promised.

Exhibit 8-2
Types of Contractual Transfer

The Ground of the Baskervilles

*A Fanciful Adaptation from Sherlock Holmes To Illustrate
Contractual Transfers for
Risk Control and Risk Financing*

Sir Henry Baskerville, wishing to remove from his property the quicksand bog that swallowed up so many characters in Sir Arthur Conan Doyle's famous saga of Sherlock Holmes, hires a landscaping engineer, Sam ("Sapper") Gollum, to fill in Baskerville's famous bog using Gollum's bulldozer. (Sir Henry could have done this himself, using his own bulldozer, but he recognizes the hazards of the bog and does not want the Baskerville bulldozer to be lost in it.) The contract between Sir Henry and Sam specifies that Sam will use his own bulldozer and will assume all responsibility for damage to the bulldozer while on Baskerville's property. For Baskerville, this is a contractual transfer for risk control—by asking Sam Gollum to fill in the bog, Baskerville (as transferor) has transferred to Gollum (as transferee) responsibility for filling in the bog and for any related damage to Gollum's bulldozer.

Five minutes after Sam begins the work, the bulldozer almost slips beneath the quicksand of the bog. Recognizing this extreme hazard, Gollum refuses to continue unless Baskerville agrees to amend their contract with a provision that, should Gollum's bulldozer be lost in the quicksand, Baskerville will pay Gollum 350 pounds sterling, the agreed fair market value of a bulldozer comparable to the one Gollum is using. From Gollum's standpoint, this indemnification amendment to their agreement is a contractual transfer for risk financing under which Gollum, as transferor/indemnitee, is entitled to compensation from Baskerville, as transferee/indemnitor, should Gollum lose his bulldozer while filling in Baskerville's bog.

Now consider the case in Exhibit 8-2 under a variety of circumstances. Assume that Sam Gollum's bulldozer slips beneath the quicksand of Baskerville's bog. If the bulldozer were lost during Gollum's first five minutes of work, before he amended the contract with a contractual transfer for risk financing protecting Gollum, the bulldozer risk would fall on Gollum. Baskerville's contractual transfer for risk control would have worked. Gollum, despite the loss of his bulldozer, would have been obligated to finish filling in the bog, and Baskerville's own bulldozer would have remained safe. As long as their contract was fairly bargained without deception or duress by either party, Gollum could not hold Baskerville responsible for Gollum's loss of his bulldozer.

Alternatively, assume that Gollum's bulldozer is lost after the revised contract had been signed, with the contractual transfer for risk financing protecting Gollum. Under this amended contract, Baskerville would be obligated to pay 350 British pounds to Gollum to indemnify him for the loss of his bulldozer. Here, Gollum's contractual transfer for risk financing would seemingly have the upper hand because the financial burden of the loss of the bulldozer would fall on Baskerville. As before, however, Baskerville's own bulldozer would still be safe— to that extent, his contractual transfer for risk control would have worked. Gollum would remain obligated to complete the job, presumably with a replacement bulldozer.

Now assume a third, somewhat more complex, scenario. Suppose that the bulldozer slips beneath the quicksand after Gollum is well into his work and thinks that, as in the second case, he is protected by the contractual transfer for risk financing in his amended agreement with Baskerville. As before, he approaches Baskerville and asks for the 350 British pounds as indemnity. But presume, as a complication, that Baskerville is suddenly deprived of his hereditary estate and, as a complete shock to both Baskerville and Gollum, Baskerville finds himself destitute and lacking any applicable insurance. In this case, the financial burden of the loss is very likely to fall on Gollum because, unless backed by insurance or some other independent guarantee, a contractual transfer for risk financing is only as good as the financial strength of the transferee/indemnitor. Baskerville's destitution makes Gollum's financial protection under the contractual transfer for risk financing virtually worthless. Despite this risk financing contract (or hold harmless or indemnity agreement) supposedly benefiting Gollum, the financial burden of the loss still falls on him. (In contrast, in the first case in which Baskerville was protected by the contractual transfer for risk control, Gollum's risk of his bulldozer falls on Gollum even though the bulldozer's destruction could impoverish Gollum. In this case, Baskerville would still have the legal right to force Gollum to fill in the bog. This absence of any expectation of indemnity distinguishes a contractual transfer for risk control from a contractual transfer for risk financing and from commercial insurance.)

Contractual transfer for risk control can easily be mistaken for exposure avoidance. Some have incorrectly said, for example, that one way to avoid the physical damage exposures inherent in operating a fireworks factory is to sell the factory to someone else so that the new buyer now faces these exposures. The seller, the former owner, is sometimes wrongly said to have avoided these exposures. This analysis is incorrect because it fails to recognize that the exposures inherent in operating the factory still exist. They have not been eliminated; they merely have been shifted to the new buyer through a contract of sale (from the seller's standpoint, a contractual transfer for risk control). True exposure avoidance requires eliminating the loss exposure for everyone, even for society as a whole, by using it for some other purpose, by abandoning this factory, or by not constructing it initially.

Contractual transfer for risk control is a frequent strategy for dealing with business risks—a strategy often called "subcontracting" or "outsourcing." Here, the organization wanting to transfer the business risks associated with a particular product or activity to another organization or individual enters into a contract under which the transferee agrees to complete that product or activity for a given price paid by the transferor. If the transferee fulfills the contract for less than the contracted price, the transferee makes a profit (generates a surplus), earning at least some of the profit or surplus that the transferor presumably would earn, had the transferor been willing to undertake the risks involved. If the transferee cannot complete the contract for the agreed price, the business loss falls on the transferee, making the transfer beneficial to the transferor, assuming that the transferee does complete the contract by providing the good or service that the transferor expects. If the transferee does not fulfill the contract, leaving the transferor still lacking the contracted product or service, both the transferee and the transferor are likely to suffer business losses.

For example, the toy manufacturer seeking to introduce a new doll might subcontract to a container manufacturer the making of an especially attractive box for each new doll. Such a subcontract relieves the doll manufacturer of the business risk of unexpected packaging design and production costs but would leave the doll manufacturer open to severe business losses if the packager failed to deliver an adequate number of suitable boxes on time.

Risk Financing Techniques

If risk control techniques do not treat a particular exposure adequately, the remaining alternatives are all risk financing techniques. Several risk financing techniques involve retention. An organization can retain loss exposures through the following:

- Current expensing of losses
- Unfunded reserves
- Funded reserves

> **What are the distinguishing characteristics of each financing control technique?**
>
> **How do risk financing techniques apply to accidental losses?**
>
> **How do risk financing techniques apply to business losses?**

- Use of borrowed funds
- Use of an affiliated "captive" insurer

Contractual transfer provides another alternative for risk financing. The final alternative is commercial insurance.

Risk Financing Through Retention

All retention techniques for risk financing share the common characteristic that they draw on funds originating within the organization suffering the loss or within that organization's economic family. The range of retention options can be arrayed, as in Exhibit 8-1, in increasing order of formality. These options are retention through current expensing of losses, retention through an unfunded reserve, retention through a funded reserve, retention through borrowed funds, and retention through an affiliated ("captive") insurer.

An organization may retain losses for either of two reasons: (1) because retention is forced (there being no transfer options) or (2) because some form of retention is more cost-effective than any form of transfer. These two types of retention may be called **forced retention** and **optional retention**, respectively. (A possible third reason for retaining losses from a particular exposure is that the organization has not recognized the exposure and therefore has made no funding arrangements. One of the most fundamental objectives of risk management is to recognize as many loss exposures as possible, thus minimizing retention through ignorance.)

Forced retention can result from a number of causes, including the following four:

1. The peril that caused the loss was uninsurable (such as wear and tear or nuclear damage to property) or otherwise nontransferable.

2. The loss was not within the scope of the organization's commercial insurance or other contractual transfer for risk financing. (Extra expenses were retained because no coverage for them was specified.)

3. All or some portion of a loss fell within a deductible that the insurer required in order to exclude coverage of relatively small, insured losses.

4. The size of the loss was such that

    (a) it exceeded the limits of the organization's insurance, and the excess had to be paid directly by the organization, or

(b) the insurer or other transferee was unwilling, or did not have the financial capacity, to pay the loss.

Similarly, optional (presumably informed and conscious) retention can be the result of any of several factors, including the following three:

1. The loss resulted from an exposure that the organization decided to fully retain—such as flood damage in a flood-prone area—through any one or a combination of the retention options previously described.

2. The size of the loss was such that only a portion of it fell within a deductible or other retention in the organization's program of insurance or other contractual transfer for risk financing.

3. The organization chose a deductible that excluded all or some portion of a loss that could have been fully insured.

Before choosing what, if any, optional retention an organization should undertake, its risk management professional, key financial executives, and perhaps other managers need to consider the extent of the organization's forced retention. Because any organization, at any given time, has a limited capacity to retain losses safely and cost-effectively, and because the organization has no choice regarding its forced retentions, its optional retentions should be regarded as a residual. That is, the organization should consider optional retentions only after it has dealt with its forced retentions for all loss exposures considered collectively, not just for each one separately.

Within its area of optional retention, an organization's decision to retain or to transfer a given exposure depends largely on the characteristics of both the losses and the organization. Generally, an organization can more safely and more cost-effectively retain exposures that generate losses that meet the following three criteria:

1. Are limited in the size of an individual loss to an amount clearly within the organization's retention capacity

2. Are unlikely to cause a large number of losses within a short period, lest the aggregate of retained losses be beyond the organization's retention capacity for that period

3. Are sufficiently frequent to be routinely budgeted

Although perhaps no loss exposure ideally fulfills all three of these criteria, those that more nearly meet them tend to be the better candidates for retention. Further, an organization's retention options are not limited to the choice of fully retaining versus fully transferring all losses from a given exposure. Between these two extremes, a wide range of possible levels of retention—through deductibles or "self-insured" retentions (SIRs)—can be combined with commercial insurance or some other transfer technique to finance losses above these levels. Small amounts of loss, within the limits that many organizations are likely to choose as their deductibles, meet these three criteria more fully than do the less predictable extremes of more severe, higher levels of loss. Thus, by choosing its deductibles and SIRs carefully, an organization can limit retention to the losses that meet these criteria.

The financial and managerial characteristics of an organization also affect the types and amounts of optional retentions that the organization should choose. More specifically, an organization's capacity to retain loss exposures is increased when one or more of the following are true:

- The organization has the ensured financial capability, both currently and in the foreseeable future, to generate funds sufficient to pay losses within its chosen retentions without unduly disrupting the organization's normal productive activities. (This financial capacity can be based on past accumulations of retained earnings or on current earnings. In either case, the organization's senior management must devote appropriate portions of accumulated or current earnings to finance recovery from accidental losses.)

- The organization's senior management (and owners in small or medium-sized organizations) are psychologically comfortable with the levels of retention that the organization adopts.

There is no one right set of retention levels for all organizations facing a particular set of loss exposures. The characteristics of the exposures do not wholly determine the appropriate retention choices; some characteristics of the organization also are important. When an organization's characteristics change—as when its financial strength is affected by swings in economic cycles or long-term persistent trends of growth or decline, when its managers' philosophies change, or when the relative costs of retention and transfer change—the uses of retention that are appropriate for that organization are also likely to change. Thus, there are no uses of retention that, even for one organization, are always fully appropriate.

For financing business risks, retention is what most organizations routinely do—absorbing (in effect paying) losses out of their own pockets. It is the hope of profits (or surpluses, for nonprofit organizations) that induces most firms to undertake business risks. Except in special cases, trying to transfer the financial burden of business losses usually eliminates all hope of business profits or surpluses. Therefore, the notion of asking a second organization to guarantee or insure a first organization's profit or addition to surplus is not conceptually or practically possible.

It is more efficient to define each of the five retention techniques before illustrating their appropriate uses. The following definitions of retention techniques, as well as of transfer techniques, will help the risk management professional to analyze feasible risk financing options. The techniques' focus is essentially managerial, and they should not be used for other (especially regulatory or other governmental) purposes. Specifically, it would be a misuse of the following definitions to cite them as evidence in a legal proceeding involving whether a particular risk financing arrangement is or is not retention or transfer. Generally, the federal Internal Revenue Code gives more favorable tax treatment to financing arrangements that are considered transfer than it does to financing arrangements that are considered retention. Because the tax status of risk financing arrangements is a public policy question, the following definitions may not apply in that context.

Retention Through Current Expensing of Losses

Retention through current expensing of losses involves paying losses when they occur, as normal, current business expenses. This financing technique is most appropriate for any losses to be paid from current revenues that will not unduly disrupt a given accounting period's financial results. For many organizations, the breaking of a windowpane or the puncturing of a single automobile tire would routinely be paid out of available cash. Depending on cash inflows and the other demands placed on those inflows, some organizations also would pay $2,500 of repairs resulting from an automobile accident as a current expense; still other organizations would consider a $25,000 or $50,000 fire loss one that could be easily absorbed with current cash flows without any special advance funding arrangements.

An organization's decision to pay losses as current expenses depends on its financial position, plans for future investment/expansion, seasonal fluctuations in cash flows, and debt commitments, as well as other factors. In evaluating these factors, the risk management professional should not attempt to make this or other financing decisions without consulting the organization's accounting and finance managers.

When determining the extent to which to treat losses as current expenses, the organization should be aware of the uncertainties that surround this technique. Specifically, current expensing may fail to provide anticipated cash sufficient to pay retained losses if any one of the following is true:

- The organization has considered separately the exposures for which it wants to retain some portion of resulting losses but has failed to consider the combined burden of paying losses arising out of several exposures, all of which may result within a short period.

- The organization's loss experience might be unexpectedly adverse. A single large loss, or a series of smaller losses in a short time, might exceed the cash that the organization can conveniently free from normal operations to restore losses.

- Anticipated cash flows from the organization's normal operations might unexpectedly decrease because of a downturn in its business. This decrease in anticipated cash flows could decrease the organization's ability to pay losses as current expenses.

- The organization's loss experience might not be sufficiently predictable for it to evaluate its ability to absorb losses as current expenses.

- The organization might face an inadequate spread of risk, creating potential catastrophe exposures. For example, one organization might reasonably believe it can retain as a current expense up to $300 in physical damage to any one of its ten vehicles. However, this does not mean that it can retain $3,000 collective damage should all ten suffer loss while garaged at one location.

Those sources of uncertainty, clearly evident when considering retention through current expensing of losses, also pervade, in differing degrees, other forms of retention. Therefore, in evaluating the extent to which it wants to use any particular type of retention, an organization should examine its overall financial position rather than consider any one retention technique or any one loss exposure in isolation. In making retention decisions, especially through current expensing, the risk management professional should focus on the total amount of uncertainty in the organization's overall risk financing plan, as well as the uncertainty associated with any particular set of exposures.

Retention Through an Unfunded Reserve

An **unfunded reserve** is a bookkeeping account to which the actual or anticipated losses from a particular exposure are charged each year (or other accounting period). Periodic additions to this reserve can be considered an expense for managerial purposes. The accumulated reserve, built up over a series of accounting periods, actually is a liability that reduces the organization's retained earnings, accumulated surplus, or other owners' equity. For managerial purposes, this unfunded reserve recognizes the effects that actual or anticipated losses for which the reserve was established would have on the organization's current profits and accumulated earnings or surplus.

Most loss reserves, whether unfunded or funded, serve essentially a managerial function, helping executives to recognize the real financial effect that anticipated or actual losses might have on their organization's financial position. However, as the IRS currently interprets the Internal Revenue Code, additions to such loss reserves cannot usually be recognized as tax-deductible business expenses. A tax deduction is allowed only when the loss is paid from the reserve. Thus, unfunded reserves are not a specific source of funds except to the extent that these reserves enforce conservatism on the organization's management and forestall the organization's use of the funds for other purposes.

Unfunded reserves might fail to provide the cash that the organization planned to have available to restore losses under either of the following two circumstances:

1. A severe loss might occur before the reserve has been built to a sufficient level. Whether funded or unfunded, additions to reserves typically are based on the average or expected value of losses, but actual losses might not conform to this expectation.

2. Because the reserve is unfunded, the organization might not have readily available cash equal to the reserve balance. Because the reserve is an accounting entry without any earmarked cash, the unfunded reserve is subject to the same weaknesses as is retention through paying losses as current expenses.

Retention Through a Funded Reserve

With a **funded reserve**, the organization does set aside—usually as an investment in a stable financial asset—cash equal to the periodic additions to the reserve in amounts that it anticipates will be sufficient to meet expected losses. The assets in a funded reserve should be liquid, that is, rapidly convertible into a highly predictable amount of cash when needed to pay losses. Even though a reserve is liquid, the cash it can provide might be inadequate under the following three conditions:

1. A severe loss occurs before the fund is sufficient to meet it.

2. Some senior executives or others, viewing the funds in the reserve as idle, use the funds for purposes not related to risk financing. This use might leave the organization unprotected against losses for which its operating management thought it held adequate funds.

3. Because of difficulties in predicting the organization's loss experience, the periodic contributions to the funded reserve (plus the investment earnings on those funds) might be too low, even in the long run, to pay for actual losses.

Funded loss reserves are relatively rare retention vehicles for at least two reasons. First, most organizations have better uses for their funds than merely to invest them in financial instruments in anticipation of future losses. Typically, an organization can earn more by devoting its funds to regular, productive operations. Second, seemingly idle reserve funds are, in most organizations, so attractive a "target" for competing managers seeking additional funding for their own operations that it is politically difficult for a risk management professional to defend these reserves.

Retention Through Borrowed Funds

In principle, an organization could borrow funds to finance recovery from accidental losses. **Borrowing** occurs by incurring debt in exchange for money currently received, such as by securing a line of credit from a financial institution, issuing bonds, slowing payments to creditors, or issuing promissory notes. The organization could borrow funds through either (1) arranging, before a loss occurs, for a line of credit or other borrowing vehicle to be activated, by the borrower's request, after a loss; or (2) arranging, after a loss, to borrow the funds it needs to recover from that particular loss.

In practice, borrowing has not been widely used as a risk financing technique, perhaps because recovering from an accidental loss might not be viewed as a fully legitimate reason for going into debt. Moreover, relying on borrowed funds involves some significant uncertainties. First, if the borrowing arrangements are made before the loss occurs, the organization must estimate in advance the funds it will need to recover from the loss. If the loss exceeds these estimates, the borrowed funds, even if available, might be inadequate. Second, if the borrowing arrangements are made after the loss occurs, the organization might find that it is not able to borrow sufficient funds on the terms anticipated. (This could be because the loss has been so severe that the lender's confidence in the borrower's ability to repay the loan has been shaken.)

One could legitimately question why borrowing is considered risk retention rather than risk transfer. If borrowing is retention, and if all retention techniques involve the use of funds that originate within the organization or its economic family, in what sense do the borrowed funds originate internally? The answer is that, when an organization borrows to restore accidental losses, it uses some part of its ability to borrow funds for other purposes. Because an organization's credit standing (its ability to borrow) is an asset to that organization, partial use of this borrowing capacity to pay for accidental losses diminishes this asset. In a real economic sense, borrowing constitutes retention.

Retention Through an Affiliated ("Captive") Insurer

Some large organizations or associations form subsidiaries to finance specified types of accidental losses that the "parent(s)" might suffer. Such a risk financing subsidiary is an **affiliated (captive) insurer**. Just as a manufacturing firm might form a corporate subsidiary through which to purchase or manufacture a component or a service, so the parent of an affiliated (captive) insurer also can form a subsidiary through which to purchase "insurance." ("Insurance" is placed in quotation marks here because the IRS, in challenging or denying the tax deductibility to the parent of premiums paid to its captive, has questioned whether the transaction constitutes "insurance.") In economic reality, although not necessarily for tax purposes, the organization's "captive" subsidiary thus becomes a highly formalized means of retention.

If a captive has only one parent, it is known as a **pure** or "traditional" **captive**. If it has several parents to which it offers financial protection, it is known as an **association** or a **group captive**. In either case, the captive is designed to function as a regular insurance company—domiciled, regulated by, and paying taxes to the state in which it is headquartered. A captive often offers financial protection to other outside organizations beyond its parents both so that it can more nearly achieve the spread of loss exposures underwritten by a typical commercial insurance company and also so that it can enhance its independence from its parents.

The line between a captive insurer and a commercial insurer is not always clear. Many United States mutual insurance companies formed in the late nineteenth and early twentieth centuries specialized in offering coverages to firms in particular industries—such as hardware stores, florists, or sawmills—that believed that they could not obtain adequate coverage at reasonable premiums from the existing insurers. In a sense, particularly in their earliest days, these specialized mutuals closely resembled some of today's association captives. The captive insurance arrangement, particularly with pure captives, closely resembles risk transfer through commercial insurance, demonstrating that the distinction between retention and transfer is not always clear.

Although this lack of clarity does not pose serious difficulties for the internal operation of an organization's risk management program, it has generated some confusion in the application of tax laws based on the retention/transfer distinction. The IRS has challenged the status of premiums paid to a captive on the bases that the captive (1) was not managed by executives who were independent of the management of the parents; (2) did not write a sufficient portion of its "insurance" portfolio on exposures that were unrelated to the business of the parents; and (3) did not reflect any valid business purpose of the parents other than reducing income tax payments.

Risk Financing Through Transfer

In addition to the various forms of retention, the other risk financing options consist of some form of transfer. As shown in Exhibit 8-1, the two major risk transferring options are contractual transfer for risk financing and commercial insurance. The two forms of risk transfer are quite similar except for the nature of the transferees. Under contractual transfer for risk financing, the transferee is some organization, individual, or entity other than a commercial insurer. Therefore, the contract is not an insurance contract, and the transferee is not regulated as an insurer. Under commercial insurance, the transferee is an insurer.

Contractual Transfer for Risk Financing

A **contractual transfer for risk financing** is a contract under which one party, the transferee/indemnitor, agrees to pay for specified types of losses. In the absence of that contract, the financial burden would fall on the transferor/indemnitee. The transferee may agree to reimburse the transferor directly, in which case the contract is often called an **indemnity contract** or clause. Alternatively, the transferee may agree to pay losses on behalf of the transferor. Consequently, the contract of transfer is often called a **hold harmless agreement** or clause because the transferee holds the transferor harmless from financial responsibility for the loss—typically a claim that a third party brings against the transferor—that is the subject of the transfer contract. The contractual transfer specifies the types of loss for which the transferee agrees to be financially responsible. The agreement also may require the transferee to maintain and give evidence of insurance adequate to fulfill its obligations under the contractual transfer for risk financing.

The example in Exhibit 8-2, "The Ground of the Baskervilles," illustrates the difference between contractual transfer for risk control and contractual transfer for risk financing. In that case, the contractual provision under which Sir Henry Baskerville agrees to indemnify Sam Gollum if Gollum's bulldozer is lost in the bog is a contractual transfer for risk financing. Baskerville's only obligation under that provision is to pay Gollum the specified 350 British pounds if the bulldozer is lost in the bog. Beyond that, Baskerville has no obligations to perform any other activities or to pay any other losses. In this example, only property loss exposures were involved.

In practice, many contractual transfers for risk financing deal with the transferor's potential liability to third parties or to the general public. As an illustration in terms of Baskerville's bog, Sir Henry might have required Gollum to hold Baskerville harmless from any liability claims that others might bring against Baskerville, as the landowner responsible for the bog, arising from any work that Gollum did there. Gollum would have been the transferee/indemnitor regarding the public liability exposure of Baskerville, the transferor/indemnitee. The contractual transfer for risk financing (or hold harmless clause) might have read as follows:

> The Contractor (Gollum) will indemnify and hold harmless the Owner (Baskerville) and his agents and employees from and against all claims, damages, losses, and expenses—including attorneys' fees—arising from and resulting from the performance of the work (on the bog), of every nature and description brought or recoverable against the Owner or his employees or agents.

Although this is a relatively broad grant of seeming protection to Baskerville, apparently covering all claims without financial limit, Baskerville's protection is, in reality, only as sound as Gollum's financial strength. For that reason, Baskerville might also have required Gollum to purchase insurance to cover Gollum's obligation to indemnify Baskerville. In fact, Baskerville might even have required that Gollum pay for such insurance, with Baskerville purchasing it in Gollum's name.

Contractual transfers for risk financing usually alter the rules of common law that would otherwise apply in allocating losses. The wording and apparent meaning of these transfers are limited only by the ingenuity of the legal profession, provided that courts are willing to enforce these contractual transfers as written. Moreover, some state statutes limit the extent to which parties can shift financial responsibility for loss. Generally, court decisions and statutes render ineffective attempted contractual transfers for risk financing that, at face value, are either unfairly bargained and unconscionable or act to deprive the public of adequate compensation for injuries. For example, if Sir Henry Baskerville were very rich and in a much better position than Sam Gollum to control the safety of the bog, the courts (or an applicable statute) might disregard Baskerville's attempt to shift financial responsibility to Gollum.

Consequently, the financial protection that a transferor/indemnitee gains under a contractual transfer for risk financing is subject to the following three uncertainties:

1. The transferee/indemnitor might not have insurance or other financial resources to meet its obligations to the transferor/indemnitee.
2. A court might find that the transfer agreement does not adequately define the transferred exposure as the parties had intended. (For example, does the above quoted agreement apply if one of Sir Henry Baskerville's employees, entitled to workers compensation benefits from Sir Henry, falls into the bog while Gollum is working on it?)
3. A court or a statute might declare that the contractual transfer is unenforceable because it is unconscionably harsh on the transferee.

Contractual transfer for risk financing typically is not feasible for business risks. This is because it usually is not possible for a potential transferor and a potential transferee to agree on what profits or surpluses the transferee should pay to the transferor to adequately compensate for the transferor's business losses. Furthermore, if the business venture that is the subject of the transferor and transferee's risk-shifting contract is not successful, it is doubtful that the transferee/indemnitor will be financially able and willing to pay the transferor/indemnitee for the latter's actual business losses. The two parties may, however, be able to negotiate some liquidated damages contract provisions that they agree would adequately compensate the transferor's losses on their shared venture.

Commercial Insurance

Although commercial insurance is perhaps the most evident and most widely used of all risk management techniques, it is the last technique described in this chapter because commercial insurance should be the last resort in a sound risk management program. It should be the alternative used when no other technique or combination of techniques is sufficient. When properly used in combination with other risk management techniques, commercial insurance fulfills its intended role of providing truly needed protection and thus both better serves the insured and generates a more reliable underwriting profit for the insurer.

As usually defined, **commercial insurance** is a contract under which one party, the insurer, agrees—in exchange for the payment of a periodic (usually) premium—to pay for specified losses that the insured might suffer, up to (usually) specified amounts, under conditions specified in the insurance contract. Other than incidental duties tangential to paying insured losses, a commercial insurer typically has few duties under the contract.

Purchasing commercial insurance is generally the most reliable form of risk financing. The only significant uncertainties facing an insured under a commercial insurance contract are the following three possibilities:

1.   The commercial insurer might become insolvent or refuse to meet its policy obligations for some other reason.

2.   The insurer and the insured might disagree about whether a loss is insured or about the amount of the loss.

3.   The amount of the loss might be so large that some portion of it exceeds the applicable limit of the commercial insurance.

The first of these three sources of uncertainty can be reduced by carefully selecting financially sound insurers. In addition, most states have guarantee funds designed to meet policy obligations of insolvent insurers. The second uncertainty, relating to the scope and limits of coverage, can be minimized through insurer/insured discussions of the meaning of the insurance contract in particular situations (or, if necessary, through litigation after a loss occurs). The third uncertainty, inadequate limits, can be forestalled through the insured's proper selection of coverage limits. Despite those precautions, some residual elements of uncertainty could linger in a commercial insurance transaction. Nonetheless, if anything can be taken as typical in risk financing, it is that, by and large, a commercial insurer will pay an insured loss.

For an organization to insure against the financial consequences of a particular loss exposure, that exposure must meet, to at least a reasonable degree, the traditional requirements of an insurable exposure. As generally recognized in the insurance business, these six requirements are as follows:

1. The exposure involves pure risk rather than speculative risk.
2. Uncertainty exists as to the time or probability of loss.
3. The happening, time, and amount of an insured loss can clearly be determined.
4. A large number of exposures are insured.
5. A loss will not simultaneously affect many insureds.
6. Insurance is economically feasible.[3]

The fact that an exposure is commercially insurable does not mean that a particular organization should choose to purchase the available insurance. Other risk financing techniques, used alone or in conjunction with insurance, might be more cost-effective and provide substantially comparable financial protection. Chapters 11 and 12 of this text present general guidelines for making decisions about when to purchase commercial insurance. The ARM 56 text, *Essentials of Risk Financing*, explores the complexities of making appropriate insurance and other transfer/retention risk financing decisions.

In principle, business risks are not normally insurable because (1) they do not meet the requirements of an insurable exposure enumerated above and (2) therefore, over the long run, the premium that an insurer would charge to guarantee an organization's continuing profits or surpluses would exceed the expected value of those profits or surpluses. Similarly, insurance premiums for covering an insured's exposures to covered accidental losses exceed the expected value of those losses to provide its insurer with underwriting profits and contingency reserves.

Hedging

For business risks created by price changes, a risk financing technique known as **hedging** enables an organization (or individual) to transfer those risks to the other party in the hedging transaction. The risk transferred is the exposure to loss from declines in the market price of a commodity, which the transferor must hold for an extended period as a normal part of doing business. Farmers, for example, are exposed to loss if the market price of a crop they are growing drops significantly between when they plant their crops and when they sell the oil made from the beans (if the price of soybeans falls because of, for example, an oversupply, the price of soybean oil will also drop with that of the beans). The same type of business risk confronts firms using natural raw material in a production process that requires significant periods of time during which prices can change.

To safeguard itself against business losses from declining commodity or other raw material prices through a hedging contract, an organization must relinquish the possibility that it could profit from rising prices of that commodity or raw material. A hedging contract insulates an organization from gains or losses caused by price changes. The organization's business gain or loss depends on its business skill, not on unpredictable fluctuations in the prices of the raw materials it buys or in the prices of the goods or services it sells.

For the hedge to provide effective risk transfer, a futures market for the commodity must exist. Such a market requires the following:

- A standardized "futures" contract. (A promise to deliver a given quantity of the commodity, of a specified level of quality, by a specified future date).

- Individuals or organizations willing to speculate by buying or selling futures contracts in hopes of making a profit by projecting future prices of the actual commodity on the specified delivery date. (The speculators are the transferees of the risk of price changes from which the farmers or other owners of the actual commodities want to insulate themselves from their risk. The farmers or other owners are the transferors of this price risk.)

- A market for trading the futures, a place where buyers and sellers (transferees and transferors of the risk of price changes) can come together, with the help of technical experts in futures trading, to buy and sell futures contracts in an orderly fashion at publicly known prices for the futures contract.

A future contract buyer estimates or speculates that the commodity price will rise. The future delivery contract seller believes or hopes that the commodity price and the future delivery contract will fall. If the future contract buyer's hopes are realized, the buyer can sell the future contract (not the underlying commodity) for a profit. The future's original seller believes that the commodity price will fall and can profit if the commodity price (and future contract) actually do fall. The seller received the future contract price when the seller originally sold it. If the commodity price and the future contract fall, the seller can then buy another future delivery contract at a lower price than the trader sold the first one, taking the difference as profit.

A futures market can facilitate transfer of the risks of price changes regardless of the commodity involved, as long as the requirements previously given for the existence of a sound futures market are fulfilled. In addition to natural raw materials, foreign currencies are other examples of commodities whose futures can be traded. For example, a United States firm contracts today to have a computer mainframe custom-made in Japan and delivered in six months. The firm will pay $300 million yen for delivery and may purchase today a futures contract for $300 million yen to be delivered in six months. If the dollar price of yen rises in six months, the importer would have to pay more dollars to buy the mainframe in six months than it would have to pay today. Consequently, the importer would incur a loss because of the adverse change in the dollar/yen exchange rate (the dollar price of yen). However, the importer should recover most of the loss with the profit it makes selling its futures contract at a higher price than it was purchased.

However, if the dollar price of yen falls during the six months, the importer would gain because fewer dollars would be needed to pay the $300 million yen for the mainframe. That gain would be balanced, however, by the loss that the importer would incur on its futures contract for the $300 million yen. In short, regardless of the dollar/yen exchange rate at the end of the six months, the futures contract insulates the American importer from any loss (or gain) from changes in the exchange rate. Futures market speculators gain or lose depending on how exchange rates change. Because this simplified example omitted the transactions costs of buying and selling futures contracts, the two transactions do not exactly balance. The importer must assume costs such as commissions, taxes, and insurance. Transaction expenses can be considered costs that the importer pays to benefit from the added peace of mind that the hedging activity provides.

Recent developments in hedging open many new possibilities for risk financing of potential and actual accidental losses. Some of those possibilities can be very positive; others can be very negative.

On the positive side, forms of hedging against possible net income losses from price changes can reduce an organization's business risk exposures. Consequently, an organization has greater capacity to retain its losses and to use other risk financing techniques. Furthermore, when an organization's managers of business risk and its managers of risks of accidental loss both recognize that all risks must be managed as a whole, managers are better positioned to manage all risks more effectively. Everyone should recognize that the actions of both groups of managers affect the other group's decisions.

Still on the positive side, many of the financial instruments now available open new investment opportunities for risk managers, pools captive operators, financial executives of traditional insurers, and others who can provide funds from new sources to finance recovery from accidental losses. Some of the new instruments can be very appropriate investment vehicles for funds that could eventually finance recovery from accidental losses. Properly selected and managed, those instruments can effectively generate risk financing funds and help reduce an organization's cost of risk.

On the negative side, however, hedging can destabilize not only an organization's general risk financing plans but also its entire financial structure. If an organization's retained earnings or surplus are seriously jeopardized by unwise speculative investments, the earnings or surpluses no longer reliably pay for retained accidental losses. Consequently, the financial security that they provide can be greatly impaired. The objective of reducing an organization's cost of risk for accidental losses by generating high returns for loss reserves must be balanced against the objective of ensuring that funds will be available when needed. New investment opportunities and investments might or might not promote that balance.

Review

> **How can you apply general risk management techniques in specific cases?**
>
> **Is there more than one way to apply a technique to an exposure?**
>
> **Can you apply several techniques simultaneously?**

The basic theme of this chapter has been that most risk management techniques apply equally well to exposures to both accidental and business losses. To better understand that theme, consider eight exposures to accidental losses—two property, two liability, two personnel, and two net income—facing Wheeler's Tire Disposal and Aunt Melinda's Cookie Company in the tire fire case presented in Chapter 1. In addition, to understand how most risk management techniques also help an organization to manage its speculative risk exposures to business losses, consider how Wheeler's and Aunt Melinda's each could apply these techniques to one of their business loss exposures. The resulting ten exposures are as follows:

Property losses to

- Wheeler's from fire damage to its buildings, equipment, inventories of scrap tires and recycled rubber products, and supplies of materials used in the recycling process at its Friendship City facility.

- Aunt Melinda's from collision damage to its trucks and to its cargoes of fresh cookies while the trucks rushed along long, unfamiliar routes around Wheeler's fire site to the Friendship City airport by 6:00 each morning.

Liability losses to

- Wheeler's for pollution damage to neighboring properties—both before and during the tire fire—and especially to Harold's Heavy-Duty Equipment

Company, onto which thousands of gallons of oil released from Wheeler's burning scrap tires flowed during, and in the week following, the tire fire.

- Aunt Melinda's, because of large legal defense costs that the cookie company incurred defending itself against, or settling for its small "nuisance value," unfounded bodily injury claims brought by passengers of Destiny Airlines who asserted that they had been sickened by eating some of Aunt Melinda's cookies. The passengers believed that the cookies had somehow become tainted, even " poisoned," in the tire fire, despite the fact that Aunt Melinda's bakery is across town from Wheeler's and the fact that Melinda's trucks followed new routes to the airport far from Wheeler's.

Personnel losses to

- Wheeler's because of Walt Wheeler's fifteen-month nervous breakdown, resulting in the company's inability to conduct business during this period and the continuing uncertainty about Walt's mental health among his family and business associates.
- Aunt Melinda's because of Melinda's automobile injury suffered while she was rushing a shipment of cookies to Destiny Airlines at the Friendship City Airport.

Net income losses to

- Wheeler's because of the heavy fire damage to its Friendship City facilities.
- Aunt Melinda's due to the company's persistent difficulties meeting the 6:00 A.M. airport delivery deadline, causing Aunt Melinda's to both incur extra expenses and lose revenue (for failing to fulfill its contract with Destiny) each day that the company had to struggle, or actually failed, to meet the airport delivery schedule.

Business losses to

- Wheeler's because of declines in the wholesale prices at which Wheeler's can sell the rubber and related byproducts it recovers from the tires that it recycles.
- Aunt Melinda's because it expects Destiny Airlines to offer it a lower price for the 1,000 dozen cookies when its contract comes up for renewal in six months. To produce cookies at a profit for the price that Destiny will probably offer to pay, Aunt Melinda's must purchase futures contracts to protect itself against increases in the wholesale prices of flour, sugar, cocoa, and several other key ingredients of its cookies.

Although somewhat random, these exposures exemplify the wide range of exposures with which risk management professionals must often deal and allow students to practice visualizing feasible uses of the range of risk control and risk financing techniques. Exhibits 8-3 through 8-7, preceding this chapter's summary, indicate how—with few exceptions—control and risk financing techniques could help manage the specific loss exposures drawn from the tire fire case. Learning how to apply various risk management techniques to exposures equips a risk management professional to be equally creative in applying these techniques to many other routine and unusual exposures.

Exhibit 8-3
Applying Risk Management Techniques to Property Loss Exposures

Applying Risk Control Techniques

Technique / Exposure	Exposure Avoidance	Loss Prevention	Loss Reduction	Segregation by Separation	Segregation by Duplication	Contractual Transfer—Risk Control
Fire at Wheeler's Friendship City Lot	Never own or lease this lot.	• Control ignition sources. • Isolate flammables.	• Reduce amount of combustible material. • Separate piles of tires. • Extinguish fires quickly.	Operate more, smaller lots.	Arrange for emergency use of others' property.	• Lease lot from another, who bears property exposure.
Collision, Aunt Melinda's Truck	Make cookies at airport (no truck transport).	• Drive cautiously. • Select drivers prudently. • Take safer route to airport.	• Drive slowly (less) damage at impact). • Use less costly trucks.	Split each day's delivery among several trucks.	Contract to use others' trucks in emergency.	• Subcontract cookie delivery to airport. • Use rented delivery trucks. • Contract for Destiny to pick up cookies at bakery.

Applying Risk Finance Techniques

Technique → / Exposure ↓	Retention—Current Expensing	Retention—Unfunded Reserving	Retention—Funded Reserving	Retention—Borrowing	Retention—Captive	Contractual Transfer—Risk Financing	Commercial Insurance	Hedging
Fire at Wheeler's Friendship City Lot	Use cash on hand to pay for minor machinery damage.	Plan to pay for budgetable spoilage of rubber-processing chemicals.	Set aside funds for anticipated workers compensation claims.	Arrange line of credit to pay for any severe, uninsured damages to property on lot.	Create or join association captive for fire or other damage.	Probably infeasible—no logical transferee.	Buy fire insurance on lot or on just tires.	No business risk.
Collision, Aunt Melinda's Truck	• Pay for minor truck collision damage. • Send extra cookies, expecting some cookie damage in transport.	Budget for average annual collision losses.	Set aside case for unforeseen, possibly uninsured, damage to trucks.	Get bank loan after collision to pay for any major insured truck damage.	Melinda's probably too small to use captive.	Destiny *might* agree to reimburse Melinda's losses.	Buy collision, perhaps also cargo insurance.	No business risk.

Exhibit 8-4
Applying Risk Management Techniques to Liability Loss Exposures

Technique / Exposure	Exposure Avoidance	Loss Prevention	Loss Reduction	Segregation by Separation	Segregation by Duplication	Contractual Transfer—Risk Control
Wheeler's Damage to Neighbors' Properties	Have no neighbors.	• Respect neighbors' property rights. • Dissuade neighbors from bringing claims.	• Fix harm to others' property. • Work to defeat others' claims. • Repair any neighbors' damages. • Treat neighbors respectfully. • Negotiate liquidated damages before incident.	Generally not applicable to liability exposures.	Usually not applicable.	Persuade neighbors in advance to waive their rights to sue Wheeler's.
Aunt Melinda's Claims of Sickened Passengers	Only if cookies or other food not sold to any airline.	• Provide only healthful cookies. • Treat sickened passengers with empathy.	• Good claims management. • Effective cookie quality control.	Make smaller lots of cookies.	Usually not applicable.	No available subcontractor or other transferee.

(Column heading group: Applying Risk Control Techniques)

Applying Risk Finance Techniques

Technique → / Exposure ↓	Retention—Current Expensing	Retention—Unfunded Reserving	Retention—Funded Reserving	Retention—Borrowing	Retention—Captive	Contractual Transfer—Risk Financing	Commercial Insurance	Hedging
Wheeler's Damage to Neighbors' Properties	Reimburse neighbors for minor damage.	Establish liability account for anticipated routine damage.	Set aside funds for known claims to be paid over time.	Borrow from bank to pay known major claims.	Join tire association captive that *might* cover these claims.	Not applicable—no apparent transferee.	General liability insurance on Wheeler's	Not applicable—no business risk.
Aunt Melinda's Claims of Sickened Passengers	Resolve very minor claims with free supply of cookies.	Establish liability account for routine defense costs.	Set aside funds for known claims to be paid over time.	Borrow from bank to pay known major claims.	Probably not applicable (loss potential too small).	Have Destiny hold Melinda's harmless, but not likely.	Melinda's products liability insurance.	Not applicable—no business risk.

Exhibit 8-5
Applying Risk Management Techniques to Personnel Loss Exposures

Technique → / Exposure ↓	Applying Risk Control Techniques					
	Exposure Avoidance	*Loss Prevention*	*Loss Reduction*	*Segregation by Separation*	*Segregation by Duplication*	*Contractual Transfer— Risk Control*
Walt Wheeler's Nervous Breakdown	Unavoidable unless Walt retires before breakdown.	• Keep Walt calm. • Frequent physical examinations.	• Get Walt's work done by others. • Rehabilitation for Walt.	Not applicable, or Walt supervises several assistants.	• Cross-training others to step in for Walt. • Succession planning for Walt.	Probably not applicable (no available transferee).
Aunt Melinda's Collision Injuries	Melinda avoids driving trucks.	• Melinda drives carefully. • Melinda takes safer routes.	• Melinda uses crash-resistant truck. • Rehabilitation for Melinda.	Not applicable.	• Cross-training others to step in for Melinda. • Hire temporary replacement driver. • Does Melinda have a sister?	Probably not applicable (no available transferee).

Applying Risk Finance Techniques

Technique / Exposure	Retention— Current Expensing	Retention— Unfunded Reserving	Retention— Funded Reserving	Retention— Borrowing	Retention— Captive	Contractual Transfer— Risk Financing	Commercial Insurance	Hedging
Walt Wheeler's Nervous Breakdown	Pay others overtime to do Walt's routine work.	Accumulate retained earning, anticipating any disability to Walt.	Self-funded employee benefit plans by Wheeler's.	Borrowing by Wheeler's or Walt personally to cover his or the firm's expenses.	Funding employee benefits through association captive.	Probably not applicable (no available transferee).	• Expenses covered by health insurance that Walt or firm can buy. • "Key person" disability insurance against firm's earnings loss.	Not applicable— no business risk.
Aunt Melinda's Collision Injuries	Hire replacement driver.	Not applicable, or personal savings by Melinda.	Self-funded employee benefit plans by Melinda's.	Borrowing by Melinda's or Melinda personally to cover her or the firm's expenses.	Funding employee benefits through association captive.	Probably not applicable (no available transferee).	• Medical expense insurance that Melinda or firm can buy. • "Key person" disability insurance for firm's earnings loss.	Not applicable— no business risk.

Exhibit 8-6

Applying Risk Management Techniques to Net Income Loss Exposures

Technique / Exposure	Exposure Avoidance	Loss Prevention	Loss Reduction	Segregation by Separation	Segregation by Duplication	Contractual Transfer—Risk Control
			Applying Risk Control Techniques			
Wheeler's Shutdown From Fire	• Abandon this lot before fire. • Abandon this business before fire.	Prevent fire damage.	• Minimize fire damage. • Reduce continuing expenses. • Hasten reopening and return to normal.	Shift operations to other Wheeler lots.	Arrange for temporary substitute facilities.	Subcontract to others very hazardous tire-processing activities that pose great fire hazards.
Aunt Melinda's Extra Costs Meeting Deadlines	• Cancel this contract and make other contracts. • Negotiate removal of all deadlines. • Unavoidable.	• Negotiate more liberal deadlines. • Work harder to meet deadlines. • Store some emergency cookies at airport.	• Reduce operating costs. • Reduce contractual penalties for missing deadlines.	Send separate shipments each morning.	Arrange to buy cookies from others, for delivery by Melinda's to Destiny, when Melinda's cannot produce.	Subcontract daily delivery operations.

Applying Risk Finance Techniques

Technique → / Exposure ↓	Retention— Current Expensing	Retention— Unfunded Reserving	Retention— Funded Reserving	Retention— Borrowing	Retention— Captive	Contractual Transfer— Risk Financing	Commercial Insurance	Hedging
Wheeler's Shutdown From Fire	Absorb losses from very brief fire-related interruptions.	Absorb any significant losses by drawing on past retained earnings.	Probably not feasible: losses too uncertain.	Retain cash by slowing payments to creditors, effectively borrowing more money from them.	Shift loss to association's captive if it covers fire-related business interruption.	Delay shipments of rubber products to buyers (after receiving their money).	Purchase business interruption insurance covering on-premises fire.	Not applicable—no business risk.
Aunt Melinda's Extra Costs Meeting Deadlines	Absorb minor extra costs of meeting deadlines.	Absorb any significant losses by drawing on past retained earnings.	Probably not feasible: losses too uncertain.	Retain cash by slowing payments to creditors, effectively borrowing more money from them.	Not applicable—exposure too small for captive treatment.	Offset extra costs by raising prices of cookies in next contract with Destiny.	Purchase extra expense coverage for consequences of off-premises events.	Not applicable—no business risk.

Exhibit 8-7
Applying Risk Management Techniques to Business Risks

Technique / Exposure	Applying Risk Control Techniques					
	Exposure Avoidance	*Loss Prevention*	*Loss Reduction*	*Segregation by Separation*	*Segregation by Duplication*	*Contractual Transfer— Risk Control*
Wheeler's Lessening Demand for Some Products	Discontinue products with uncertain futures.	Focus on products whose prices are firm.	• Warehouse products with low selling prices until prices rise. • Reduce dependence on uncertain products. • Sell in small quantities.	Diversify variety of products.	Probably not applicable.	Establish long-term, fixed price selling contracts (buyer takes price risk).
Aunt Melinda's Rising Flour Prices	Make only products that require no flour.	Stockpile flour when price is favorable.	• Reduce amount of flour required. • Purchase large supplies of flour when prices are relatively low.	Diversify products, emphasizing those that need no flour.	Probably not applicable.	Establish long-term, fixed-price buying contracts (seller takes much of price risk).

Applying Risk Finance Techniques

Technique → / Exposure →

Exposure	Retention—Current Expensing	Retention—Unfunded Reserving	Retention—Funded Reserving	Retention—Borrowing	Retention—Captive	Contractual Transfer—Risk Financing	Commercial Insurance	Hedging
Wheeler's Lessening Demand for Some Products	Absorb gains and losses through fluctuating earnings.	Establish bookkeeping account that reflects gains and losses from price fluctuations.	Probably not applicable unless other products' rising demand generates extra money for fund.	Use line of bank credit to stabilize cash inflows when product prices fall.	Not applicable—business risk not subject to insurance principles.	Not applicable—no available transferee.	Not applicable—business risk not subject to insurance principles.	Not applicable—no futures market for raw recycled rubber or its products.
Aunt Melinda's Rising Flour Prices	Absorb gains and losses through fluctuating earnings.	Establish bookkeeping account that reflects gains and losses from price fluctuations.	Establish fund to absorb gains and losses from flour price fluctuations.	Delay payments to creditors to keep cash when outflows to buy flour rise.	Not applicable—business risk not subject to insurance principles.	Not applicable—no available transferee.	Not applicable—business risk not subject to insurance principles.	Earn profits buying wheat futures to offset losses from rising wheat flour prices.

Summary

This chapter focused on the second step of the risk management process, examining alternative risk management techniques that may be applied to—individually or in combination with—property, liability, personnel, net income, and business loss exposures. The various techniques, charted in Exhibit 8-1, fall into two broad categories: risk control techniques to prevent losses from occurring (or to minimize their size) and risk financing techniques to pay for those losses that, despite even the best risk control efforts, inevitably occur.

Except where exposure avoidance completely eliminates any possibility of loss, sound risk management calls for combining some risk control techniques with some risk financing techniques for each significant loss exposure that an organization might face. Without risk financing, risk control techniques are not sufficient because some losses are almost bound to occur, and recovery from these losses must be financed. Without effective risk control, risk financing techniques typically do not constitute effective risk management. Merely paying for losses as they occur, rather than trying to stop them or minimize their size, is wasteful, both of an organization's funds and of the entire economy's overall resources.

With alternative risk management techniques and their possible applications clearly in mind, risk management professionals should turn to the next step in the risk management decision process: selecting the most cost-effective technique or combination of techniques. This third step is the focus of Chapters 9 through 12 of this text.

Chapter Notes

1. H.W. Heinrich, Dan Petersen, and Nestor Roos, *Industrial Accident Prevention*, 5th ed. (New York, NY: McGraw-Hill Book Company, 1980), pp. 20-31.
2. Dan Bailey and Greg Tokle, "Wildland Fire Management," in Arthur E. Cote (ed.), *Fire Protection Handbook*, 17th ed. (Quincy, MA: National Fire Protection Association, 1991), pp. 8-223 to 8-225.
3. Robert J. Gibbons, George E. Rejda, and Michael W. Elliott, *Insurance Perspectives* (Malvern, PA: American Institute for CPCU, 1992), pp. 61-66.

Chapter 9

Forecasting: The Basis for Risk Management Decisions

Educational Objectives

1. Given a situation and appropriate data, forecast the expected value of the losses that an organization or individual will incur during a given time interval.

   In support of the above educational objective, you should be able to do the following:

   a. Explain when it is appropriate to use probability analysis, and when it is appropriate to use trend analysis, to forecast accidental losses.

   b. Adjust historical losses for changes in price levels.

   c. Perform time series analysis and regression analysis for trending loss data.

   d. State from memory the general formulas for each of the following:
      (1) arithmetic means
      (2) medians
      (3) standard deviations
      (4) coefficients of variation
      (5) slope and y-intercept for

Outline

Developing Data on Past Losses
   Complete Data
   Consistent Data
   Relevant Data
   Organized Data

Probability Analysis
   The Nature of Probability
   Sources of Probability Data
   Constructing Probability Distributions
   Characteristics of Probability Distributions

Trend Analysis
   Intuitive Trending
   Arithmetic Trending Techniques

Summary

(a) linear time series trend lines

(b) linear regression lines

e. Given a set of loss data (amounts of losses or numbers of losses), construct or compute each of the following for those data:

(1) an array of losses

(2) arithmetic mean

(3) median

(4) mode

(5) standard deviation

(6) coefficient of variation

2. Explain the importance of forecasts of losses and of the costs and benefits of risk management alternatives in making risk management decisions.

3. Explain the importance of, and procedures for developing, loss data that are complete, consistent, relevant, and organized for making risk management decisions.

4. Use the standard deviation of a normal probability distribution to compute probabilities based on integer values (whole numbers) of standard deviations.

5. Describe intuitive methods of trending loss data.

6. Define or describe each of the Key Words and Phrases for this assignment.

Forecasting: The Basis for Risk Management Decisions

Risk management decisions rely on forecasts of future losses. A **forecast** is a projection of some future value, amount, or quantity calculated from some current value by mathematical techniques or by intuition. Those forecasts help determine the demands that will be placed on the risk management department as it works to protect the organization against accidental losses. As a foundation for the description in subsequent chapters of proper procedures for selecting risk management techniques, this chapter uses arithmetic and common-sense explanations of loss forecasting techniques that should help the risk management professional work with others in making better decisions.

The unpredictability of accidental losses—the mere fact that they are accidental—has been said to be the most challenging part of risk management. Many say that if an organization's property, liability, personnel, and net income losses were as predictable as its sales or production costs, then risk management would be no different than any other specialty within general management. Many claim that cost-effective risk management decisions would then be made like any other type of business decision—by finding the presumably known benefits and costs of each alternative and then choosing the option whose benefits most exceed its costs.

However, those experienced in forecasting an organization's sales, costs, or profits face uncertainty at least as great as those who would forecast future losses. The same forecasting techniques applied throughout general management are equally valid for projecting future accidental losses. In the aggregate, over a substantial period, those losses are as predictable as many other costs.

> **Why is it important to forecast accidental losses?**
>
> **How can a risk management professional develop data on past losses?**

Developing Data on Past Losses

Forecasting accidental losses, like any other future event, requires detecting patterns in the past and projecting them into the future. Those patterns might be as simple as "no change." For example, more often than not, tomorrow's weather will be the same as today's. There also may be much truth in saying that this year's accidental losses for a particular organization will be about the same as last year's.

Alternatively, a pattern for the future might be one of change. The advance of a cold front might signal more severe weather tomorrow. Plans to increase factory output might foretell a greater number of injuries to employees. Furthermore, if inflation is projected to continue, each of those employee injuries might be more costly next year. Even when the pattern is one of change, some elements are constant: the frequency of work injuries might be predictably related to output levels, and the rate at which inflation increases the financial effect of a given injury or property loss might be a continuation of past inflationary trends.

Thus, forecasting future accidental losses by finding these patterns begins with deciding which of two basic patterns, "no change" or "change in a predictable way," applies. Finding these patterns requires careful study of the numbers, amounts, causes, and other circumstances of past losses. With adequate data in hand, a risk management professional can then look for patterns.

To find patterns in past losses, a risk management professional should attempt to find data that are (1) complete, (2) consistent, (3) relevant, and (4) organized. These data should be obtained by a reasonable expenditure of money, effort, and time.

Consider, for example, the situation faced by the risk management consultant whom Walt Wheeler's family hired to evaluate insurance and safety matters at Wheeler's Tire Disposal. This consultant recognized the special importance for tire-recycling firms of property and net income loss exposures from the breakdown of the mechanized conveyors, lifters, and other heavy machinery. Organizations like Wheeler's used such machinery to move large quantities of scrap tires or unusually heavy individual tires. This consultant also wondered how accurate, consistent, meaningful, and complete Wheeler's records of its past losses were. Therefore, the consultant asked Wheeler's accounting department to provide a listing of the dates and historical dollar amounts of major machinery damage or breakdown losses at Wheeler's during the period including Year 1 through Year 4.

Complete Data

Because risk management professionals must rely on others to gather much, perhaps most, of the information for making risk management decisions, Wheeler's risk management consultant Ruth Sanders was thankful to have these data from the accounting department. She knew that she would have to gather from others not only the amounts of the losses arising from these employee injuries, such as data in Exhibit 9-1, but also information on the circumstances surrounding each loss. Factors such as the experience and training of the involved employees, the time of day that each machinery damage or breakdown occurred, the task being performed, and the supervisor on duty at the time of injury might be helpful in isolating and correcting the true causes of each machinery damage or breakdown loss. Furthermore, the consultant knew that she would need the best available data or reliable estimates of the dollar amounts of the various elements of each loss, the cost of repairing or replacing the damaged or inoperative machinery, the resulting loss of revenue, any extra expense to Wheeler's, and any overtime wages to Wheeler's employees to deal with each machinery-related accident.

Exhibit 9-1
Calendar of Historical Losses

Date	Historical Amount
Year 1	
April 21	$ 1,008
May 3	4,651
September 29	155
December 4	1,783
Year 2	
March 18	$ 1,271[†]
July 12	6,271[†]
August 15	7,119[†]
November 1	13,208[†]
Year 3	
February 8	$ 5,189
May 17	7,834
July 27	2,100[††]
August 4	15,000[††]
December 19	12,830
Year 4	
January 2	$ 6,782
January 9	21,425
April 22	4,483
June 10	9,059
June 14	4,224
October 23	35,508

[†] Originally omitted from listing by Accounting Department.
[††] Upon further inquiry, these two reported amounts proved to be estimates that should have been $3,774 and $12,295, respectively.

A risk management professional must rely on personal insight and judgment to recognize when crucial data are missing. For example, when Wheeler's risk management consultant first examined the accounting department's report, he found that the report did not show any machinery damage or breakdown for Year 2. The losses whose amounts are marked with a single dagger in Exhibit 9-1 were omitted from the original report. Because such losses had occurred in each of the other three years, it seemed reasonable to ask accounting to verify that machinery-related losses had occurred in Year 2.

After checking, accounting found that the clerk who had been recording these machinery losses for Wheeler's during Year 1 had been replaced in Year 2 with a new clerk who had not been aware of the need to post this type of loss to the summary account, which was the basis of the risk management professional's report. Through insight and a cooperative spirit, needed data were obtained.

Consistent Data

To reflect past patterns, loss data must be consistent in at least two respects. First, the loss data must be collected on a consistent basis for all recorded losses. Second, to adjust for differences in price levels, all losses must be expressed in constant dollars, which, for Wheeler's in early Year 5, might well have been Year 4 dollars.

Consistent Basis for Data Collection

Loss data might hide patterns useful in forecasting future losses. If the loss data are collected from different sources using different techniques, the possible sources of inconsistency are numerous. For example, in examining the amounts in the "Historical Amount" column of Exhibit 9-1, Wheeler's risk management consultant noticed that two losses, those whose amounts are marked with double daggers, were reported in even hundreds of dollars.

Although a dollar amount ending in "00" or "000" is just as likely as an amount ending in any other two or three digits, a risk management professional should be aware of the common tendency to use approximate, round numbers—numbers that might not be as accurate as others. An inquiry to accounting revealed that these double-dagger amounts were estimates, made either by Wheeler's machinery maintenance department or by the supervisor on duty at the time of the accident. Therefore, while not to be ignored, these amounts are likely to be less credible than the other loss figures in Exhibit 9-1.

To make these two estimates more useful in forecasting future losses, Wheeler's risk management consultant asked for the property, revenue, and extra expense consequences resulting directly from these two incidents. Thus reconstructed to be consistent with the other data, these amounts were changed from $2,100 to $3,774 and from $15,000 to $12,925. These revised figures are used in all subsequent calculations involving these two losses.

Amounts of Loss Adjusted for Price Level Changes

Property damage and reductions in net income, like all other losses expressed in historical amounts, should be adjusted (or indexed) for price level changes. Otherwise, the reported amounts of two physically identical losses occurring in different years probably will be different. Inflation will make the later loss appear larger because it is measured in less valuable dollars. To prevent this distortion, the loss data must express all losses in constant dollars. A **constant dollar** is a measure of value that remains unchanged despite changes in price level. In standard practice, the price level for the most recent complete year—in this case, Year 4—is used for expressing all losses in constant dollars.

For example, the value of a Year 1 loss would have to be increased to reflect the change in the relevant price index since Year 1. A **price index** is the ratio of the current price of some goods or services expressed as a decimal fraction of the price of comparable goods or services in some earlier base time. It is necessary to "inflate" the historical amounts of all past losses to current (Year 4) levels by multiplying the historical amount of each loss in a given year by an indexing factor appropriate for that year. The **indexing factor** appropriate for a given year is equal to the price level in that given year divided by the price level in some base year. For instance, the indexing factor to bring Year 1 losses up to Year 4 price levels is computed as follows:

$$\text{Indexing factor (Year 4)} \; = \; \frac{\text{Current (Year 4) price index}}{\text{Price index for a given year (Year 1)}}$$

The best approach to indexing past losses is to apply separate inflators to each element of cost in each loss—for example, separate indexes for machinery replacement costs and overtime wage rates. With a suitable price index, indexing mechanics are straightforward. Exhibit 9-2 shows how an appropriate indexing factor for each year should be computed. Because the price index stood at 115.2 in Year 1 and at 148.6 in Year 4, Year 1 losses should be multiplied by the ratio of 148.6/115.2 (yielding an index of 1.29). Similarly, computing the indexing factors for other years involves dividing the Year 4 price index by the price index for each year (shown in the second column of Exhibit 9-2). This results in the following factors: 1.18 for Year 2 losses, 1.06 for Year 3 losses, and 1.00 for Year 4 losses (historical and constant dollars being the same in Year 4).

Exhibit 9-2
Indexing Factors for Losses to Year 4 "Current Dollars"

Year	Price Index $(P_{\text{Year }0} = 100)$	Indexing Factors Computed as	Figure
1	115.2	P_4/P_1	1.29
2	125.9	P_4/P_2	1.18
3	140.2	P_4/P_3	1.06
4	148.6	P_4/P_4	1.00

Exhibit 9-3 shows both the historical and adjusted amounts for each loss. The adjusted amount of each loss has been computed by a two-step process: (1) multiply each loss by the indexing factor for the year in which the loss occurred and (2) round the result to the nearest $100 to simplify later calculations. The gain in simplicity is well worth the slight loss of precision through rounding.

To illustrate, the first loss in Exhibit 9-3 (or in Exhibit 9-1) had a historical value of $1,008 on April 21 of Year 1. When multiplied by the Year 1 indexing factor of 1.29, the adjusted amount of this loss becomes $1,300.32. After rounding to the nearest $100, the loss becomes $1,300, shown in the "Adjusted Amount" column of Exhibit 9-3. Similarly, the November 1 Year 2 loss, with a historical value of $13,208, adjusts to $15,600.

Those calculations involve some assumptions about the timing of losses, which, while customary, are somewhat arbitrary, and thus should be carefully noted. For the year in which a loss occurs, adjusting its historical amount by the full rate of inflation during that year is technically correct only if it is assumed that the loss occurred on the last day of the year. Otherwise, if the loss is assumed to have occurred sometime earlier during that year, only a portion of the entire price level change during that year should be used to adjust the historical loss figure to adjust it to the price level existing at the end of the year in which the loss occurred.

A reasonable, more realistic assumption would be that all losses occur in the middle of the year and that only half of that year's inflation rate would bring those losses to year-end price levels. Even this assumption is realistic only if it can be further assumed that the rate of change (increase or decrease) in prices was uniform throughout the year. Thus, if the inflation rate during Year 3 were 6 percent, some additional accuracy could be gained by inflating these losses by only 3 percent (instead of 6 percent) to bring losses up to price levels existing at the beginning of Year 4 on the assumption that these losses presumably occurred in mid-Year 3.

Exhibit 9-3

Adjustment of Historical Losses to Year 4 Price Levels

Date	Historical Amount	Adjusted Amount	Annual Total	Annual Number
		Year 1		
April 21	$ 1,008	$ 1,300		
May 3	4,651	6,000		
September 29	155	200		
December 4	1,783	2,300	$ 9,800	4
		Year 2		
March 18	$ 1,271	$ 1,500		
July 12	6,271	7,400		
August 15	7,119	8,400		
November 1	13,208	15,600	$ 32,900	4
		Year 3		
February 8	$ 5,189	$ 5,500		
May 17	7,834	8,300		
July 27	3,774	4,000		
August 4	12,925	13,700		
December 19	2,830	13,600	$ 45,100	5
		Year 4		
January 2	$ 6,782	$ 6,800		
January 9	21,425	21,400		
April 22	4,483	4,500		
June 10	9,059	9,100		
June 14	4,224	4,200		
October 23	35,508	35,500	$ 81,500	6
		Total	$169,300	Arithmetic Mean
			$ 8,911	(Total/19)

Arithmetic mean amount of losses $169,300/19 = $8,911

Arithmetic mean number of losses 19/4 = 4.75

However, because additional accuracy is gained only if the rate of price change was uniform throughout the year (for example, one-half of 1 percent during each month of Year 3) and because this approach is rarely used when only annual price index figures are available, this discussion follows the more usual practice of applying all indexing factors on an annual, rather than a semiannual, basis. If monthly price index figures are available, improved accuracy could be gained by applying this indexing procedure on a monthly basis, starting with the month in which each loss occurred.

Relevant Data

The amounts of past losses should be valued on the basis most relevant to risk management—usually the cost to the organization of restoring the loss. For property losses, these **relevant data** are the repair or replacement cost of the property at the time it is to be restored, not the property's historical "book" value. For liability losses, the loss should include not only any claims paid but also the cost of investigating and defending or settling the claim. Both personnel and net income losses must include not only reductions in revenue from any disruption of operations but also any additional expenses that an organization incurs while trying to return the business to normalcy.

For Wheeler's machinery damage and breakdown losses, the risk management consultant was happy to learn that the values reported by accounting covered the full amounts of these property and net income losses, including the then current repair or replacement cost of the machinery involved, and the estimates of Wheeler's revenue and extra expense losses stemming from these machinery losses (again, expressed in historical dollars). Thus, once adjusted for inflation, the amounts provided by accounting were, in this fortunate case, appropriate for risk management. Had the data not been appropriate, the risk management consultant probably would have had to confer with experts in accounting, statistics, and tire recycling to value these losses properly or to make adjustments for any machinery-related losses that had to be omitted because they could not be properly valued.

Organized Data

Listing losses by calendar dates, as in Exhibits 9-1 and 9-3, may fail to disclose patterns that could be revealed by listing losses by size. An **array** of losses—amounts of losses listed in increasing or decreasing value—might reveal clusterings of losses by severity and also might focus attention on large losses, which are often the most important in making risk management decisions. Organizing losses is the first step in charting losses by size to develop loss severity distributions or loss trends over time.

An array of the nineteen major machinery damage or breakdown losses that Wheeler's suffered in Year 1 through Year 4 appears in Exhibit 9-4. The third column from the left is the adjusted amounts, with the other columns showing the dates, historical (unadjusted) amounts, and the rank of each arrayed loss. Notice that the numbers in the far right-hand column, "Rank," of Exhibit 9-4 are arranged so that the largest loss, presumably the most important, has a rank of "1" (first), while the smallest loss has a rank of "19" (last). Finally, notice that ranking losses by adjusted price-indexed amounts rather than historical amounts eliminates distortions caused by mere price level changes and is therefore more useful in identifying the true effect of each loss.

Exhibit 9-4
Array of Historical and Adjusted Losses

Date	Historical Amount	Adjusted Amount	Rank
September 29, Year 1	$ 155	$ 200	19
April 21, Year 1	1,008	1,300	18
March 18, Year 2	1,271	1,500	17
December 4, Year 1	1,783	2,300	16
July 27, Year 3	3,774	4,000	15
June 14, Year 4	4,224	4,200	14
April 22, Year 4	4,483	4,500	13
February 8, Year 3	5,189[†]	5,500	12
May 3, Year 1	4,651	6,000	11
January 2, Year 4	6,782[†]	6,800	10
July 12, Year 2	6,271	7,400	9
May 17, Year 3	7,834[†]	8,300	8
August 15, Year 2	7,119	8,400	7
June 10, Year 4	9,059	9,100	6
December 19, Year 3	12,830	13,600	5
August 4, Year 3	12,925	13,700	4
November 1, Year 2	13,208	15,600	3
January 9, Year 4	21,425	21,400	2
October 23, Year 4	35,508	35,500	1

[†] Loss for which adjustment of historical amount to Year 4 constant dollars changes ranking in array

Thus adjusted and organized, historical loss data provide an important basis for forecasting future losses. The following discussion explains how to make such forecasts, first by using probability analysis (of a presumably unchanging world) and then by using trend analysis (of a presumably changing world, but changing in a predictable manner).

Probability Analysis

> *How is probability analysis used to predict future accidental losses?*
>
> *What are some of the sources of probability data?*

Probability analysis is a technique for forecasting future events, such as accidental and business losses, on the assumption that these events are governed by an unchanging probability distribution. Probability analysis is particularly effective for predicting future accidental losses in organizations that (1) have a substantial volume of data on past losses and (2) have fairly stable operations so that (except for price level changes) patterns of past losses presumably will continue in the future. In such an unchanging environment, past losses can be viewed as a sample of all possible losses that the organization might suffer in the future. The larger this sample of losses and the more stable the environment that produces those losses, the more reliable will be the forecasts of future losses.

The Nature of Probability

Probability is the relative frequency with which an event can be expected to occur in the long run in a stable environment. For example, given many tosses, a coin can be expected to come up heads as often as it comes up tails. Given many rolls of one die from a pair of dice, a 4 can be expected to come up one-sixth of the time. According to one standard mortality table, slightly over 2 percent of males aged sixty-two can be expected to die before reaching age sixty-three.[1] Finally, of the many automobiles now on the road, insurance company statistics in 1993 indicated that 1 out of every 127 could be expected to be stolen within the year.[2]

Any probability can be expressed as a fraction, percent, or percentage. The probability of a head on a coin toss can be expressed as 1/2, 50 percent, or 0.50. The probability of a 4 on one roll of one die can be written as 1/6, 16.66 percent, or 0.167. Similarly, 1/127, 0.787 percent, and 0.00787 are all proper ways of indicating the probability that a particular automobile would be stolen during 1993.

The probability of an event that is totally impossible is 0, the probability of an absolutely certain event is 1.0, and the probabilities of all events that are neither totally impossible nor absolutely certain are greater than 0 but less than 1.0.

Probabilities can be developed either from historical data or from theoretical considerations. Probabilities associated with coin tosses or dice throws can be developed theoretically and are totally unchanging. From a description of a fair coin or die, a person who has never seen either of them could calculate the probability of, say, a head or a 4. Such probabilities are known as **theoretical probabilities** because they are based on theoretical principles rather than on actual experience.

[handwritten note: ROLLING A DIE]

In contrast, the empirical probability that a sixty-two-year-old male will die or that a particular car will be stolen during a particular year cannot be deduced theoretically but must be estimated by studying the loss experience of a sample of men aged sixty-two or a sample of cars. The **empirical probabilities** deduced solely from historical data might change as new data are discovered or as the environment that produces these events changes. In contrast to theoretical probabilities, empirical probabilities are only estimates whose accuracy depends on the size and representatives of the samples being studied. Moreover, empirical probabilities can change, whereas *theoretical* probabilities are constant as long as the physical conditions that generate them remain unchanged. For example, the same source cited above indicating that in 1993, 1 vehicle in 127 could expect to be stolen within the year also reported that in 1970, this ratio was 1 in 121.

[handwritten note: ESTABLISH BASED OLD DATA]

Sources of Probability Data

Risk management professionals often have significant difficulty developing data on probability distributions of accidental losses. The organization's own loss data often are not substantial enough to be reliable, and the data on the combined experience of other organizations, if available at all, frequently are not sufficiently specific or current to be particularly useful.

Therefore, although probability analysis is an important forecasting tool, most probabilities of particular types of losses are, at best, estimates based on a number of sources: the organization's own loss experience; loss experience of similar organizations; and perhaps nationwide loss experience from insurance companies, insurance rating organizations, or such organizations as the National Safety Council, the National Fire Protection Association, or (for Wheeler's) the National Tire Dealers and Retreaders Association. Because the underlying chances of loss are empirical probabilities that must be estimated and are subject to change, a risk management professional must pay close attention to the sources of loss data.

Constructing Probability Distributions

A **probability distribution** is a presentation, in a table or in a graph, of all possible outcomes of a particular set of circumstances and of the probability of each possible outcome. Because every such distribution includes the probability of every possible outcome, making it certain that one of these outcomes—and only one—will occur, the sum of the probabilities in a probability distribution *must* be 1.0.

This definition of a probability distribution applies to both *theoretical* probabilities (such as those involved in tossing coins or rolling dice) and empirical probabilities (such as of the number or size of accidental losses). For example, in flipping a fair coin, each of the two possible outcomes, heads or tails, has an equal probability of one-half, or 50 percent. Since, on a particular flip of a coin, only one outcome is possible, these outcomes are described as **mutually exclusive**. Similarly, since these two outcomes are the only possible results and therefore exhaust all possibilities, they are said to be **collectively exhaustive**. A properly constructed probability distribution always contains outcomes that are both mutually exclusive and collectively exhaustive.

A chart and diagram of the probability distribution of the outcomes of a single flip of a fair coin appear in Exhibit 9-5. Note that the sum of the probabilities, in both the chart and the diagram, is 1.0, and that both the chart and the diagram include all possible outcomes. By using these formats and by keeping in mind that all valid probability distributions contain events that are mutually exclusive and collectively exhaustive, one can chart and diagram other probability distributions.

Exhibit 9-5
Probability Distribution for One Coin Toss

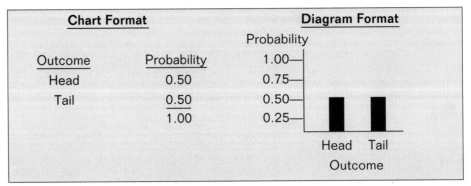

Consider now a slightly more complex probability distribution: a distribution of the total number of points on one throw of two dice, one red and one green. The thirty-six equally likely outcomes (green 1, red 1; green 1, red 2; . . . green 6, red 6)

Exhibit 9-6
Probability Distribution of Total Points on One Roll of Two Dice

(a)

Table of Outcomes

Red Die

G r e e n D i e		1	2	3	4	5	6
	1	2	3	4	5	6	7
	2	3	4	5	6	7	8
	3	4	5	6	7	8	9
	4	5	6	7	8	9	10
	5	6	7	8	9	10	11
	6	7	8	9	10	11	12

$5 \times : 36$

(b)

Chart Format

Total Points— Both Dice		Probability		
2	1/36	or	0.028	or	2.8%
3	2/36	or	0.056	or	5.6%
4	3/36	or	0.083	or	8.3%
5	4/36	or	0.111	or	11.1%
6	5/36	or	0.139	or	13.9%
7	6/36	or	0.167	or	16.7%
8	5/36	or	0.139	or	13.9%
9	4/36	or	0.111	or	11.1%
10	3/36	or	0.083	or	8.3%
11	2/36	or	0.056	or	5.6%
12	1/36	or	0.028	or	2.8%
Total	36/36	or	1.001[†]	or	100.1%[†]

[†] Separate probabilities do not add to 1.000 or 100.0% because of rounding.

(c)

Diagram Format

Probability

Total Points

are shown in Exhibit 9-6. Eleven outcomes are possible (ranging from a total of two points to a total of twelve points), and the probability of each of these eleven possible outcomes is proportional to the number of times each point value appears in the table of outcomes. As the chart indicates, the probability of a total of two points is 1/36 because only one of the thirty-six possible ways that the dice might fall (green 1, red 1) produces a total of two points. Similarly, 1/36 is the probability of a total of twelve points. The most likely total point value, seven points, has a probability of 6/36, represented in the table of outcomes by the diagonal southwest-northeast row of sevens.

In the diagram showing each possible outcome, the height of the vertical line above each outcome is proportional to the probability of that outcome. Exhibit 9-6 presents three views of a complete probability distribution: all possible outcomes are accounted for (they are collectively exhaustive), and the occurrence of any possible outcome (such as green 1, red 1, or alternatively, a point total of 4) makes impossible (or excludes) any other outcome.

Tossing coins and rolling dice involve theoretical probabilities that are readily apparent to most people familiar with these devices. Empirical probabilities derived from experience follow the same rules as the distributions of theoretical probabilities. For example, the data on loss size in Exhibit 9-7 include in Column 3 a probability distribution of the sizes of Wheeler's machinery damage and breakdown property and net income losses based on its Year 1—Year 4 loss experience. Given the array of losses by size in Exhibit 9-4, one can group these losses into the size categories presented in Column 1 of Exhibit 9-7 (or into any other convenient size categories) and determine by count, shown in Column 2, how many losses fall into each category. Given nineteen losses over four years, the probability of losses in each category is computed by dividing the number of losses in that category by nineteen. The sum of the resulting decimal fractions is 1.000, with any given loss falling into only one category. Thus, the probability distribution in Column 3 of Exhibit 9-7 meets the requirements of including outcomes that are both mutually exclusive and collectively exhaustive.

Columns 4 and 5 of Exhibit 9-7 present some additional information that a risk management professional may develop to supplement the probability distribution in Column 3. Each dollar amount in Column 4 shows the total of the losses in the size category in Column 1. The adjusted amounts of these losses, which total $169,300, are taken from Exhibit 9-3. Column 5 of Exhibit 9-7 expresses the dollar amounts in Column 4 as percentages of this $169,300 total.

Columns 4 and 5 show that, although large dollar losses are individually infrequent, they usually account for the bulk of the dollar total of losses. For example, the three losses that are greater than $10,000 but less than $20,000 total

Exhibit 9-7
Probability Distribution of Loss Severity Developed From
Wheeler's Tire Disposal 1991-1994 Machinery Losses

(1) Size Category	(2) Number of Losses	(3) Percentage of Number of Losses	(4) Amount of Losses ($\times$ 1,000)	(5) Percentage of Dollars in Category
>$0 but not > $1,000	1	5.26	$ 0.2	0.12
>$1,000 but not > $5,000	6	31.58	17.8	10.51
>$5,000 but not > $10,000	7	36.84	51.5	30.42
>$10,000 but not > $20,000	3	15.79	42.9	25.34
>$20,000 but not > $30,000	1	5.26	21.4	12.60
>$30,000	1	5.26	35.5	20.97
	19	100.00	$169.3[†]	100.00

[†] This total, $169,300, is also the sum of the four amounts shown in the "Annual Total" column of Exhibit 9-3.

$42,900, or about 25 percent of the total dollar amount of losses. The five losses that exceed $10,000 total $99,800, about 59 percent of the total dollar volume of machinery losses.

The probability distribution of these machinery loss sizes in Column 3 differs in two ways from the probability distributions of coin tosses and dice rolls developed earlier. First, the outcomes shown in Column 1, size categories of losses, are somewhat arbitrary and are not as self-evident as the heads/tails outcomes in tossing coins or the two through twelve total point scores in rolling two dice. Second, the highest possible dice total is twelve, while the highest size category of machinery losses, "> $30,000," (read as "greater than $30,000") is open-ended, with no evident upper limit.

Having more losses generates a more complete and reliable probability distribution only if these added losses permit better use of the law of large numbers. Developed by eighteenth-century mathematicians and perhaps more aptly labeled "the stability of statistical frequencies" by the British economist John Maynard Keynes, the **law of large numbers** applies, under certain circumstances, to events that can have several outcomes. The law states the following:

> As the number of independent events increases, the actual relative frequency (percentage) of each of the possible outcomes more nearly approaches the theoretically expected relative frequency (percentage) of that outcome.

To understand that the law of large numbers applies to relative (or percentage) differences between actual and theoretically predicted results—not absolute differences between actual and forecasted results—consider an example involving multiple throws of two dice. Suppose the objective (or a "success") is to roll a total of 9 points on a given throw of these dice. Exhibit 9-6 shows that the theoretical probability of this result is 4/36, or 0.11. Therefore, theoretically, 100 rolls of these dice should yield 11 outcomes of 9 points. In practice, however, throwing these dice 100 times might yield only 8 outcomes of 9 points. Here, the absolute difference between the expected 11 "successes" and the actual 8 "successes" is 3, or 27.3 percent, computed as (11-8)/11.

In contrast, suppose, in another trial of throwing these dice 1,000 times, in which the theoretically expected number of 9-point outcomes would be 111, that the actual number of "successes" is 95. In this second, larger trial, the absolute difference between the expected 111 and the actual 95 "successes" is 16, larger than before. However, the percentage difference between the actual and the expected result is smaller with the larger number of throws: only 14.4 percent, computed as (111-95)/111. The law of large numbers holds that this will tend to be the general case: As the number of trials increases, the percentage (or relative) difference between actual and expected results decreases. In risk management settings, trials can be exposure units, losses, time periods (such as days, months, or years), or other units that are essentially similar to one another.

The law of large numbers applies to forecasts of future events only when the events whose outcomes are being forecast meet all three of the following criteria:

1. The events have occurred in the past under substantially identical conditions and have resulted from unchanging, basic causal forces.

2. The events can be expected to occur in the future under the same, unchanging conditions.

3. The events have been, and will continue to be, both independent of one another and sufficiently numerous.

With accidental losses, the law of large numbers—when it can be applied—implies that, as the number of losses increases, the actual relative frequency of losses (as a percentage of units exposed to loss) more nearly approaches the theoretically expected relative frequency of losses. Note that this law becomes more meaningful as the number of *losses*, not the number of exposure units suffering no losses, increases. Similarly, the distribution of the size of losses also more nearly approaches the theoretically expected loss severity distribution. For the law to apply to forecasts of future losses, both the past losses on which the forecast is based and the future losses that it projects must have struck exposure units that *have been* and *will remain* (1) essentially identical, involving comparable values exposed to comparable hazards and (2) numerous and independent so that no one occurrence of a peril can simultaneously strike a substantial percentage of exposure units.

The real world meets these conditions only in degree, usually partially, but rarely wholly. When gathering data on past losses to use in forecasting future losses, a risk management professional should have data that reflect circumstances closely approaching those two conditions. In short, the more losses that enter into a forecast—if drawn from a large number of substantially identical, independent exposures comparable to future exposures—the more reliable is the resulting forecast of future losses.

Characteristics of Probability Distributions

One important characteristic of all probability distributions has already been noted: every distribution must assign relative frequencies to all possible outcomes of a particular event. No possible outcome can be omitted; consequently, the probabilities in a valid probability distribution must be mutually exclusive and collectively exhaustive.

Probability distributions also are described in terms of three additional characteristics: skewness, central tendency, and dispersion.

Skewness

Skewness pertains to whether a probability distribution is balanced, or symmetrical, with a hump located in the center of its range, or whether the hump is located to one side (left or right) of its range, with a long, thin tail extending to the other side. A probability of distribution is **symmetrical** if its left half is the mirror image of its right half when the distribution is "folded" at its midpoint on its horizontal axis.

The Three General Possibilities

There are three general possibilities with respect to skewness. First, a balanced, or symmetrical, distribution has no skewness. The hump in such a distribution, showing the most likely outcomes, is in the center. Therefore, the probabilities of less likely outcomes decline at the same rate on both sides of this central value in the distribution. The diagram in Exhibit 9-6 of a probability distribution of the total points on a single roll of two dice illustrates such a symmetrical distribution. This symmetrical distribution is one of the three general possibilities shown in Exhibit 9-8.

Notice the curves shown in Exhibit 9-8 differ from the vertical lines depicted in Exhibit 9-6. The curves in Exhibit 9-8 are created by joining with a smooth (not jagged) curve the tops of the vertical lines in the previous exhibits so that the

Exhibit 9-8
Typical Shapes of Symmetrical and Skewed Distributions
Showing Relative Locations of Mean, Median, and Mode

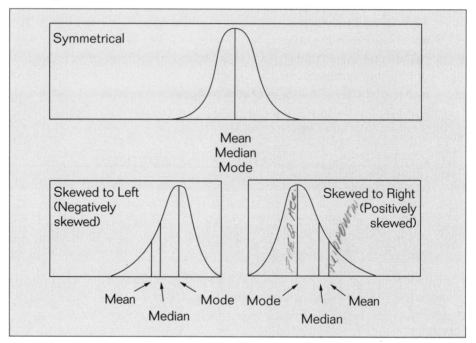

height of the curve indicates the probabilities of various outcomes. In this format, the area under the probability curve, representing a summation of all the probabilities of all the possible outcomes, totals 1.0.

The second general possibility is negative skewness. In a **negatively skewed** probability distribution, the outcome with the highest probability is above the center of the range of outcomes covered in that distribution, and the thin tail of low probability outcomes extends to the left. Although relatively rare in risk management, such distributions could apply to unprotected properties where, for example, most losses caused by fire, explosion, or flood are generally presumed to be total rather than partial. For such perils, a probability distribution of loss size to an unprotected property might follow the general shape of the negatively skewed distribution shown in Exhibit 9-8.

The third general possibility is a **positively skewed** distribution, in which the most frequent outcome is below (to the left of) the center of the range of the distribution, and the relatively long tail (indicating low probabilities) extends to the high values in the distribution. For example, with protected properties, a distribution of loss size by fire, theft, or flood is generally presumed to follow the shape of the positively skewed distribution in Exhibit 9-8 because small losses tend to be more frequent than large ones.

Skewed probability distributions are sometimes described by the direction in which their tails point. Thus, a distribution that is "skewed right" is a positively skewed distribution, while a distribution that is "skewed left" is a negatively skewed distribution.

The Special Case of the "Normal" Distribution

A special kind of symmetrical distribution is often called the **normal distribution**. This particular probability distribution applies to many physical phenomena that involve chance variations around some central, average, or expected value. The normal distribution applies to many real-world situations when the number of separate events is large and the factors that influence each separate outcome remain unchanged.

As an example for Wheeler's scrap tire recycling activities, the six large ovens used at Wheeler's three facilities to liquefy and extract useable rubber from tires are heated by a total of 600 electrical elements. The reliable useful life of each element is limited, and an element used too long poses a substantial danger of exploding, starting an electrical fire—fueled by flying droplets of super-heated rubber—that could cause a serious fire loss for Wheeler at that entire facility.

Suppose, for example, that the average life of such an electric heating element is 5,000 hours. Although 5,000 might be a valid average, some elements will become hazardous at 4,500 hours, some at 5,500 hours, and still others earlier or later. Because a normal probability distribution applies, however, the deviations around the 5,000-hour average life will be symmetrically distributed around this average in a predictable pattern.

In more precise terminology, the actual life of a given heating element in one of Wheeler's ovens is normally distributed around the 5,000-hour average or expected value. Fortunately for fire safety at each of Wheeler's facilities, the characteristics of the normal probability distribution provide a way of scheduling oven maintenance so that the likelihood of an element becoming very dangerous before it is replaced can be kept below any margin of safety that Wheeler's wants to specify. To see how this can be done, one must first understand more about the other two characteristics of all probability distributions: central tendency and dispersion.

Central Tendency

The **central tendency** of a probability distribution is the single outcome within the distribution that, in some sense, is the most representative of all possible outcomes. Many probability distributions cluster around a particular value, which might or might not be in the exact center of the range of values in the distribution. This central value is often used as the most representative of the outcomes included within the distribution. The three most widely accepted ways of identifying this most representative outcome are the arithmetic mean, the median, and the mode. For any particular distribution, the relationship of these points to one another and to the hump of the distribution depends on the distribution's skewness.

The Arithmetic Mean

The **arithmetic mean** of a distribution is a more precise name for the common **average**, which is the sum of the values in the distribution divided by the number of values. For example, the arithmetic mean for the annual number of machinery losses that Wheeler's suffered in Friendship City between Year 1 and Year 4 is the sum of 4 losses in Year 1, plus 4 losses in Year 2, plus 5 losses in Year 3, plus 6 losses in Year 4—the entire total of 19 being divided by 4 to compute the arithmetic mean of 4.75 losses per year. Most authors use the term "mean" by itself as shorthand for "arithmetic mean." (An equivalent term is **expected value.**)

Any series of numbers can be averaged. For example, the data in Exhibit 9-3 show that the average adjusted dollar amount of the five machinery losses that Wheeler's suffered in Friendship City in Year 3 was $9,020 ($5,500 + $8,300 + $4,000 + $13,700 + $13,600 = $45,100/5 = $9,020). Similarly, the average adjusted amount of each machinery loss over all four years was, to the nearest dollar, $8,911 (computed as $9,800 + $32,900 + $45,100 + $81,500 = $169,300/ 19 = $8,911).

The procedure for calculating the arithmetic mean of a probability distribution is only slightly more complex than the above procedure for calculating the arithmetic mean of any series of numbers. For a probability distribution, the only difference is that, instead of dividing by the number of values, each value in the distribution is multiplied by its respective probability to obtain a product, and the sum of these products is the mean of the distribution. In other words, each value in the distribution is weighted by its probability, and the arithmetic mean of the distribution is the weighted average.

Thus, if the values in the probability distribution are symbolized as $X_1, X_2, X_3, \ldots X_n$ (X_n represents the last value in the series), having respective probabilities of $p_1, p_2, p_3, \ldots p_n$, the arithmetic mean, or expected value, of the distribution is the sum of $(p_1 X_1) + (p_2 X_2) + (p_3 X_3) + \ldots (p_n X_n)$. For the dice example, the arithmetic mean of the distribution could be computed as shown in Exhibit 9-9. This

Exhibit 9-9
Computing the Mean (Expected Value) of a Probability Distribution—
the Example of Two Dice

(1) Points (X)	(2) Probability (p)	(3) Col. (1) × Col. (2) (pX)
2	1/36	2/36
3	2/36	6/36
4	3/36	12/36
5	4/36	20/36
6	5/36	30/36
7	6/36	42/36
8	5/36	40/36
9	4/36	36/36
10	3/36	30/36
11	2/36	22/36
12	1/36	12/36
Totals:	36/36	252/36

Arithmetic Mean = 252/36 = 7.0

procedure for calculating an arithmetic mean applies to all probability distributions regardless of their skewness or dispersion.

Median and Cumulative Probabilities

The **median** of a series of numbers or of a probability distribution is the "value in the middle," the value for which the number of lower observations or outcomes equals the number of higher observations or outcomes. Thus, in the array of nineteen losses in Exhibit 9-4, the median loss has an adjusted amount of $6,800. This tenth loss (counting from either the top or the bottom of the array) is the median because nine losses are smaller and nine losses are larger. For the five Year 3 losses in Exhibit 9-3, the median loss is $8,300. Inspection of the exhibit shows that two losses are smaller and two are larger.

When the number of observations or outcomes is an even number, the median is the arithmetic average of the middle two observations or outcomes. Thus, among the four Year 2 losses in Exhibit 9-3, the median is the mean of $7,400 and $8,400, or $7,900. This is true for the median of any even number of outcomes, even if two or more of them are the same. For example, for the six Year 4 losses shown in Exhibit 9-3, the median is the average of the third and fourth losses *when they have been arrayed by size, not when listed chronologically*. The fourth and fifth losses in this array are $6,800 and $9,100, so the median of all six Year 4 losses is $7,950, computed as ($6,800 + $9,100)/2. If two or more of these six losses had been the same, such as if the $21,400 loss had instead also been $9,100, the median still would have been computed as ($6,800 + $9,100)/2 or $7,950.

The median of a probability distribution is again the "value in the middle," the value for which the total probability of all higher observations is equal to the total probability of all lower observations. This median value can be found by summing the cumulative probabilities in the distribution to find the value for which a cumulative probability of 50 percent is reached. For example, 7 is the median of the probability distribution of points in rolling two dice because 7 is the only number of points for which the probability of higher observations (15/36) is equal to the probability of lower observations. That is, there are fifteen equally probable ways of getting a result higher than 7, and fifteen equally probable ways of getting a result lower than 7.

This same result can be confirmed by cumulating the probabilities of outcomes equal to or less than a given number of points in rolling two dice, as in Exhibit 9-10. The cumulative 50 percent probability (18/36) is reached with 7 points (actually, in the middle of the 7-point class of results). Therefore, 7 is the median of this distribution.

The cumulative probabilities in Column 3 of Exhibit 9-10 indicate the probability of a roll yielding a certain number of points or less. For example, the probability of rolling a 3 or less is 3/36 (or the sum of 1/36 for rolling a 2 plus 2/36 for rolling a 3). Similarly, the probability of rolling a 10 or less is 33/36, computed by adding the individual Column 2 probabilities of outcomes of 10 points or less. When one works with probability distributions of losses, computing probabilities of losses equal to or less than a given number of losses or dollar amounts of losses, individually and cumulatively, can be helpful in selecting retention levels. Similarly, computing individual and cumulative probabilities of losses equal to or greater than a given number of losses or dollar amounts can help in selecting upper limits of insurance coverage.

Exhibit 9-11 shows how to derive a **cumulative probability distribution** of loss sizes from the individual probabilities of loss size in Exhibit 9-7. Column 3 indicates that, on the basis of the available data, 5.26 percent of all losses are less than $1,000 and that another 31.58 percent are greater than $1,000 but less than $5,000. Thus, the probabilities of a loss being $5,000 or less is the sum of these two probabilities, or 36.84 percent as shown in Column 3. Similarly, as shown in Column 5, losses of $5,000 or less can be expected to account for 10.63 percent of the total dollar amount of all losses.

The cumulated probabilities in Column 3 indicate that the median individual loss is between $5,000 and $10,000, the category in which the 50 percent cumulative probability is reached. This result is consistent with the $6,800 median loss found earlier by inspection of Exhibit 9-4.

Beyond locating the median loss, Exhibit 9-7 and Exhibit 9-11 have some implications for risk management decisions. For example, if Wheeler's Tire Disposal were to insure its machinery losses subject to a $5,000 per accident deductible, the firm could expect to retain the full amount of more than one out of every three losses (36.84 percent of the number of losses in Column 3 of Exhibit 9-11). The firm would also retain the first $5,000 of every larger loss (an additional $60,000 for the twelve losses in Column 2 of Exhibit 9-7 that exceed $5,000). Thus, Wheeler's total expected annual retention of machinery losses with a $5,000 deductible would be the expected value of the full amount of all

Exhibit 9-10
Cumulative Probability Distribution of Total Points in Rolling Two Dice

(1) Number of Points (X)	(2) Probability ("p")	(3) Cumulative Probability (sum of "p"s)
2	1/36	1/36
3	2/36	= 3/36
4	3/36	= 6/36
5	4/36	= 10/36
6	5/36	= 15/36
7	6/36	= 21/36
8	5/36	= 26/36
9	4/36	= 30/36
10	3/36	= 33/36
11	2/36	= 35/36
12	1/36	= 36/36

The cumulative probability of rolling a 3 or less is 3/36, or the sum of 1/36 for rolling a 2 plus 2/36 for rolling a 3.

Exhibit 9-11
Cumulative Probabilities That Machinery Losses Will Not
Exceed Specified Amounts

(1) Size Category	(2) Percentage of Number in Category	(3) Cumulative Percentage of Number of Losses Not Exceeding Category	(4) Percentage of Value in Category	(5) Cumulative Percentage of Dollars of Loss Not Exceeding Category
> $0 but not > $1,000	5.26	5.26	0.12	0.12
> $1,000 but not > $5,000	31.58 + = 36.84	36.84	10.51	10.63
> $5,000 but not > $10,000	36.84 + = 73.68	73.68	30.42	41.05
> $10,000 but not > $20,000	15.79 + = 89.47	89.47	25.34	66.39
> $20,000 but not > $30,000	5.26 + = 94.73	94.73	12.64	79.03
> $30,000	5.26 + = 100.00	100.00	20.97	100.00
	100.00		100.00	

Column 3 indicates that, on the basis of the available data, 5.26 percent of all losses are less than $1,000 and that another 31.58 percent are greater than $1,000 but less than $5,000. The probabilities of a loss being $5,000 or less is the sum of these two probabilities, or 36.84 percent.

losses not exceeding $5,000 ($18,000, computed as $0.2 + $17.8, from Exhibit 9-7, Column 4, × 1,000) plus $60,000 ($5,000 × 12, the number of such larger losses from Exhibit 9-7, Column 2). This makes a total of $78,000. This expected retention would be about 46 percent of the $169,300 total of all of Wheeler's annual expected machinery losses. This is the amount that Wheeler's might budget annually for retained machinery losses or use as a comparison against an insurance premium credit for a $5,000 deductible.

If, on the other hand, Wheeler's were to adopt a $10,000 deductible, it could expect to retain the full amount of more than seven out of every ten losses (73.68 percent of the number of losses in Exhibit 9-11, Column 3), or from Exhibit 9-7, $119,500 of annual losses (consisting of the $69,500 full expected value of losses not exceeding $10,000 plus $10,000 for each of the five expected larger losses). This expected retention would be approximately 74 percent of the total amount of all expected machinery losses.

Mode

The **mode** of a distribution is the single value that is most likely to occur. With a distribution that has a single hump, the mode is the value of the outcome directly beneath the peak of that hump. In the distribution of total points of throws of two dice, the mode is seven points. In the distribution of the sizes of Wheeler's machinery losses, the mode falls within the largest size class (in Exhibit 9-7, Column 2, $5,000-$10,000, with seven losses). The fact that both the mode and the median fall in the same class does *not* imply that the mode and the median are the same dollar amount.

The actual array of Wheeler's adjusted machinery loss sizes (Exhibit 9-4) shows that, because no particular dollar amount of loss occurred more than once, no specific dollar amount can be said to be the mode. However, it is reasonable to assume that losses will occur more frequently in the $5,000-$10,000 size category. That is, this category will have more losses than will any other category.

In one sense, $0 or "no loss" is the most frequent *outcome* suggested by the four years' data on Wheeler's machinery losses. For any particular day, week, or month, the most frequent outcome is that there were no machinery losses. This is true in many risk management situations: "no loss" is the most frequent outcome. The mode, the mean, and the median of the machinery loss distribution are actually measures of the central tendency of *losses* rather than *outcomes* (both losses and no losses). Yet risk management focuses on accidental losses and how best to cope with them. Therefore, even though "no loss" is often the most likely single outcome, planning for "no loss" is poor risk management.

Relationships of Mean, Median, and Mode to Skewness

In a distribution that has only one hump (technically, a **unimodal distribution**), the direction of skewness determines the relative locations of its mean, median, and mode.

In a positively skewed distribution, the "long tail" extends to the right, and the three measures of central tendency are positioned in mode-median-mean order when reading from left to right. In a negatively skewed distribution, the "long tail" extends to the left and the three measures of central tendency are positioned in mean-median-mode order when reading from left to right.

Generally, the mode of a skewed unimodal distribution is at the hump of the distribution, the mean is the measure of central tendency most pulled by extremely high or low values toward the tail of the distribution, and the median typically falls between the mode and the mean.

In a symmetrical unimodal distribution, the mean, median, and mode typically have the same value.

Dispersion (Variability)

Dispersion, or **variability**, describes the extent to which the distribution is spread out rather than concentrated around a single outcome. It is the degree of variability from the mean of the distribution. The less the dispersion around the mean of a distribution, the greater the likelihood that actual results will fall within a given range of that mean. With less dispersion, there is less uncertainty involved in predicting that a result close to the mean actually will materialize.

There are two widely used measures of dispersion. One is the standard deviation of a distribution; the other is its coefficient of variation.

Standard Deviation

A **standard deviation** of a set of values is the square root of the average of the squared deviation of each value from the arithmetic mean of those values. A standard deviation is a special kind of average, an average of deviations (or differences) between individual, varied values and the arithmetic mean of those values.

The precise method for computing a standard deviation depends on whether the items are individual observations (such as the amounts of individual losses) or are the values within a probability distribution (like the probabilities of points in throwing two dice).

Following are the steps for calculating the standard deviation of a set of individual observations not involving probabilities:

1. Find the arithmetic mean of the observations (the sum of the observations divided by the number of observations).

2. Subtract the mean from each of the observations (with the result being positive for each observation larger than the mean, and negative for each observation smaller than the mean).

3. Square each of the resulting differences (the rules of algebra making all resulting squares positive).

4. Sum these squares.

5. Divide this sum by the number of observations minus one. (The answer to a division problem is called a quotient.)

6. Find the square root of the quotient. (The **square root** of any number is another number that when multiplied by itself equals the original number. For example, the square root of 16 is 4.)

Exhibit 9-12 shows how to apply this procedure to the adjusted dollar amounts of the four machinery losses at Wheeler's suffered in Year 2, with the amount of

Exhibit 9-12

Computing a Standard Deviation—Individual Observations

	(1) Loss (× 1,000)	(2) Deviation From Mean (X – M)	(3) Squared Deviation (X – M)²
1.	1.50 – 8.2 =	– 6.70	44.89
2.	7.40	– 0.80	0.64
3.	8.40	0.20	0.04
4	15.60	7.40	54.76
	32.90		100.33

(n = 4)

Mean = M = 32.9 ÷ 4 = 8.225, rounded to 8.2

S.D. = $\sqrt{\text{sum } (X - M)^2 / N - 1}$

= $\sqrt{100.33/3}$, or $\sqrt{33.44}$

= 5.78

each loss being expressed in thousands of dollars. This brief example demonstrates the procedure for computing the standard deviation of any number of observations of any size.

In Exhibit 9-12, Step 1 of finding the standard deviation requires dividing the total amount of the four losses in Column 1 by 4 to find the arithmetic mean loss, which, rounded, is 8.2. Step 2 is done in Column 2, which shows the result of subtracting this mean from each loss. Step 3, shown in Column 3, involves squaring each number in Column 2. Step 4 requires finding the total, 100.33, of the squared values in Column 3. Steps 4 and 5 appear at the bottom of the exhibit, where the standard deviation (S.D.) is computed by first dividing 100.33 by 3 (the number of observations, N, minus 1) to find the quotient (33.44) and then extracting the square root of this quotient.

For a probability distribution, in contrast to a set of observations, the comparable procedure for finding the standard deviation is as follows:

1. Find the expected value (or mean) of the distribution.
2. Subtract this expected value from each outcome included in the distribution.
3. Square each of the resulting differences.
4. Multiply each resulting square by the probability associated with the outcome for which the squared difference was computed in Step 3 (the answer to a multiplication problem is called a "product").

Exhibit 9-13

Computation of the Standard Deviation of a Probability Distribution—
the Example of Two Dice

(1) Points (X)	(2) Probability (p)	(3) (X – M)	(4) (X – M)^2	(5) p(X – M)^2		
2	1/36	– 5	25	(1/36)(25)	=	25/36
3	2/36	– 4	16	(2/36)(16)	=	32/36
4	3/36	– 3	9	(3/36)(9)	=	27/36
5	4/36	– 2	4	(4/36)(4)	=	16/36
6	5/36	– 1	1	(5/36)(1)	=	5/36
7	6/36	0	0	(6/36)(0)	=	0
8	5/36	+ 1	1	(5/36)(1)	=	5/36
9	4/36	+ 2	4	(4/36)(4)	=	16/36
10	3/36	+ 3	9	(3/36)(9)	=	27/36
11	2/36	+ 4	16	(2/36)(16)	=	32/36
12	1/36	+ 5	25	(1/36)(25)	=	25/36
						210/36

M   = mean of distribution = 7, previously computed

S.D. = $\sqrt{210/36}$

   = $\sqrt{5.83}$

   = 2.4 approximately

5. Sum the products.
6. Find the square root of the sum.

Exhibit 9-13 shows this procedure for the standard deviation of the points in rolling two dice. M, the mean of this distribution, was computed in Exhibit 9-9 to be 7 points. Column 3 of Exhibit 9-13 subtracts 7 from the values arrayed in Column 1, Column 4 squares the differences shown in Column 3, and Column 5 multiplies each of these differences by the probability of the respective number of points. The sum of the products in Column 5, 210/36, or 5.83, is the square of the standard deviation. Therefore, the standard deviation is approximately 2.4 points.

Exhibit 9-14 applies the same steps for computing a standard deviation to the probability distribution of the dollar amounts of Wheeler's machinery losses for Year 1 through Year 4. To compute the standard deviation of a probability distribution, however, one must know the mean of the probability distribution, which, for Wheeler's losses, is computed in Exhibit 9-14 from grouped data, comparable to the mean computed in Exhibit 9-3 from individual loss data. Exhibit 9-15 indicates the respective probabilities of the various sizes of loss. The

Exhibit 9-14
Calculation of Standard Deviation of Probability Distribution of the Size
of Machinery Losses

Size Category (X 1,000)	Midpoint (x)	Probability (p)	(X – M)	(X – M)²	p(X – M)²
> $0	0.5	0.0526	– 8.4	70.56	3.711
> $1.0	3.0	0.3158	– 5.9	34.81	10.993
> $5.0	7.5	0.3684	– 1.4	1.96	0.722
> $10.0	15.0	0.1579	6.1	37.21	5.875
> $20.0	25.0	0.0526	16.1	259.21	13.634
> $30.0	35.5[†]	0.0526	26.6	707.56	37.218
Totals:		100.0000			72.153

M = 8.9 (or $8,900), rounded from Exhibit 9-3.
[†] Arithmetic mean of losses in this open-ended class
S.D. = $\sqrt{72.153}$ = 8.494 (approx.), or $8,494

Exhibit 9-15
Calculation of Expected Value (Mean) of Probability Distribution of the Size
of a Machinery Loss

Size Category (x 1,000)	Midpoint X(x 1,000)	Probability (p)	(p)X
> $0 but not > $1	0.5	0.0526	0.0263
> $1 but not > $5	3.0	0.3158	0.9474
> $5 but not >$10	7.5	0.3684	2.7630
> $10 but not > $20	15.0	0.1579	2.3680
> $20 but not > $30	25.0	0.0526	1.3150
> $30	35.5[†]	0.0526	1.8673
			9.2870

Mean X = 9.287 (or $9,287), rounded

[†] Note: For an open-ended class, the class midpoint is assumed to be
the mean of the actual observations in this class.

procedures in Exhibits 9-14 (losses) and 9-13 (dice) are identical. However, the
possible different dollar amounts of accidental losses are much more numerous
(potentially unlimited) than the point values on two dice, and the probability
distribution is expressed in terms of categories of loss size, not precise dollar
amounts.

Exhibits 9-14 and 9-15 make two adjustments for differences in the underlying data: (1) all the losses in a given size category are assumed to equal the midpoint (x) of that class (for example, all losses greater than $1,000 up to $5,000 are assumed to be $3,000 in this calculation) and (2) the arithmetic mean of all of the actual losses in the open-ended size category "> $30,000" is used to represent the value of all losses in this top category. Exhibits 9-14 and 9-15 express all losses in thousands of dollars to simplify the calculations (for example, a $500 loss is expressed as $0.5).

With the adjustments just mentioned, Exhibit 9-14 computes the standard deviation of the size of Wheeler's machinery losses following the same steps as in Exhibit 9-13 to be approximately $8,494. The mean and standard deviation computed from the nineteen individual losses differ from the mean and standard deviation derived from the probability distribution because that distribution uses the midpoint of each size class to represent all losses in that size class. (The arithmetic mean used in calculating the standard deviation in Exhibit 9-14 has been rounded in thousands to $8.9—computed directly from the individual losses as explained under the previous heading, "The Arithmetic Mean"—not the $9.287 (or $9.3) in thousands computed in Exhibit 9-15 from the grouped loss data. A mean, or any other statistic that has been computed directly from individual data, can be expected to be more accurate than a mean computed from grouped data.)

Standard Deviation of a Normal Distribution

As indicated, the variability of many real-world events can be accurately forecast through a symmetrical probability distribution, which statisticians call a "normal distribution." Exhibit 9-16 illustrates the typical bell-shaped curve of a normal distribution. This diagram looks much like the previous diagram of a symmetrical probability distribution, but with one significant difference: the normal curve never touches the horizontal line at the base of the diagram. In theory, the normal distribution assigns some probability for every outcome regardless of its distance from the mean. The probability of a given outcome depends on the number of standard deviations that separate that outcome from the mean of the distribution. This is true both above and below the mean, for all normal distributions, regardless of the size of the mean or of the standard deviation.

In all normal distributions, certain percentages of all outcomes fall within a given number of standard deviations above or below the mean of a distribution. For example, 34.13 percent of all outcomes are within one standard deviation *above* the mean. Similarly, since every normal distribution is symmetrical, another 34.13 percent of all outcomes fall within one standard deviation *below* the mean. By addition, 68.26 percent of all outcomes are within one standard

Exhibit 9-16
The Normal Distribution—Percentages of Outcomes Within
Specified Standard Deviations of the Mean

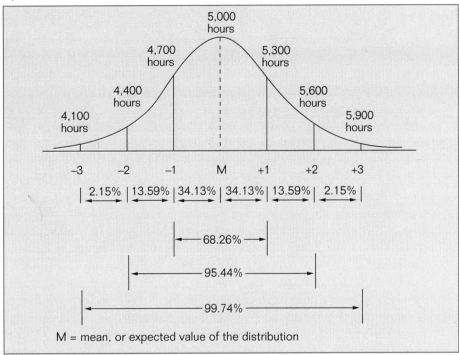

M = mean, or expected value of the distribution

deviation above or below the mean. The portion of a normal distribution that is between one and two standard deviations above the mean contains 13.59 percent of all outcomes, as does the portion between one and two standard deviations below the mean. Hence, the area between the mean and two standard deviations above the mean contains 47.72 percent (34.13 percent + 13.59 percent) of the outcomes, and another 47.72 percent are two standard deviations or less below the mean. Consequently, 95.44 percent of all outcomes are within two standard deviations above or below the mean.

Similarly, 2.15 percent of all outcomes are between two and three standard deviations above the mean, and another 2.15 percent are between two and three standard deviations below the mean. Thus, 49.87 percent (34.13 percent + 13.59 percent + 2.15 percent) of all outcomes are three standard deviations or less above the mean, and an equal percentage are three standard deviations or less below the mean. The portion of the distribution between three standard deviations above the mean and three standard deviations below it contains 99.74 percent (49.87 percent × 2) of all outcomes. Only 0.26 percent (100 percent–99.74 percent) of all outcomes lie *beyond* three standard deviations from the mean, and these are divided equally—0.13 percent above the mean and 0.13 percent below it.

These relationships involving standard deviation can be applied to the previous example involving the heating elements in the ovens in which Wheeler's processes scrap tires. The expected safe life of each element conforms to a normal distribution having a mean of 5,000 hours and a standard deviation of 300 hours. Wheeler's maintenance crews try to replace the elements before they become unsafe. However, even if the maintenance schedule requires replacing each element after it has been in service only 5,000 hours (the mean, or expected, safe life), there is a 50 percent chance that it will become unsafe before being changed, since 50 percent of the normal distribution is below this 5,000-hour mean. If each element is changed after having been used only 4,700 hours (one standard deviation below the mean), there is still a 15.87 percent (50 percent–34.13 percent) chance that an element will become unsafe before being changed. If this probability of high hazard is still too high, changing each element after 4,400 hours (two standard deviations below the mean) reduces the probability of high hazard to only 2.28 percent, the portion of a normal distribution that is more than two standard deviations below the mean. This probability can be calculated as 50 percent – (34.13 percent + 13.59 percent). A still more cautious practice would be to change elements routinely after only 4,100 hours (three standard deviations below the mean), so that the probability of an element becoming highly hazardous before replacement would be only 0.13 percent, slightly more than one chance in 1,000.

Using this same analysis, Wheeler's management may select an acceptable probability that a heating element will become unsafe before being replaced and can therefore schedule maintenance accordingly. Suppose, for example, that management accepts one chance in ten that an element would become dangerous before being replaced. That is, 90 percent of the elements should be replaced before they became overly dangerous. In terms of Exhibit 9-16, achieving this goal requires finding the point along the bottom of the diagram where 10 percent of the entire distribution (the portion of heating elements whose hazard could be tolerated) is below (to the left of) the time of replacement and the remaining 90 percent is above this point. This point is between one and two standard deviations below the mean—that is, between 15.87 percent of the total distribution and 2.28 percent. Statisticians have shown that a value of 1.65 standard deviations below the mean cuts off the lowest 10 percent of any normal distribution. Thus, scheduling replacement of each element after 4,505 hours of use— computed as 5,000 – (1.65 × 300)—would ensure that only 10 percent of the elements became hazardous before replacement. For still greater assurance, say, 95 percent (instead of 90 percent), one must move 1.96 standard deviations below the mean or replace each element after 4,412 hours of use.

Coefficient of Variation

Given two distributions that have the same mean, the one with the larger standard deviation has the greater variability. However, when two distributions have different means, another measure of variability—the coefficient of variation—should be used to compare their degree of variability.

The **coefficient of variation** of any probability distribution or other set of values is the quotient obtained by dividing that distribution's standard deviation by its arithmetic mean. For example, the coefficient of variation for the distribution of total points in rolling two dice equals 2.4 points divided by 7.0 points, or 0.34. For Wheeler's, heating elements in the coefficient of variation is 300 divided by 5,000, or 0.060. Notice the coefficient of variation is a ratio; like an index number, it does not measure any tangible quantity.

For the dollar amount of Wheeler's machinery losses, a coefficient of variation can be computed from either the adjusted dollar amounts of individual losses as shown in Exhibit 9-4 or from the grouped data in Exhibit 9-15. Using individual loss data generates a mean loss of $8,911 and a standard deviation in loss amount of $8,231. Therefore, from these individual loss data, the coefficient of variation is $8,231 divided by $8,911, or 0.924. From the grouped data, the coefficient of variation is 0.915, computed as $8,494 divided by $9,287. The difference between those two computations of the coefficient of variation might or might not be significant. It is therefore important to know whether such a coefficient is computed from grouped data or from the generally more reliable individual loss data. Individual loss figures might, however, be too expensive or even impossible to obtain.

The coefficient is useful in comparing the variability of dissimilar distributions that have different shapes, means, or standard deviations. The distribution with the largest coefficient of variation has the greatest relative variability. The higher the variability within a distribution, the more difficult it is to make an accurate forecast of an individual outcome.

Trend Analysis

If—with respect to the forces that occasionally combine to cause "accidental losses"—the world can be assumed to be stable, then all past losses are only a sample of all possible losses, and that sample might or might not be representative. However, the greater the number of past losses, the larger the sample and the more reliable the forecasts of future losses that both common sense (intuition) and statistical techniques can draw from that sample. The preceding discussion of probability analysis has assumed such a stable world. The following explanation of how to forecast losses by trending assumes a more dynamic world.

> **What is the difference between trend analysis and probability analysis?**
>
> **How is intuitive trending used in forecasting?**
>
> **How are arithmetic trending techniques used in forecasting?**

Like probability analysis, **trend analysis** looks for patterns in past losses and then projects these patterns into the future. Unlike probability analysis, however, trend analysis looks for patterns of *movement*—that is, changes in loss frequency or severity that might coincide with changes in some other variable (such as production) that is easier to forecast accurately—not patterns of rigid *stability*.

Estimates of the likelihood or the potential severity of losses derived from probability concepts discussed previously assume a static, unchanging world. Those estimates assume, for example, that the frequency or severity of a particular type of loss has remained constant during both the period over which loss data have been gathered and the future period for which the loss is being forecast.

This assumption is true only in a limited sense. The assumptions that the future will repeat the past, and that data on all past losses have been drawn from a wholly static world, often are not justified. Past or future changes in an organization's operations, in technology, or in underlying economic or social factors (such as inflation, demographics, or crime rates) are likely to invalidate a projection based solely on historical data.

To improve projections of future losses, many risk management professionals use trend analysis to adjust loss data for anticipated changes in factors presumed to affect the frequency or severity of accidental losses. Although this trending must rest on informed judgment, trended projections can be more realistic than the results of probability analysis alone. A simple example is an adjustment of forecasted future dollar amounts of losses for the anticipated inflation rate.

Judgment often must temper trend projections when extending far beyond the range of any past experience. Automatic use of any mathematical technique can produce unrealistic results. Used with discretion, however, these techniques permit some useful analysis.

For example, in estimating the property losses that an organization will need to finance through retention if it adopts a particular deductible, an alert risk management professional will recognize that projected inflationary trends will increase the monetary value of a given amount of future physical damage. Installing a sprinkler system in a particular building is likely to produce increasingly significant savings in expected fire losses as the physical volume or financial value of the property in that building increases. Hence, inflation and growing concentrations of property values might increase the deductibles and

Exhibit 9-17
Generalized Hand-Drawn Linear Intuitive Trend Line

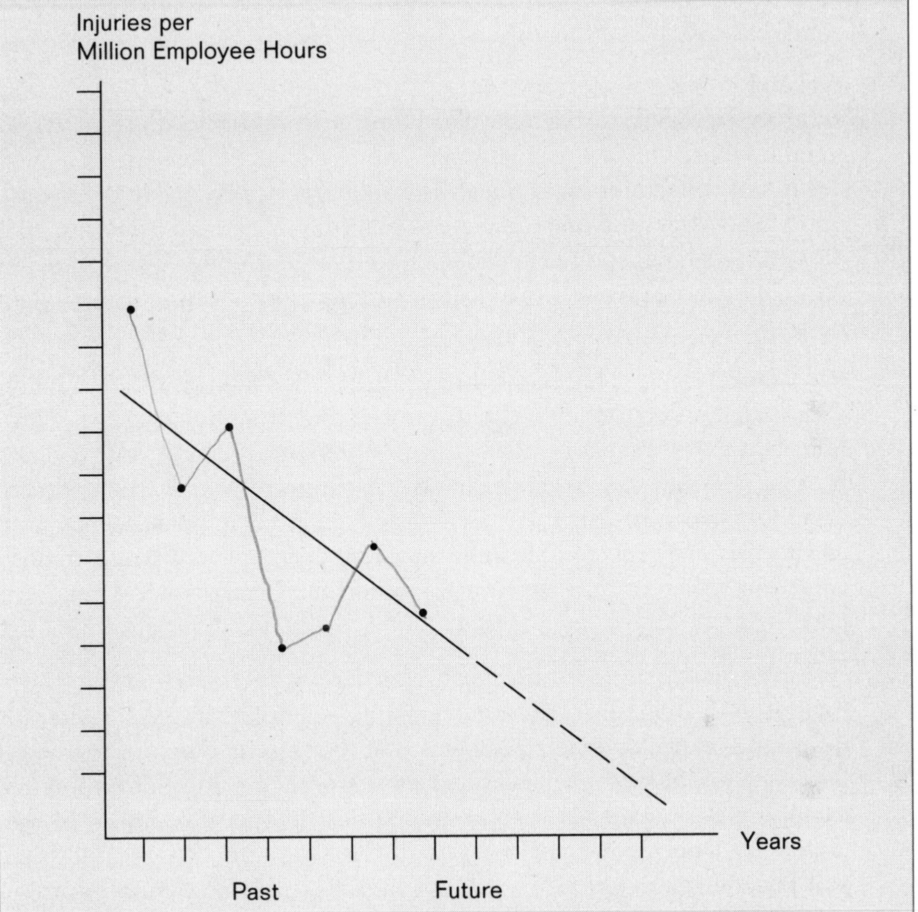

Injuries per
Million Employee Hours

Years

Past   Future

A common-sense way of representing this trend uses a ruler to draw a line
passing as nearly as possible through the data points. Extending the dotted
portion of the trend line into the future gives some intuitive basis for forecasting a continued decline in work injuries.

investments in property loss prevention that an organization decides to make.
Reaching sound decisions on such matters requires trend analysis.

Intuitive Trending

Some trends in losses, or in other variables such as price levels, can be discerned
by **intuitive trending,** which refers to making projections mentally or by sketch-
ing. As an example of intuitive trending, consider Exhibit 9-17, which shows the
number of disabling injuries that the employees of Wheeler's Tire Disposal have

suffered per million employee hours worked (graphed vertically) over a period of seven years (graphed horizontally). Each dot (**data point**) in the chart indicates the rate, or frequency, of injuries in a given year. The downward trend of these data points clearly indicates that the organization's work injury record is improving.

A common-sense way of representing this trend uses a ruler to draw a line passing as nearly as possible through the data points. Extending the dotted portion of the trend line into the future gives some intuitive basis for forecasting a continued decline in work injuries, although it would not be reasonable to expect a zero injury rate. The **trend line** is the eye's best estimate, drawn to minimize the total distances of all data points from the trend line. Arithmetic trending techniques only define more precisely the location of this distance-minimizing straight line.

The straightness of this trend line implies that the work injury record has been improving steadily. That is, the injury rate has been falling by a constant number each year. This constancy accounts for the straight, or linear, shape of the trend line. However, in many situations, a totally **linear trend line** is unrealistic because it would suggest, for example, that injuries would eventually cease to occur. In this and other situations, a curved trend line might reflect past loss data and reasonably expected future losses more accurately. When a trend line is curved, it is known as a **curvilinear trend line**. Because many trend lines are curvilinear, it is common practice to refer to all trend lines, including straight-line ones, as **curves**.

Exhibit 9-18 shows how to estimate a curvilinear trend line—again solely on intuition—that closely approximates past losses. The curvilinear trend line is located to minimize the total of the distances of each of the plotted dots from the trend line. Risk management professionals can plot past losses in this way and then judge whether a linear or a curvilinear trend line most accurately projects past losses into the future.

Arithmetic Trending Techniques

Because computing a curvilinear trend line is complex, most risk management professionals turn to a trained statistician when the need arises. However, linear trending, which is more straightforward and has many uses, is a procedure that should be within the analytic repertoire of every risk management professional.

Exhibit 9-19 presents data suitable for linear trending. Arithmetic trending techniques can develop an equation that precisely locates a linear trend line like that in Exhibit 9-17. Exhibit 9-19 shows the number of machinery losses that Wheeler's suffered and the number of ton-miles of cargo (in hundreds of thousands) in each year from Year 1 to Year 4. This information can be used to project trends that relate the number of machinery losses to (1) time (through a process

Exhibit 9-18
Generalized Hand-Drawn Curvilinear Trend Line

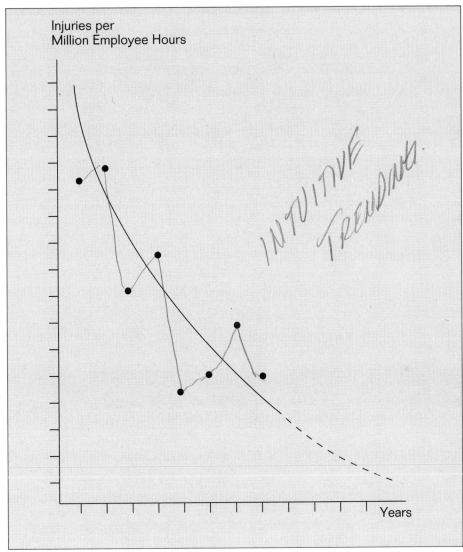

known as "time series analysis") and (2) annual ton-miles carried (through a process known as "regression analysis").

Time Series Analysis

Time series analysis assumes that the variable to be forecast (known as the **dependent variable**) varies predictably with time (the **independent variable**). **Linear time series analysis** also assumes that the change in the dependent

Exhibit 9-19
Relationships of Losses to Exposure (Tons of Output)

Year	Annual Number of Losses	Tons of Output (× 100,000)
1991	4	35
1992	4	60
1993	5	72
1994	6	95
	19	262

This information can be used to project trends that relate the number of machinery losses to time and to annual tons of rubber output.

Exhibit 9-20
Diagram of Linear Time Series Analysis Trend Line

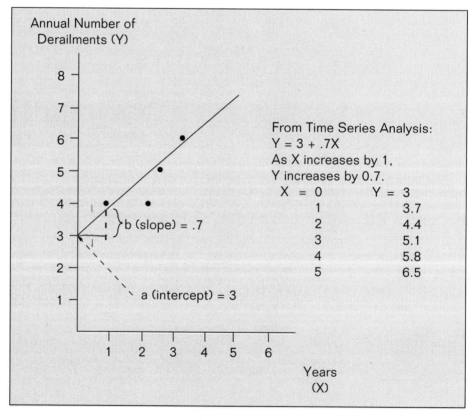

variable is constant for each unit of change in the independent variable (the change is the same from year to year), so that the projected trend line is straight (or linear), not curved.

Exhibit 9-20 plots Wheeler's annual machinery losses on a graph. The dependent variable (annual number of losses) is charted on the vertical (y) axis; the independent variable (years) is charted on the horizontal (x) axis. The heavy dots in the body of the exhibit show that 4, 4, 5, and 6 losses occurred, respectively, in each of the years Year 1 through Year 4 (which, for convenience, can be simply labeled 1, 2, 3, and 4). The objective of time series analysis is to find the equation for the linear trend line that best fits these four data points and to project this line to forecast the number of future losses.

A good first step in calculating a linear trend line is to plot the data points and sketch an approximate trend line. Such a sketch helps to intuitively estimate the two determinants of any linear trend line. The first determinant is the point where the line crosses the vertical y axis, labeled "a" in the diagram and technically known as the **y-intercept**, or the value of y when x equals zero. The second determinant is the "slope" of the line, the amount by which y increases or decreases with a one-unit increase in x. The length of the dashed line labeled "b" signifies the slope. A line slanting upward from left to right has **positive slope**; a line slanting downward has **negative slope**. The values of a and b depend on the values of the dependent and independent variables represented by the four plotted data points. The general equations for a and b follow:

$$a = \frac{(\text{Sum } y)(\text{Sum } x^2) - (\text{Sum } x)(\text{Sum } xy)}{n(\text{Sum } x^2) - (\text{Sum } x)^2}$$

$$b = \frac{n(\text{Sum } xy) - (\text{Sum } x)(\text{Sum } y)}{n(\text{Sum } x^2) - (\text{Sum } x)^2}$$

In these equations, n indicates the number of data points, or the number of paired x and y values, which is four in this case. For clarity, these formulas also use "Sum" to mean the sum of the variable following the symbol. For example, "Sum y" means the sum of the annual numbers of losses, 19 in all.

Exhibit 9-21 shows the calculation of a linear trend line of the annual number of Wheeler's machinery losses, using the above formulas. Columns 1 and 2 simply repeat the data from Exhibit 9-19, showing the years as single digits (for example, 1 rather than Year 1). Each figure in Column 3 represents the product of multiplying each x value by the y value on the same line. Column 4 squares the figures in Column 1. The totals of these four columns—10, 19, 51, and 30—permit solving for a and b, as shown.

Exhibit 9-21

Computation of Linear Time Series Trend Line

(1) Years x	(2) Losses y	(3) xy	(4) x^2
1	4	4	1
2	4	8	4
3	5	15	9
4	6	24	16
10	19	51	30

$$a = \frac{(\text{Sum } y)(\text{Sum } x^2) - (\text{Sum } x)(\text{Sum } xy)}{n(\text{Sum } x^2) - (\text{Sum } x)^2}$$

$$b = \frac{n(\text{Sum } xy) - (\text{Sum } x)(\text{Sum } y)}{n(\text{Sum } x^2) - (\text{Sum } x)^2}$$

$$a = \frac{(19)(30) - (10)(51)}{4(30) - (10)^2}$$

$$= \frac{4(51) - (10)(19)}{4(30) - (10)^2}$$

$$= \frac{570 - 510}{120 - 100}$$

$$= \frac{204 - 190}{120 - 100}$$

$$= \frac{60}{20}$$

$$= \frac{14}{20}$$

$$= 3$$

$$= 0.70$$

Interpreting these results is, for the most part, straightforward. The value of 3 for a in the equation indicates that, at the y-intercept when x equals zero (Year 0), y would be 3. The value of 0.70 for b means that the number of losses can be expected to increase by seven-tenths of a loss each year. (Had b been negative, the number of losses would have been forecast to decrease each year, as they do in Exhibit 9-17). Furthermore, if this trend or pattern continues, the number of losses in Year 5 could be forecast as 3 + 5(0.7) = 6.5, making it reasonable to forecast either 6 or 7 losses in Year 5, and 7—actually, 7.2, losses, computed as 3 + (6 × 0.7)—in Year 6.

The equation for such a linear time series trend is y = a + bx. In this case, the dependent variable, y, is the forecast number of Wheeler's machinery losses; the independent variable, x, is the number of years beyond year zero; a is the y-intercept; and b is the slope of the line.

Two potentially confusing aspects of interpreting linear trend lines need to be recognized. First, a linear trend line might not be accurate when it approaches the horizontal x axis. Despite the linearity of the equation and the line, the dependent variable that is graphed vertically usually does not approach zero in the real world.

Second, for any past year, the value of the dependent variable computed by the linear trend line is not likely to exactly equal the historical value for that past year. Any trend line represents a "best fit," on the average, of a straight or smoothly curved line to actual historical data for all past years. For any given year, the projected trend value will probably differ from the actual outcome, both in the past and in the future. The size of this difference between actual and projected values will also vary. For example, in Exhibit 9-20, the historical outcome for Year 1 is farther from the projected trend line than is the outcome for Year 2.

Regression Analysis

Regression analysis is—in most respects, and especially in the computational steps—just like time series analysis. From the standpoint of risk management, the only important difference between them lies in the assumptions that characterize each.

Time series analysis assumes that the dependent variable (such as the annual number of losses) varies only with the passage of time. Given any future year, the trend line can be extended to forecast the expected number of losses in that year.

In contrast, regression analysis assumes that many other independent variables may be useful predictors of the dependent variable. For example, the annual number of Wheeler's machinery losses might be affected by such variables as the volume of scrap tires processed, the number of inches of snow (or some other measure of adverse weather conditions), or the wholesale price of scrap rubber.

Regression analysis substitutes one of these other variables (volume of output, weather, or prices) for time as the independent variable that predicts the number of future machinery losses. In fact, time series analysis is nothing more than a special case of regression analysis in which time is the independent variable.

Therefore, any reasonable causative factor that can be measured and predicted with more accuracy than accidental losses can be an independent variable. Regardless of the variables used, the procedures for computing the a and b determinants of the linear trend line remain the same. (By turning to an expert statistician, a risk management professional can develop either curvilinear or linear trend lines, which take account of many variables simultaneously. An example is an equation that would forecast the number or dollar amounts of losses in a future year based on combined effects of forecast freight volumes, weather conditions, price levels, and perhaps other independent variables more easily predictable than the losses themselves.)

Exhibit 9-22
Diagram of Linear Regression Line

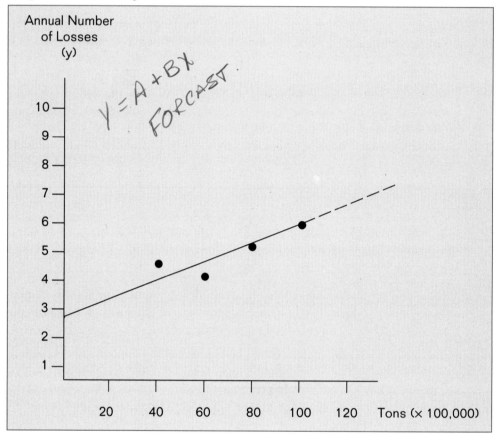

If, for example, Wheeler's risk management consultant wished to use the annual output of recycled rubber products (in 100,000-ton-units) as a predictor of the annual number of machinery losses, a diagram might be developed. Exhibit 9-22 graphs annual tons of output horizontally on the x axis as the independent variable and annual number of machinery losses vertically on the y axis as the dependent variable. The four data points in the exhibit correspond to the pairs of numbers of losses and tons of output shown in Exhibit 9-19, and the solid portion of the linear regression line approximates the trend of the historical data. The dashed extension of the regression line projects annual numbers of machinery losses for levels of output (in units of 100,000) beyond the range of this particular historical data. Developing such a diagram and approximating a regression line help in visualizing and confirming the results obtained by computing the values of a and b for the actual linear regression line.

Exhibit 9-23
Computation of Linear Regression Line

(1) Output (Tons × 100,000)	(2) Losses (y)	(3) (xy)	(4) $(x)^2$
35	4	140	1,225
60	4	240	3,600
72	5	360	5,184
95	6	570	9,025
262	19	1,310	19,034

$$a = \frac{(19)(19,034) - (262)(1,310)}{4(19,034) - (262)^2} \qquad b = \frac{4(1,310) - (262)(19)}{4(19,034) - (262)^2}$$

$$= \frac{361,646 - 343,220}{76,136 - 68,644} \qquad = \frac{5,240 - 4,978}{76,136 - 68,644}$$

$$= \frac{18,426}{7,492} \qquad = \frac{262}{7,492}$$

$$= 2.46 \qquad = 0.035$$

The procedure for calculating values for a (y-intercept) and b (slope) determinants of the regression line relating losses to output, as seen in Exhibit 9-23, is the same procedure for computing a time series analysis trend line. As computed at the bottom of Exhibit 9-23, the indicated value for a is 2.46 machinery losses, and the value for b is 0.035. If the number of losses is linearly related to output for all possible levels of output, the 2.46 value for a means that, even if annual output were zero (that is, Wheeler's was not operating), it would still suffer 2.46 (actually 2 or 3) machinery losses each year. The 0.035 value for b implies that, with each 100,000 ton increase in output, 0.035 additional machinery losses can be expected. One could also say that one additional machinery loss can be expected with approximately each additional 2,857,000 tons of Wheeler's output (computed as 100,000 ton-miles × 1/0.035).

Although arithmetically correct, these values may not be valid for very low or very high volumes of output, again indicating the need to temper mathematics with reason. One should not extend a regression line too far beyond the bounds of past experience.

To forecast losses from these regression results, assume Wheeler's expects to produce 10 million (or 100 hundred thousand) tons of recycled rubber products next year. The expected number of machinery losses next year then can be computed as follows:

$$y \quad = \quad 2.46 + 100(0.035)$$
$$= \quad 2.46 + 3.50$$
$$= \quad 5.96 \text{ losses}$$

Fractional numbers of losses being impossible—there could be five or six losses, but nothing in between—a reasonable forecast would be for six machinery losses in a year when Wheeler's produces 10 million tons of recycled rubber products.

This forecast, like the others described in this chapter, should be accepted only if the underlying assumptions are valid. Therefore, it is important to know these assumptions and recognize the potential limitations in these forecasting techniques.

Probability and trend analyses can be very powerful tools for forecasting future losses, but they must be used with care. Their results must be interpreted with reason and not with blind acceptance just because they are mathematically based. Furthermore, perhaps more for risk management than for some other uses of these forecasting techniques, the seeming scarcity of loss data, when compared with the apparent wealth of data in other management specialties, makes forecasts of accidental losses more difficult.

Summary

Risk management decisions rest on forecasts of future losses. Those forecasts help determine the demands that will be placed on the risk management department as it works to protect the organization against accidental losses.

Forecasting accidental losses, like any other future event, requires detecting patterns in the past and projecting them into the future. Forecasting future accidental losses begins with deciding which of two basic patterns, "no change" or "change in a predictable way," applies. To find patterns that might be discovered in past losses, a risk management professional should attempt to find data that are complete, consistent, relevant, and organized.

Probability analysis is particularly effective for forecasting future accidental losses in organizations that have a substantial volume of data on past losses and that have fairly stable operations, with patterns of past losses that presumably will continue in the future. The larger volume of data on past losses and the more stable the environment that produces those losses, the more reliable will be the forecasts of future losses.

Probability is the relative frequency with which an event can be expected to occur in the long run in a stable environment. Probability can be developed either from historical data or from theoretical considerations.

Most probability estimates are compiled from several sources, including the organization's own loss experience, that of similar organizations, and nationwide data from companies in the same industry.

A probability distribution is a tabular or graphic presentation of all possible outcomes of a particular set of circumstances and of the relative frequency of each possible outcome.

As noted in the chapter, probability distributions are described in terms of skewness, central tendency, and dispersion.

Trend analysis, like probability analysis, involves looking for patterns in past losses and then projecting those patterns into the future. In addition, trend analysis looks for changes in loss frequency or severity that might coincide with changes in some other variable that is easier to forecast accurately. Many risk management professionals use trend analysis to adjust loss data for anticipated changes in factors presumed to affect the frequency or severity of accidental losses.

Some loss trends can be discerned only by intuitive judgment, not by charts and graphs. There are two types of arithmetic trending techniques: time series analysis and regression analysis. Time series analysis assumes that the variable to be forecast varies predictably with time. Regression analysis assumes that many other independent variables could be useful predictors of the dependent variable.

Chapter Notes

1. The Commissioners 1980 Standard Ordinary Male Mortality Table, 1970-1975, available in many standard insurance references.
2. Federal Bureau of Investigation and Federal Highway Administration data reported in MVMA *Motor Vehicle Facts and Figures* (Detroit: Motor Vehicle Manufacturers Association, 1995), p. 63.

Chapter 10

Risk Management Applications of Forecasts

      (2) alternative probability of
         (i) two mutually exclusive
         events and (ii) two events
         that are not mutually
         exclusive
  e. Compute trend lines showing
     the following:
     (1) combined effects of two or
         more trends that can
         properly be added
     (2) constant-percentage rate
         of change
2. Define or describe each of the
Key Words and Phrases for this
assignment.

Risk Management Applications of Forecasts

Applying probability and trend analysis to loss forecasting involves making realistic forecasts in situations somewhat more complex than the elementary cases described in Chapter 9. This chapter describes how to recognize those more complex situations and how to analyze them for closer scrutiny and, therefore, more precise forecasts.

This chapter describes elementary models and examples of forecasting techniques to illustrate their significance and their mechanics. The discussion draws on examples from Schneller Transport, one of the firms affected by the tire fire case. Understanding the computational procedures that these forecasting techniques use is important. With this understanding, the risk management professional can, when working with large quantities of real-world data, rely on much more rapid and sophisticated computers and data processing equipment that might be available to develop these and other forecasts.

Some Further Calculations Involving Probabilities

What symbols are used to make probability calculations?

What are joint probabilities, and how do you calculate them?

What are alternative probabilities, and how do you calculate them?

Chapter 9 introduced two basic types of forecasting tools: (1) probability analysis for situations in which the world is presumed to be stable and the future is expected to repeat the past without change and (2) trend analysis for situations involving change, when several variables move together and can predict others. Somewhat more advanced aspects of each of these two types of analysis help in dealing with more complex situations. For example, probability analysis can be extended to multiple combinations of events, and trend analysis can be extended to situations in which combining the effects of several independent variables permits more accurate forecasting of dependent variables.

Chapter 9 defined the concept of probability and explained how to develop probability distributions to estimate the probabilities of specific individual events.

The probability calculations that follow extend this analysis to determine the probabilities of various combinations of events.

Basic Notation

Probability calculations are usually expressed using symbols. The symbol p( ) means "probability of" the item in parentheses, so that **p(A)** means "the probability of A" occurring in a given period, where A represents any specified event. Similarly, **p(A and B)** is a shorthand expression for "the probability of A and B," both occurring in a given period. The symbol **p(A or B)** stands for "the probability that either A or B, or possibly both," will occur within a specified period. This notation is flexible because any event or combination of events can be designated in the parentheses.

The symbol **n** also appears frequently in probability calculations to designate the number of separate units from which a probability is developed or to which it is applied. For example, if Schneller Transport made 20,000 trips, or "runs," in Years 1 through 4, when the railroad suffered nineteen major collisions to its trucks, then the probability of a derailment on any particular run could be computed as 19/20,000, which equals 0.000950. More generally, the symbol "n" typically designates the number of trials or exposures (here, runs) from which an empirical probability is derived. The symbol "m" designates the number of occurrences of the event whose probability is sought, 19 in this case. Thus, the general equation for the probability of a collision that is significant is expressed as follows:

$$p(\text{collision}) = m/n = 19/20{,}000 = 0.000950$$

and, by algebraic manipulation,

$$m = np = (20{,}000)(0.000950) = 19$$

In a slightly different, predictive context, "n" can represent the number of truck runs that Schneller Transport plans for Year 5. Since p is the best estimate (based on the available data) of the probability of a collision on any one run, then n times p, (np), is the number of collisions that Schneller's can expect in Year 5. Given that p equals 0.000950, if Schneller's forecasts making 7,000 runs in Year 5 , this company can expect seven collisions that year (6.65 to be precise, but fractional collisions are impossible). Symbolically, expected collisions equal the number of runs times the probability of collisions on one run, expressed as follows:

$$\text{Expected collisions} = (np) = 0.000950 \times 7{,}000 = 6.65$$

"Expected collisions per year" can be interpreted as the average (arithmetic mean) number of collisions expected to occur annually in the long run, not necessarily the number that *will* occur in the next twelve months.

The concept of expected value is so common in working with probabilities that a symbol, **E( )**, is used as shorthand for "the expected number or value" of the event specified in the parentheses. If C stands for the annual number of collisions in the year in which Schneller's makes n runs, then

$$E(C) = np$$

That equation can be read as "the expected annual number of collisions equals the number of runs times the probability of collision on any one run." The following probability calculation would be used for the first collision example:

$$E(C) = np = (20,000)(0.000950) = 19$$

Most probability calculations rest on two assumptions, which, while usually obvious, should be made explicit to avoid mistakes when these assumptions are not true. The first assumption is that the probability, p, remains constant and is valid for the future events whose probability is being calculated. This is true whether the value for p is derived from experience (as for collisions) or wholly from logic (like the *a priori* probabilities involved in rolling dice). In other words, the world that has generated any particular value for p is assumed to remain unchanged so that p also applies to the future.

The second assumption is that an event either occurs or does not occur. No other possibilities exist. The occur/not occur possibilities are mutually exclusive (meaning that one or the other, but not both, must occur), and together they exhaust all possibilities. Therefore, the probability of any event occurring, p(A), and the probability of it not occurring, p(not A), add up to one. For example, since the probability of a collision on any one run is 0.000950, then the probability of no collision on that run is 0.999050. Generally, the following is true:

$$p(A) + p(\text{not } A) = 1, \text{ and, by algebraic manipulation,}$$
$$p(A) = 1 - p(\text{not } A), \text{ and}$$
$$p(\text{not } A) = 1 - p(A)$$

In those equations, A may represent a single event or a set of events. Those equations are useful when the probability of A is unknown and might be difficult to compute directly. Consequently, it is often easier to find the probability calculations of A by computing p(not A) and subtracting the result from one.

This basic equation applies to all probability analyses. Two probability calculations most useful in risk management are calculations of joint probabilities (the probability that two or more events will occur together in a given time period) and of alternative probabilities (the probability that any one of two or more events will occur in a given time period).

Joint Probabilities

A **joint probability**, also often called a *compound probability*, is the probability that two or more events will all happen within a given period. Examples are the probability that two collisions involving Schneller's trucks will occur in a particular month, that eight men will all die within one year, or that Schneller's will suffer both a fire loss and a theft loss within one month.

Before computing the joint probability of two or more events, one must determine whether these events are independent. Two events, A and B, are independent if the occurrence or nonoccurrence of one does not affect the probability of the occurrence of the other. If A and B are independent, the probability of A is unchanged by the occurrence or nonoccurrence of B. Similarly, the probability of B is unchanged by the occurrence or nonoccurrence of A. For example, the probabilities that two of Schneller's trucks, widely distant from one another, will burn, are independent of each other, because a fire at one will not endanger the other. However, if the two trucks are close enough that fire can spread from one to the other, their probabilities of fire loss are not independent. Specifically, each truck alone may have a 2 percent chance of fire in a given year, but if the trucks are close together, a fire in one of them will raise the probability of fire in the other.

For Independent Events

If two or more events are independent, the joint probability that all the events will occur is the product of their separate probabilities. That is, if the two trucks previously mentioned are widely distant, the probability that they will both burn in one year, p(2 fires), is equal to the probability of fire in one, p(F1), times the probability of fire in the other, p(F2), expressed as follows:

$$p(2 \text{ fires}) = p(F1)p(F2)$$
$$p(2 \text{ fires}) = (0.02)(0.02) = 0.0004$$

For Dependent Events

If the two trucks are close enough to be affected by one fire, the joint probability that both will burn is determined by multiplying the probability of fire in one times the probability of fire in the second, given that the first truck is already on fire. The probability of fire in the second truck is known as **conditional probability** because this probability is conditioned on the occurrence of another event, or in this case, the existence of fire in the first truck. Generally, if the probability of event B is conditional on event A, the notation for "the probability of B, given A" is **p(B | A).**

Assume, for example, that the two trucks previously mentioned are sufficiently close that fire could spread from one to the other or that a fire from an outside source could strike both trucks. Assume further that it has been observed over the years (creating an empirical probability) that on 40 percent of the occasions when one truck catches fire, a nearby truck also catches fire. Then, even though the probability of fire in one or the other remains at 2 percent, leaving $p(F1) = 0.02$, the conditional probability of fire in the second truck, given fire in the first, increases to 40 percent in notation, $p(F2 \mid F1) = 0.40$.

With conditional probabilities—when the probability of one event changes depending on whether another event has already occurred—it is especially important to specify not only the nature but also the sequence of the events whose joint probability is being computed. Assume, for example, that Truck One is much older than Truck Two and therefore more likely to catch fire. Assume also that the probability of fire in Truck One—denoted as $p(F1)$—is 0.05, while the corresponding probability for Truck Two is 0.01. Furthermore, perhaps because Truck One contains a more flammable cargo than does Truck Two or because Truck One is upwind from Truck Two, let the probability of a fire spreading from Truck One to Truck Two be 0.60, while the probability of fire spreading in the other direction is 0.10. That is, $p(F2 \mid F1) = 0.60$, while $p(F1 \mid F2) = 0.10$. Then, the probability that Truck Two will catch fire after and as a result of a fire in Truck One is equal to the probability that Truck One will catch fire times the probability that this fire will spread to Truck Two, expressed as follows:

$$p(F1 \text{ followed by } F2) = p(F1)p(F2 \mid F1) = (0.05)(0.60) = 0.03$$

Conversely, the probability that a fire will begin in Truck Two and spread to Truck One is computed as follows:

$$p(F2 \text{ followed by } F1) = p(F2)p(F1 \mid F2) = (0.01)(0.10) = 0.001$$

Notice that each of those calculations derives the probability of a particular sequence of events and does not include any allowance for any other sequence (such as both trucks simultaneously being ignited by a fire whose origin is outside either one).

The General Case

Specifying the sequence in which events occur is important in dealing with events whose probabilities depend on one another. Sequence is unimportant with events whose probabilities are independent because the occurrence or nonoccurrence of one event does not affect the probability of the other. Therefore, the formula for the joint probability of two events that are not independent is also the general formula for all joint probabilities regardless of independence.

This formula follows:

$$p(A \text{ followed by } B) = p(A)p(B \mid A)$$

This formula is applicable to independent events because if A and B are independent, $p(B \mid A) = p(B)$.

This general formula for the joint probability of two events can be extended to find the joint probability of any number of events. However, the formula rapidly becomes lengthy as the number of separate events increases. The key point is that joint probabilities are computed by multiplying either unconditional or conditional probabilities depending on whether the events are independent or dependent.

To illustrate this general formula further, the probability of rolling 8 fours in 8 rolls of one die (independent events) is 1/6 (the probability of a four on each roll) multiplied by itself as follows:

$$p(8 \text{ fours}) = (1/6)(1/6)(1/6)(1/6)(1/6)(1/6)(1/6)(1/6)$$

$$= (1/6)^8$$

$$= 1/1,679,616$$

Other Joint Probability Calculations

As another illustration, if the probability that one of Schneller's warehouses will suffer a fire, $p(F)$, is 0.005 and if the probability that the contents of the warehouse will be looted if fire occurs, $p(L \mid F)$, or "the probability of looting given a fire," is 0.60, then the probability that the warehouse will burn and then be looted in the wake of the fire is as follows:

$$p(F \text{ followed by } L) = p(F)p(L \mid F) = (0.005)(0.60) = 0.003$$

Notice that this is the probability of fire followed by looting, which is not the same as the probability of looting followed by fire or the probability of looting and fire occurring in two unrelated events. The equation does not calculate those latter two probabilities. Generally, great care should be taken in defining the events whose joint probability is being computed.

Joint probabilities can also be used to compute the likelihood that an organization will *not* suffer a loss. Suppose that the probability that one of Schneller's truck drivers will be injured in a job-related traffic accident during the next year is 0.03. Because $p(\text{not } A) = 1 - p(A)$, the probability of no injury to the driver is 0.97. For two drivers whose probabilities of injury are assumed to be independent, that is, that the drivers will not endanger one another and that their vehicles will not collide with one another, the probability that neither will be injured is $(0.97)(0.97)$, or $(0.97)^2$, which is 0.9409, or roughly 94 percent.

As the number of drivers increases, the probability that none will suffer injury decreases until, with 76 drivers, the probability of *no* injuries among these drivers falls to less than 10 percent (because 0.97^{76} is less than 0.10). To generalize, it follows that any organization with even a moderate number of employees is likely to experience at least one workers compensation claim in a given year, even though the probability of injury to any one employee is relatively small.

With extremely small probabilities of some loss (extremely large probabilities of no loss), the number of separate exposure units must become quite large before some loss is virtually certain. For Schneller Transport, for example, the 0.999050 probability that any one truck will reach its destination *without* a significant collision means that, for any two trucks, there is a 0.998101 probability that both will reach their destinations without a collision, this probability being computed as $(0.999050)^2$. As the number of truck runs increases, however, the probability of *no* collisions falls (though not as rapidly as in the previous work injury example). It is not until Schneller's has 2,423 separate truck trips that the probability of no significant collisions falls to less than 10 percent because $(0.999050)^{2423}$ is less than 0.10.

Those examples illustrate two basic points. First, as the number of exposure units (here, workers or trucks) increases, some loss eventually becomes virtually certain. Second, the smaller the probability of loss to any one exposure unit, the greater is the number of units required to reach a given probability (here, more than 90 percent) that some loss will occur in a given year or other time period.

What is true for the probability of loss within a given number of exposure units in one year is also true for a single exposure unit over a number of years. Some loss is likely to occur. For example, assume that the probability is 1 in 8 (0.125 or 12.5 percent) that, during a given winter, Bigh Pass, a crucial mountain road for Schneller's, will be closed by heavy snow at least once. The equation to compute the probability that Bigh Pass will *not,* during four consecutive years, ever be closed by snow follows:

$$p(\text{no snow closure for 4 years}) = (1 - 0.125)^4$$
$$= (0.875)^4$$
$$= 0.586$$

or slightly less than 59 percent.

The probability that Bigh Pass will not be closed by snow in a decade is $(0.875)^{10}$, which is approximately 26.3 percent. In other words, there is an almost 74 percent chance $(1 - 0.263 = 0.737)$ that, unless special measures are taken to keep Bigh Pass open, it will be closed by snow at least once every ten years. The higher that probability, the more consideration Schneller Transport may wish to give to stationing its own snowplows near Bigh Pass.

Alternative Probabilities

An **alternative probability** is the probability that any *one* of two or more events will occur within a given time. Examples are the probability that either a three or a five will come up in one roll of one die, the probability that a card drawn from a deck will be either a five or a club, and the probability that Schneller's Transport will suffer either a fire loss or a burglary loss within the next year.

To compute alternative probabilities, the first step is to determine whether the events involved are mutually exclusive. Two or more events are *mutually exclu-sive* only if the occurrence of one makes the other *impossible*. For example, rolling a three on a die makes it impossible to roll a five (or any other number) on the same roll, so three and five on one roll of one die are mutually exclusive events. A truck driver involved in an accident can be uninjured, injured, or killed immediately. Because his or her physical condition cannot fall into two of those categories, the three are mutually exclusive.

Similarly, the probabilities that Schneller's trucks will suffer no collision loss in a particular year, that it will suffer one collision loss, that it will suffer two collision losses, and that it will suffer more than two collision losses are prob-abilities of four mutually exclusive events because in no one year can the number of collision losses fall into any two of these categories.

Events that are not mutually exclusive include drawing a five or a club from a deck on one draw (because the five of clubs may be drawn) and Schneller's, suffering both collision and snow closure losses in a particular year.

For Mutually Exclusive Events

For **mutually exclusive events** (the occurrence of one event making the other event impossible), the probability that any one of them will occur is the sum of their separate probabilities. Thus, the probability of rolling either a 3 or a 5 on one roll of one die is $p(3 \text{ or } 5) = 1/6 + 1/6 = 2/6 = 1/3$.

Another set of mutually exclusive events concerns the dollar amounts of indi-vidual losses. Since a given loss measured by a specified valuation standard can be only one particular dollar amount, no individual loss can fall into two catego-ries of loss size. A loss is, for example, either (1) less than $5,000 or (2) equal to or more than $5,000. In a probability distribution of losses by size, the probability of a loss equal to or less than a given figure is the sum of the probabilities of losses up to this figure (see Column 3 of Exhibit 9-7). Generally, the sum of the probabilities of all possible mutually exclusive events—events that are both mutually exclusive and collectively exhaustive—is always one.

Probabilities of mutually exclusive events are also germane to those risk manage-ment situations in which loss can be caused by one of two perils, but not by more than one. For example, Schneller Transport might lose a particular truck by fire or by flood, but not by both perils. Suppose that the probability that a given truck will be destroyed by fire in a given year is 0.04 and that the probability of this truck being lost to flood in that year is 0.06. Thus, the probability of the truck being lost to either fire or flood during that year is expressed as follows:

$$p(\text{flood or fire}) = 0.04 + 0.06 = 0.10$$

That computation assumes that the probabilities of flood and of fire are independent—that the occurrence of flood does not affect the probability that fire will occur, and vice versa.

For Non-Mutually Exclusive Events

When two or more events can occur within a specified time, they are not mutually exclusive. For such events, the probability that at least one, and possibly both or all, of them will occur is the sum of their separate probabilities minus the joint probability that they will both or all occur. (With more than two events that are not mutually exclusive, the computations become quite complex. This discussion of alternative probabilities for non-mutually exclusive events is therefore restricted to cases involving only two events.)

For example, the probability of drawing a five from a deck of cards without jokers is 1/13, the probability of drawing a club is 1/4, and the probability of drawing the five of clubs is 1/52. Therefore, the probability of drawing a five or a club is computed as follows:

$$
\begin{aligned}
p(\text{5 or club}) &= 1/13 + 1/4 - 1/52 \\
&= 4/52 + 13/52 - 1/52 \\
&= 16/52 \\
&= 4/13
\end{aligned}
$$

Subtracting the joint probability of events that are not mutually exclusive is necessary to avoid overstating the probability of the alternative events by double-counting the five of clubs as both a five and a club.

The problem of double-counting becomes more serious with events having large probabilities. Suppose that the climate in a particular area is such that the probability of rain at noon on any given day is 50 percent and that the probability that the noon temperature will exceed 70 degrees is 80 percent. On some days, it is both raining and over 70 degrees at noon, so rain and heat (above 70 degrees) are not mutually exclusive. If the joint probability of rain and heat is not subtracted, the probability of either rain or heat, or both, is mistakenly calculated as p(rain or heat) = 0.50 + 0.80 = 1.30. This is an impossible result because, by definition, no probability can exceed 1.0. The following is the proper calculation:

$$p(\text{rain or heat or both}) = 0.50 + 0.80 - (0.50)(0.80)$$
$$= 0.50 + 0.80 - 0.40$$
$$= 0.90$$

Thus, a 90 percent probability exists that at noon it will be raining or that the temperature will exceed 70 degrees, or *both*.

Calculating the alternative probability of two events, but *not* both, involves (1) identifying each of the mutually exclusive ways that the events may occur, (2) computing the probability of each of these ways, and (3) adding the resulting probabilities. For example, the probability of heat or rain but not both at noon on a particular day is equal to the probability of heat and no rain plus the probability of rain and no heat. Those two combinations of circumstances are the only two ways of having rain or heat but not both. Because the probability of rain is 0.50 and the probability of heat is 0.80, the alternative probability of the two events is calculated as follows:

$$p(\text{rain and no heat}) = (0.50)(1 - 0.80)$$
$$= (0.50)(0.20)$$
$$= 0.10$$
$$p(\text{no rain and heat}) = (1 - 0.50)(0.80)$$
$$= (0.50)(0.80)$$
$$= 0.40$$
$$p(\text{rain or heat but not both}) = 0.10 + 0.40 = 0.50$$

In risk management, alternative probabilities of events that are not mutually exclusive arise when dealing with two or more perils that can each cause loss, either operating independently or occurring simultaneously. For example, the cargo inside one of Schneller's Transport trucks could be struck by both water damage (by less than total flooding) and pilferage (theft of less than an entire truck load). A given shipper's property, a given truck, or even the contents of all of Schneller trucks in a caravan could suffer both water damage and pilferage losses on a single run. The occurrence of one peril is not likely to change the probability of the occurrence of the other (thus making water damage and pilferage independent events). Here, Schneller's risk management professional might want to know the probability that a given shipment will suffer either water damage or pilferage loss, or perhaps both.

Assume, for example, that the probability of pilferage loss to a shipment is 0.09 and that the probability of flood loss is 0.06. The probability of loss by pilferage or water damage or *both* is therefore computed as follows:

$$p(\text{pilferage or water damage or both}) = 0.09 + 0.06 - (0.09)(0.06)$$

$$= 0.15 - 0.0054$$

$$= 0.1446$$

Computing the probability of pilferage or water damage *but not both* requires summing the probabilities of the two mutually exclusive ways that this result can occur. Those are the probabilities of (1) pilferage but no water damage and (2) water damage but no pilferage. Computing those two probabilities and finding their sum yields the following:

$$p(\text{pilferage but no water damage}) = (0.09)(1 - 0.06)$$

$$= (0.09)(0.94)$$

$$= 0.0846$$

$$p(\text{water damage but no pilferage}) = (0.06)(1 - 0.09)$$

$$= (0.06)(0.91)$$

$$= 0.0546$$

$$p(\text{pilferage or water damage but not both}) = 0.0846 + 0.0546 = 0.1392$$

The probability of either kind of damage but not both is smaller than the probability of either kind of damage and possibly both because the first probability excludes the chance of their both happening.

Some Further Trend Analysis

How can two or more trends be combined?

How can such trends be used to forecast losses?

As noted in Chapter 9, probability analysis assumes that the world is stable. Trend analysis assumes that it is dynamic—that whatever stability exists lies in the constancy of the patterns of movement, the trends of change. In such a presumably dynamic world, the losses that a risk management professional seeks to forecast frequently are analyzed as the joint result of several trends, all acting simultaneously. Therefore, a risk management professional often may want to use trend analysis to forecast levels of exposures, numbers or sizes of losses, or the costs of insurance or retention—any of which could be the joint result of several trends operating independently. Forecasting any such variable requires combining those trends to find the net result.

For example, the risk management professional for an organization that retains its automobile physical damage losses may, for forecasting purposes, envision each year's losses as the joint result of three trends in (1) the number of vehicles that the organization operates, (2) the frequency of losses per 100 vehicles, and (3) the costs of repairing a given amount of physical damage. Forecasting each of those trends separately and combining the results is likely to generate a more accurate forecast of annual vehicle losses than trying to predict annual losses directly.

Similarly, an organization wanting to budget its annual aggregate workers compensation premiums for each of the next four years might find little predictable pattern in these annual aggregate costs. Without some clear pattern, a reliable forecast might not be feasible. Meaningful patterns might emerge when the organization's risk management professional analyzes annual aggregate workers compensation costs as the combined result of separate, more predictable trends in (1) the size of the organization's work force, (2) the changes in the wage and salary rates that the organization pays its employees, and (3) the levels of workers compensation benefits mandated by the states in which the organization's employees work. A relatively simple procedure can be used to determine, or at least estimate, the combined effects of such trends.

The procedure involved is essentially addition: two or more trends are combined by being applied in sequence. In the Schneller Transport example, annual dollars of loss of net income and loss from serious truck collisions are presumed to be the joint result of two trends. The first trend relates annual amounts of Schneller's net income losses from collision losses (in constant dollars) to output (in ton-miles of freight). The second is the trend of common carrier truck-freight rates per ton-mile of a given cargo shipped along this route (which converts constant dollars to current dollars of net income loss).

In this example, constant dollar losses are forecast through regression analysis against output (with dollars of loss being the dependent variable and forecast ton-miles the independent variable). As a second step, these trended constant dollar losses are inflated by a forecast of truck common carrier freight rates.

This approach to forecasting the combined effects of two or more trends rests on an important assumption: the two trends are independent. In this case, ton-mileages and the general level of freight rates are not related to one another in any defined pattern. If this were not the case—that is, if these two trends were interrelated—then this additive, sequential combining of trends would not be valid.

Combining Trends—Defining the Model

Business forecasters often develop *models* (systems of graphs, equations, or other relationships) that describe, in a simplified way, how the real world appears to work. When used for forecasting, a model identifies and describes the effects of all relevant causes of the dependent variable being forecast.

The elementary model presented here assumes that the two independent variables are ton-miles of freight carried and changes in freight charges, which are useful predictors of annual dollar totals of Schneller Transport's net income losses from collisions on a particular route. Those losses are the dependent variable. Because this is an elementary model, it does not consider important factors such as weather (for which low temperatures and high levels of precipitation tend to increase collision losses), expenditures on private truck and public highway maintenance (for which higher expenditures presumably mean fewer collisions), years of experience of the truck drivers and maintenance personnel (more years usually meaning fewer or less severe collision losses), the time interval since the last major collision (for which the shorter this interval, perhaps the more likely the drivers are to be particularly careful, thus reducing collisions), and even the mere passage of time (which might change the conditions that generate these two trends). Those are just some of the factors that might reasonably be used as predictors of annual dollar amounts of net income losses from truck collisions, assuming that these predictors could themselves be reasonably forecast. But, for understanding the procedure and for practicing how to apply it, two independent variables (ton-miles and rail cargo rates) are sufficient.

The First Predictor: Ton-Miles

It is reasonable to assume that the frequency and annual totals of collision losses that a common carrier trucking company suffers each year will increase or decrease as the volume of its freight hauling increases or decreases. To test this assumption, Exhibit 10-1 computes the regression equation that relates Schneller Transport's annual collision losses to its annual ton-miles of cargo carried during Years 1 through 4. (A ton-mile is one ton carried for one mile. For example, a truck carrying sixteen tons that travels eighty miles produces 1,280—16×80—ton-miles of cargo.) In this exhibit and in the equation it derives, ton-miles is the independent variable (X, expressed in hundreds of thousands of miles), and the annual dollar amount of collision losses is the dependent variable (Y, expressed in thousands of constant Year 4 dollars).

The ton-mileages in Column 1 of Exhibit 10-1 are taken directly from Exhibit 9-23. The dollar losses in Column 2 are from Exhibit 9-3. The remaining columns and computations in Exhibit 10-1 parallel those in Exhibit 9-23.

Exhibit 10-1
Regression of Annual Collision Losses Against Annual Ton-Miles

(1) Ton-Miles (× 100,000) (X)	(2) Losses (× $1,000) (Y)	(3) XY	(4) X²
35	9.8	343.0	1,225
60	32.9	1,974.0	3,600
72	45.1	3,247.2	5,184
95	82.0	7,790.0	9,025
Totals: 262	169.8	13,354.2	19,034

$$a = \frac{(\text{sum } Y)(\text{sum } X^2) - (\text{sum } X)(\text{sum } XY)}{n\,(\text{sum } X^2) - (\text{sum } X)^2}$$

$$= \frac{(169.8)(19,034) - (262)(13,354.2)}{4(19,034) - (262)^2}$$

$$= \frac{3,231,973.2 - 3,498,800.4}{76,136 - 68,644}$$

$$= -\frac{266,827.2}{7,492}$$

$$= \underline{-35.61}$$

$$b = \frac{n(\text{sum } XY) - (\text{sum } X)(\text{sum } Y)}{n\,(\text{sum } X^2) - (\text{sum } X)^2}$$

$$= \frac{4(13,354.2) - (262)(169.8)}{4(19,034) - (262)^2}$$

$$= \frac{53,416.8 - 44,487.6}{76,136 - 68,644}$$

$$= \frac{8,929.2}{7,492}$$

$$= \underline{1.192}$$

$$Y = -35.61 + 1.192X$$

$$\text{Losses } (\times \$1,000) = -35.61 + 1.192 \text{ Ton-Miles } (\times 100,000)$$

The resulting equation for the regression line indicates that the annual dollar total of losses (Y) can be expected to increase by $1,192 for each 100,000 ton-mile increase in cargo carried.

The negative $35,610 value for "a" in the equation erroneously suggests that net income losses from collisions would be less than zero if Schneller ceased to operate and if ton-mileages were zero. Because a linear regression line often creates distortions at its extremes, this result can be ignored for practical purposes. This regression equation should not be used for making predictions significantly beyond the range of ton-mileages (3,500,000 through 9,500,000) from which it was computed.

It is important not to ascribe false accuracy to the results shown in any exhibits in the remainder of this chapter. The forecast that expected, annual dollar totals of loss will rise or fall by $1,192 each time that annual ton-mileages rise or fall by 100,000 is only a best estimate, based on available data and the assumptions underlying the model. To the extent that those assumptions are not true, and to the extent that other causal factors are ignored in the model, the accuracy of this forecast is limited. At best, actual results can only be expected to fall within a range of this single-value forecast. The width of this range depends on many factors, analysis of which requires statistical expertise beyond the scope of this text.

The Second Predictor: Cargo Rates

Changes in the general level of prices are usually forecast through time series analysis. Exhibit 10-2 computes a linear trend line of changes in historic truck common carrier cargo rates from Year 1 through Year 4. (These cargo rates are the dollar amounts that a regulated common carrier, such as a trucker like Schneller's, is permitted to charge for each ton or other specified amount of cargo transported. A state or federal regulator typically publishes a schedule of allowable cargo rates. The cargo rate for a ton of any given cargo multiplied by the number of tons of a particular shipment is the freight charge for that shipment.) The actual index figures in Column 2 are taken from Exhibit 9-2, and the computation follows the procedure portrayed in Exhibit 9-2. The resulting equations suggest that if the economic conditions of Year 1 through Year 4 do not change and price levels move linearly, then the price index can be projected to increase by 11.45 index points each year.

Many forecasting models assume that price levels change by a constant, curvilinear *rate* (or percentage) from year to year rather than by a constant *number* of index points. The assumption of a constant percentage rate of change yields a curvilinear (or curving), rather than a linear (or straight), trend line. As years pass, any positive or upward rate of change means larger annual increases, while

Exhibit 10-2
Linear Trend of Truck Common Carrier Cargo Rates

	(1) Years (X)	(2) Index (Y)	(3) XY	(4) X^2
	1	115.2	115.2	1
	2	125.9	251.8	4
	3	140.2	420.6	9
	4	148.6	594.4	16
Totals:	10	529.9	1,382.0	30

$$a = \frac{(\text{sum } Y)(\text{sum } X^2) - (\text{sum } X)(\text{sum } XY)}{n(\text{sum } X^2) - (\text{sum } X)^2}$$

$$= \frac{(529.9)(30) - (10)(1,382.0)}{4(30) - (10)^2}$$

$$= \frac{15,897.0 - 13,820.0}{120 - 100}$$

$$= \frac{2,077}{20}$$

$$= 103.85$$

$$b = \frac{n(\text{sum } XY) - (\text{sum } X)(\text{sum } Y)}{n(\text{sum } X^2) - (\text{sum } X)^2}$$

$$= \frac{4(1,382.0) - (10)(529.9)}{4(30) - (10)^2}$$

$$= \frac{5,528 - 5,299}{120 - 100}$$

$$= \frac{229}{20}$$

$$= 11.45$$

$$\text{Index} = Y = a + bX$$

$$= 103.85 + 11.45 \text{ (Year)}$$

a persistent negative or downward rate of change implies an increasingly rapid fall. Because rates of change can vary, projecting a constant-rate curvilinear trend over many years can lead to unrealistic results.

Exhibit 10-3 demonstrates that linear and curvilinear trends can forecast strikingly different results, especially in more distant years. (The cargo rates in this exhibit are hypothetical, unrelated to Schneller's actual experience.) In the linear projection, each succeeding year's forecast is 11.45 ton-mile units greater than the last. In the percentage projection, each year's forecast is 8.86 percent greater than the last. As more years pass, the 8.86 percent growth is much more rapid than the 11.45 ton-mile growth. Because those two types of trending techniques produce such markedly different results, long-range forecasts can prove quite inaccurate. To improve accuracy, both in the long and the short run, a risk management professional or other qualified person must do the following:

- Obtain as much relevant data as possible for computing trends, especially current data that can be particularly valuable in making short-term forecasts.

- Experiment with both linear and curvilinear trending techniques to see which approach better fits actual historical data and presumably will better project the future. (A simple way to experiment is to graph both the historical data and the linear or curvilinear trend lines, as shown in Chapter 9, to make an intuitive judgment as to the better "fit." Alternatively, a statistician can be consulted, especially for crucial forecasts whose importance justifies the cost of such special expertise.)

- Redraw or recalculate trend lines to incorporate new data, either adding to the total volume of data on which the trends are based or, if conditions are changing so that the earliest data no longer reflect existing conditions, deleting any inapplicable earlier loss data.

Those steps help refine the forecasting model by adding to the historical data on which the model is founded and clarifying the patterns of change on which it relies. To illustrate the principles involved, this discussion purposely focuses on a most elementary model. The model here involves only four years' data and two variables. A large organization with many years' experience might want to use a model with five or six trended variables and perhaps two decades of accumulated data. For the risk management professionals in small organizations, however, even such a simple model as the one explained here can sharpen forecasts of future losses.

An Illustrative Forecast

Exhibit 10-4 illustrates one technique for forecasting Schneller's annual collision losses in both constant Year 4 and current dollars based on the following:

Exhibit 10-3

Comparison of Linear and Constant Percentage—Change
Projection of Cargo Rates

Year	Linear Projection (11.45 points/yr.)	Constant Percentage Projection[†] (8.86%/yr.)
1	148.60	148.60
2	160.05	161.76
3	171.50	176.10
4	182.95	191.70
5	194.40	208.69
6	205.85	227.17
7	217.30	247.30
8	228.75	269.21
9	240.20	293.07
10	251.65	319.03

1. The regression equation in Exhibit 10-1 that relates collision losses to ton-miles

2. A forecast from Schneller's senior management that, because of an expected general economic decline in the region that Schneller's serves, ton-mileages will be 8 million in Year 5, 5.5 million in Year 6, and 4.3 million in Year 7

3. A forecast from Schneller's finance department that the 8.86 percent increase in the motor truck common carrier cargo rates will continue for Year 5 but that the price level will increase only 7.00 percent in year 6 and, in Year 7, the general level of prices will fall 5.00 percent from their Year 6 level

The forecasts in 2. and 3. just mentioned should enhance the accuracy of the forecasts that the risk management professional could make. Without this information from other departments, these risk management forecasts might have to rely on linear or curvilinear projections of both future ton-mileages and future cargo rates.

Exhibit 10-4 recaps these trends and performs the computations that apply the regression equation for Years 5, 6, and 7. These computations involve two separate steps. The first is to compute losses in constant dollars based on projected ton-mileages. These computations are similar for all three years, involving only substitution of different ton-mileage figures for each of the three years. The resulting loss projections—$59,750 in Year 5, $29,950 in Year 6, and $15,650 in Year 7—are in constant Year 4 dollars.

The second step in the computations for each of these three years converts these constant dollar losses to current dollars, reflecting Year 5, 6, and 7 projected rate levels. These rate-adjusting computations differ among the three years because of different projected percentages in price level changes and because of the differing number of years for which the constant Year 4 dollar losses need to be adjusted.

Thus, for Year 5, the price level change merely involves multiplying $59.75 by (1 + 0.0886), reflecting an 8.86 percent increase in cargo rates from Year 4 to Year 5. Consequently, Year 5 losses are forecast to be $65,040 in Year 5 dollars. For Year 6, the rate level adjustment involves multiplying the amount of losses in constant dollars by two factors: (1 + 0.0886) to bring these losses to Year 5 levels and (1 + 0.0700) to reflect the 7.00 percent rate level increase from Year 5 to Year 6. By this procedure, expressed in Year 6 dollars, losses are projected to be $34,890 in Year 6. For Year 7, when cargo rates are projected to fall by 5.00 percent, three factors are needed to adjust to the Year 7 rate level: (1 + 0.0886) to reach the Year 5 rate level, (1 + 0.0700) to reach the Year 6 rate level, and (1 − 0.0500) to reflect the Year 7 projected price level decrease.

Exhibit 10-4
Forecasts of Annual Collision Losses for Years 5, 6, and 7

Assumptions

For Year 5
1. Ton-Miles = 8,000,000 (or 80 × 100,000)
2. Cargo rates continue to rise at 8.86% over Year 4 level

For Year 6
1. Ton-Miles = 5,500,000 (or 55 × 100,000)
2. Rates rise at 7.00% over Year 5 level

For Year 7
1. Ton-Miles = 4,300,000 (or 43 × 100,000)
2. Rates fall 5.00% from Year 6 level

Computations

For Year 5
1. Losses (in thousands of constant Year 4 dollars)
   L = −$35.61 + 1.192(80)
   = −$35.61 + $95.360
   = $59.75
2. Adjusted for cargo rate change (8.86% increase for Year 4)
   Losses = ($59.75)(1 + 0.0886)
   = $65.04

For Year 6
1. Losses (in thousands of constant Year 4 dollars)
   L = −$35.61 + $1.192(55)
   = −$35.61 + $65.56
   = $29.95
2. Adjusted for cargo rate change (7.00% increase over Year 5)
   Losses = ($29.95)(1 + 0.0886)(1 + 0.0700)
   = $34.89

For Year 7
1. Losses (in thousands of constant Year 4 dollars)
   L = −$35.61 + 1.192(43)
   = −$35.61 + $51.256
   = $15.65
2. Adjusted for cargo rate change (5.00% decrease from Year 6)
   Losses = ($15.65)(1 + 0.0886)(1 + 0.07)(1 − 0.05)
   = $17.32

Weighted by these three factors, Year 7 losses in then-current dollars can be forecast as $17,320. (These price-adjustment factors are equivalent to 1.0886, 1.0700, and 0.9500, respectively. Had the projected changes in cargo rate levels been a constant 8.86 percent for each of the three years, the respective rate level adjustment factors could have been expressed as 1.0886, 1.0886^2, and 1.0886^3.)

Summary

A risk management professional can calculate probabilities and trends that improve forecasts of potential accidental losses and of the costs of preventing or paying for such losses by applying the concepts of probability and trending.

Essential notations for calculating the probabilities of one or more of several events—calculations using the "algebra of probability"—involve computing joint probabilities and alternative probabilities. A joint probability is the likelihood that both (or all) of two (or more) events will occur in a given time period. To compute a joint probability, one must know the separate probability of each event alone, and then also know (or judge intelligently) whether the happening of one event changes the probabilities of the other events (making these probabilities independent). The algebra for joint probabilities of independent events differs from that of dependent events.

For alternative probabilities of one or more of several events occurring within a specified time period, one must determine whether the events are mutually exclusive—that is, whether the happening of one event does, or does not, make the happening of other events impossible. Again, the algebra for the alternative probabilities of events that are mutually exclusive differs from that for events that are not mutually exclusive.

Those calculations enable a risk management professional to determine or estimate the likelihood that an organization will experience various combinations of numbers or amounts of losses in a year or other time period. Arithmetic trending techniques also can improve these loss forecasts.

The trending concepts discussed in Chapter 9 help in determining how several separate trends can be projected in isolation and then combined to develop loss forecasts that recognize the combined effects of several trends influencing an organization's loss experience from a particular exposure.

Chapter 11

Cash Flow Analysis as a Decision Criterion

Educational Objectives

1. Apply basic concepts of managerial finance to forecast the cash flow effects of alternative risk management measures.

   In support of the above educational objective, you should be able to do the following:

   a. Explain (i) why money has a "time value" and (ii) the factors that determine the size of that value.

   b. Use tables to find the present values of future single payments and of streams of future payments.

   c. Identify elements of cash inflows and outflows from capital investment proposals.

   d. Apply and explain the logic of the net present value method and the time-adjusted rate of return method of evaluating capital investment proposals.

2. Define or describe each of the Key Words and Phrases for this assignment.

Outline

Cash Flow Analysis as a Decision Criterion

This chapter discusses a criterion for selecting risk management techniques or combinations of techniques. Applied to the forecasts of losses developed in Chapters 9 and 10, this criterion allocates an organization's risk management resources to meet most cost-effectively the demands that potential and actual accidental losses impose on that organization.

This criterion requires maximizing the present value of an organization's long-term, after-tax net cash flows. Most organizations use this same requirement to guide business decisions. For both profit-seeking and nonprofit organizations, maximizing the present value of net cash flows is the decision guideline that best enhances the organization's ability to apply resources to fulfill its basic objectives.

Using cash flow analysis to select risk management techniques allows risk management decisions to be made on the same basis, applying the same logic, as most other decisions in well-managed organizations. Cash flow logic unifies risk management with other management specialties by enabling the risk management professional to make and defend choices of risk management techniques in the same way that other managers make their decisions. Specifically, cash flow analysis enables the risk management professional to do the following:

- Explain how any proposal, including a proposed risk management technique, would affect the flows of cash into and out of an organization.
- Compute the present value of the net cash flows of proposals that require an organization to commit resources to an asset or activity.
- Express and evaluate proposals, including alternative risk management techniques, according to their net cash flows and rates of return.

The Importance of Cash Flows

What is the importance of managing cash flows?

How do cash flows determine what an organization does?

An organization's **net cash flow (NCF)** during any period is its cash receipts minus its cash disbursements during that period. If receipts exceed disbursements, net cash flow is positive. If disbursements exceed receipts, cash flow is negative. Net cash flow—plus any credit that the organization can use as a substitute for cash—allows the organization to commit resources to pursue its objectives. Projecting net cash flows likely to be generated by alternative assets or activities gives management a valid criterion for choosing those assets or activities that promise the most benefit to the organization.

Command Over Resources

Cash, in hand or in the bank, enables an organization to obtain resources to fulfill its objectives. Cash—more precisely, purchasing power, from equity or debt capital—is a means to other ends, indeed usually a *necessary* means to *all* other ends. The greater an organization's positive net cash flow, the more it can do. In contrast, negative cash flow reduces an organization's ability to pursue its goals. Thus, net cash flow serves as a barometer of an organization's strength, a measure of its short-range capabilities and of its long-range value to its owners and to those whom it serves.

Net cash flow measures an organization's ability to function effectively better than its accounting profits or surpluses measured by accrued revenues and expenses. Unlike profits or budget surpluses (which can be affected by changes in accounting receivables), payables, or other accruals that are not means of paying for things, net cash flow measures an organization's ability to buy or otherwise command needed resources.

Using present values of net cash flows as a decision criterion also promotes other organizational objectives (such as profits, public service, or humanitarian or political objectives) that guide an organization's decisions. Seeking cash is not a final objective in itself. It is only a means to the organization's more meaningful goals, virtually all of which require cash. Because cash flow is a means to so many other (usually higher) ends, a decision rule based on maximizing the present value of an organization's net cash flows is, in a sense, "objective-neutral." The greater the present value of the purchasing power that an organization can command in the long run, the more fully it can realize its organizational objectives. The risk management professional should coordinate the cash needs of risk management techniques with the organization's other cash needs.

Evaluating Alternative Uses of Resources

In selecting assets or activities to which to commit an organization's resources, senior management should give priority to those alternatives that promise the net cash flows having the greatest present value. The simplicity of this decision rule is often complicated by situations in which an asset or an activity requires immediate cash expenditures (as well as perhaps further expenditures in the future), especially on assets or activities that can be expected to generate cash receipts only in future periods. Such situations, in which cash expenditures or cash receipts are spread over several accounting periods, can best be dealt with by a procedure known as **capital budgeting**, which facilitates decisions based on net cash flows.

Capital budgeting distinguishes between operating expenditures and capital expenditures. **Operating expenditures** involve acquiring resources that will be consumed in a relatively short period, usually one year or less. **Capital expenditures** involve acquiring resources that are relatively long-lived and should generate cash receipts or require cash disbursements in future accounting periods. For example, when Wheeler's Tire Disposal acquires a new rubber processing machine, the cash receipts attributable to that machine will be received over the entire useful life of the equipment—perhaps twenty or even fifty years depending on technology, maintenance, and whether the expected life of the machine is shortened by an unexpected accident. If Wheeler's were to build a new yard, the benefits it would generate might be received over a period of forty, fifty, or more years.

Capital budgeting is making decisions about an organization's purchase of long-term assets. (A long-term asset is one that has an anticipated useful life of more than one accounting period, usually more than one year.) In order to make proper decisions about purchasing such assets, one must compare present values (discussed further in this chapter) of future cash inflows and outflows with the initial costs of the assets purchased in the present accounting period.

A capital budget is a plan for making long-term **capital investments** (acquisitions of long-term assets) to achieve an organization's objectives. Capital budgeting is the decision-making process involving the evaluation of various alternative capital investment proposals in terms of the cash outlays that they require and the present values of the cash inflows that they are likely to generate. Because most organizations have more worthwhile investment opportunities than they have available cash to invest, priority should be given to those uses of cash that promise to be most productive, that is, the uses for which the organization projects the greatest present value of future net cash flows.

The Time Value of Money

Capital budgeting techniques recognize that money has a time value. This **time value of money** arises because investing money over time in a project or in a financial investment generates ("earns") money. The amount of money earned by a given dollar over a given time period is the *time value* of that dollar over that period. Computing the present value of a sum of money to be received in the future incorporates its time value.

How does time affect the value of money?

What is the time value of money concept?

What is the present value of money concept?

How are present values computed?

The Present Value Concept

A *present value* is the current equivalent of some present or future dollar amount. A dollar currently available, "in hand," has a greater time value than does a dollar to be received in the future because the dollar in hand can be invested to start earning money immediately. In contrast, a dollar to be received in the future cannot be invested to generate earnings until that future date. The greater the **rate of return** (which is an asset's or activity's annual profit or surplus, expressed as a percentage of its original cost) that a dollar in hand can earn, the greater is its value relative to a future dollar. Conversely, the longer the time period until a future dollar is to be received, the lesser is its present value when compared with the value of a dollar in hand. The two factors that determine the present value of a particular amount of money are the appropriate interest rate and the length of time before that amount becomes available for use.

Interest Rate

The appropriate interest rate is the cost associated with the use of money, normally expressed as a percentage rate for each year that the money is being used. Except in cases in which money has been borrowed from an outside lender, this time value cost does not usually entail any explicit outlay for the use of money. Instead, this time value cost is an implied cost, an "opportunity cost," of using money for one purpose rather than for another. Selecting one use for money necessarily commits funds that could otherwise have been invested in an alternative project. Expressed as an interest rate, the cost of money used for one purpose is the rate of return that money could have earned had it been put to the best alternative use.

An organization typically earns an after-tax rate of return on funds put to use in its normal operations. For illustrative purposes, assume that an organization can internally generate 18 percent after taxes from its normal operations. Putting money to a use other than normal operations involves a sacrifice, an opportunity cost, of this 18 percent. This 18 percent is this organization's time value of this money.

In contrast, when an organization borrows funds at, for example, an after-tax cost of 10 percent per year, its cost of using these particular funds for one year is the after-tax 10 percent charged by the lender. Notice that in this case interest cost is not the same as opportunity cost. The organization's time value of money for evaluating proposed uses of cash remains 18 percent, not the 10 percent charged by the lender. Because the organization can earn 18 percent on money from any source, the opportunity cost of putting this money to any use remains 18 percent.

When funds are used over several years—as is often the case in risk management, particularly for loss prevention devices—this opportunity cost rate applies to each year that the funds are used. Therefore, on the basis of the organization's opportunity cost, its financial officer usually specifies a minimum rate of return, a "hurdle rate" that all acceptable proposals must meet or exceed.

Length of Time

The second determinant of the time value of money is the length of time (the number of years or units of time) for which that money could be invested at a specified interest rate. To illustrate, if money can earn a rate of 10 percent per year, the use of $100 has a time value of $10 for that one-year period—$100 earns $10 in one year at a 10 percent interest rate. With a 10 percent interest rate, an initial sum of $100 increases to $110 at the end of one year. Expressed differently, $110 in hand one year from now has a present value of $100 if the interest rate is 10 percent per year.

Computations of Present Values

Computations of present value can involve any of the following:

1. A present payment
2. A single future payment
3. A series of equal future payments
4. A series of unequal future payments

A Present Payment

The present value of a present payment (either a receipt or a disbursement) is the face amount of that payment. No discounting is required to account for the use value of that current payment before it is received or disbursed because there is no time period before receipt or disbursement. For example, $100 received or disbursed now—in a present accounting period—has both a face value and a present value of $100. The present payment most frequently encountered in capital budgeting situations is the initial outlay required by a proposed asset or activity, such as purchasing fire extinguishers and training employees in their use.

A Single Future Payment

Appendix A, located at the end of this chapter and entitled "Present Value of $1 Received at the End of Period," gives present values of $1 received at the end of various periods of time at various rates of interest. This appendix shows present value factors for each pair of determinants of the time value of money: the interest rate and time period. The **present value factor** for any investment in an asset or activity is the present value of its future net cash flows divided by the initial cost of the investment. Present value factors indicate the amount that must be invested today at a given interest rate for a given number of years to receive $1 as a single payment at the end of that number of years.

For example, using a 10 percent annual interest rate, the present value of $1 received at the end of one year is $0.909, or about 91 cents. This result is obtained by multiplying $1 by the present value factor, 0.909, in the one-year row of the 10 percent column of Appendix A. This factor is equal to the present value of $1 one year from now, divided by the present value of $1 one year from now, all discounted at 10 percent. Conversely, if approximately 91 cents is invested today for one year—earning 10 percent interest per year—the interest is 9 cents, and the amount resulting at the end of that year is $1.

If interest is compounded annually for two years, a little more than 82 cents must be invested initially to produce an ending amount of $1. Appendix A indicates that the present value factor is 0.826, indicating that 82.6 cents is needed initially if the ending amount is to be $1 after two years at 10 percent annual interest. At the end of one year, 82 cents grows to 91 cents, and at the end of the second year, the 91 cents grows to $1. Viewed prospectively, the present value of $1 to be received two years hence at interest compounded annually at the rate of 10 percent per year is 82.6 cents.

Notice the inverse relationship between the present value of $1 and the number of years during which money initially invested earns interest. As one increases, the other decreases. For example, with interest compounded annually at the rate of 10 percent, $1 in hand today has a present value of $1. The $1 in hand one year from now has a present value of about 91 cents. The $1 in hand ten years from now has a present value of about 38 cents, and $1 in hand fifty years from now has a present value of about a penny. These present values can be confirmed by applying the appropriate present value factors from Appendix A to $1.

An inverse relationship also exists between the present value of $1 and the interest rate. The higher the interest rate for any given time period, the lower the present value, and vice versa. For example, at 10 percent interest, the present value of $1 received at the end of one year is about 91 cents because at 10 percent interest, 91 cents earns 9 cents. At 12 percent, the present value of $1 under the same conditions is only about 89 cents ($0.893), and at 20 percent the present value is about 83 cents ($0.833). As an extreme example, at a 50 percent annual interest rate, the present value of $1 to be received one year from now is about 67 cents ($0.667) because 67 cents will earn 33 cents in interest if the interest rate is 50 percent for one year.

A Series of Equal Future Payments

The present value of a series of future payments is equal to the sum of the present values of each of the separate payments. Exhibit 11-1 shows the present values for a series of three payments of $1 received at the end of one, two, and three years when the interest rate is 10 percent per year compounded annually. The present value of a single payment of $1 at the end of one year under these conditions is $0.909. Similarly, the present value of $1 received at the end of two years is $0.826, and the present value of $1 received at the end of three years is $0.751. These present values are computed from the present value factors in Appendix A, using the 10 percent column, lines 1, 2, and 3, respectively. If the three present values are added, the sum of $2.486 is the present value of $1 received at the end of *each* year for a period of three years at interest compounded annually at the rate of 10 percent. Stated differently, $2.486 is the amount that must be invested today at 10 percent interest per year compounded annually to receive $1 at the end of each of the next three years, after which the investment is exhausted.

Appendix B, located at the end of this chapter and entitled "Present Value of $1 Received Annually at the End of Each Period for N Periods," provides the same result without requiring the summing of the separate present values from Appendix A. Appendix B presents these sums directly. For example, Appendix B can be used to determine the present value of $1 received annually for a period of three years at interest compounded annually at the rate of 10 percent. In the 10 percent column of Appendix B, where n, the number of years, equals 3, the present value factor is 2.487. This present value factor, applied to future payments of $1 each, yields a present value of $2.487 (or $1 × 2.487). Except for the slight difference due to rounding, this amount is the same as the $2.486 calculated by adding the three separate present value factors from Appendix A.

The present value factors in Appendix B are derived from those in Appendix A. The top line is the same in both tables because $1 is received at the end of only one year, and the present value factors in the first row of each table are the same for each rate of interest. The values on line 2 of Appendix B equal the sums of the present values shown on lines 1 and 2 in Appendix A. For example, at 10 percent interest in Appendix A, the figures for the first and second years are 0.909 and 0.826. The present value at 10 percent on line 2 in Appendix B is the sum of those two figures, 1.736. Because the present value factors are rounded to three decimal places, comparisons between the two tables might differ by one thousandth or several thousandths in the far right decimal place.

Exhibit 11-1
Present Value of a Stream of Equal Payments at 10 Percent Interest

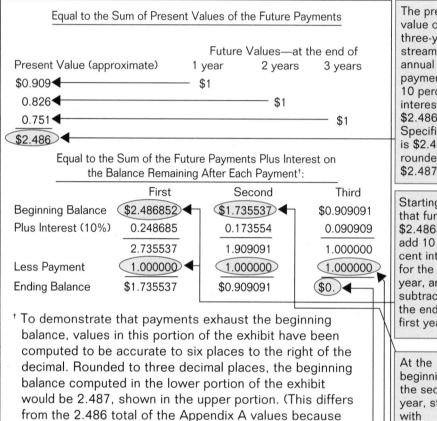

Equal to the Sum of Present Values of the Future Payments

	Future Values—at the end of		
Present Value (approximate)	1 year	2 years	3 years
$0.909	$1		
0.826		$1	
0.751			$1
$2.486			

Equal to the Sum of the Future Payments Plus Interest on the Balance Remaining After Each Payment[†]:

	First	Second	Third
Beginning Balance	$2.486852	$1.735537	$0.909091
Plus Interest (10%)	0.248685	0.173554	0.090909
	2.735537	1.909091	1.000000
Less Payment	1.000000	1.000000	1.000000
Ending Balance	$1.735537	$0.909091	$0.

The present value of a three-year stream of $1 annual payments at 10 percent interest is $2.486. Specifically, it is $2.486852, rounded to $2.487

Starting with that fund of $2.486852, add 10 percent interest for the first year, and subtract $1 at the end of the first year.

At the beginning of the second year, start with $1.735537

[†] To demonstrate that payments exhaust the beginning balance, values in this portion of the exhibit have been computed to be accurate to six places to the right of the decimal. Rounded to three decimal places, the beginning balance computed in the lower portion of the exhibit would be 2.487, shown in the upper portion. (This differs from the 2.486 total of the Appendix A values because Appendix A presents rounded values.)

When the third dollar is subtracted, the amount remaining in the fund is $0. This computation demonstrates that investing approximately $2.49 at 10 percent interest enables one to pay $1 at the end of each year over a three-year period.

The difference represents the interest earned by the investment, a total of approximately 51 cents ($3.00 − $2.49 = $0.51). Invested for a one-year period at 10 percent, 91 cents earns about 9 cents interest. Similarly, 82.6 cents invested for a two-year period earns about 17 cents, and 75 cents invested for a three-year period earns about 25 cents. Those earnings add to 51 cents.

Repeat the process of adding interest and subtracting $1 at the end of each year for the second and third years.

Exhibit 11-1 also shows another perspective for determining the present value of a stream of equal annual payments. The present value of a three-year payment stream of $1 annually at 10 percent interest is $2.487, rounded from $2.486852. Starting with that fund of $2.486852, add 10 percent interest for the first year and subtract $1 at the end of the first year. At the beginning of the second year, start with $1.735537. Repeat the process of adding interest and subtracting $1 at the end of each year for the second and third years. When the third dollar is subtracted, the amount remaining in the fund is $0. That computation demonstrates that investing approximately $2.49 at 10 percent interest enables one to pay $1 at the end of each year over a three-year period.

The difference represents the interest earned by the investment, a total of approximately 51 cents ($3.00 − $2.49 = $0.51). Exhibit 11-1 shows that 91 cents invested for a one-year period at 10 percent earns about 9 cents interest. Similarly, 82.6 cents invested for a two-year period earns about 17 cents, and 75 cents invested for a three-year period earns about 25 cents. Those earnings add to 51 cents.

Notice that the present values are for future payments of $1. If the future payments differ from $1, their present value is calculated by multiplying each future payment by the present value factor for the specified interest rate and time period. For example, to calculate the present value of a single payment of $100 to be received at the end of three years at interest compounded annually at the rate of 10 percent, determine the present value factor for $1 to be received under these conditions. The correct factor from Appendix A is 0.751. Multiplying this factor by $100 indicates that $75.10 is the present value of $100 to be received at the end of three years at interest compounded annually at the rate of 10 percent. Similarly, if the interest rate remains 10 percent, but the single payment to be received at the end of three years is $7,800, the present value of that future payment is $7,800 times the present value factor, 0.751, or $5,857.80.

To calculate the present value of $100 received annually at the end of each year for three years at interest compounded annually at the rate of 10 percent, use Appendix B to find the present value factor for a stream of $1 payments for three years at 10 percent interest. The factor is 2.487. Multiplying this factor by $100 indicates that the present value of the stream of equal $100 annual payments is $248.70. If the payment were $7,800 each instead of $100, the present value of this stream of payments would be 2.487 times $7,800, or $19,398.60.

A Series of Unequal Future Payments

When different dollar amounts are to be received at the end of different periods, each period's cash inflow must be separately valued, using the present values for single payments in Appendix A. The present value of the entire stream of unequal payments is the sum of the present values of the individual payments.

Exhibit 11-2 shows the present values of a stream of unequal payments ($2, $3, and $4) at 10 percent interest. The present value of the $2 to be received at the end of the first year is 2 times $0.909, or $1.818. Similarly, the value of $3 to be received at the end of the second year is three times the value of $1 to be received at the end of that period, or $2.478. The present value of $4 at the end of three years is $3.004, making the present value of the three years' payments $7.300.

Methods for Evaluating Cash Flows

> **What are the two basic methods of evaluating cash flows?**
>
> **How can these methods rank proposed investments?**

Capital budgeting decisions apply cash flow criteria in either of two ways. One involves determining whether a particular investment proposal is expected to meet some predetermined minimum acceptable level of performance. For example, a particular organization's overall financial policy might specify that any proposed capital investment (such as a new building or machine) must be expected to earn a minimum rate of return of 20 percent annually during its expected useful life for that project to be considered. The rate of return that an organization considers minimally acceptable often represents the interest rates it must pay to borrow funds or the interest rates it can earn by investing its funds in a financial instrument rather than its own activities.

The second way that capital budgeting decisions apply cash flow criteria involves selecting the most promising proposal by computing the rate of return that each proposal promises to earn on the investment it requires. For example, assume that three capital investment proposals that an organization is considering exceed its predetermined minimum acceptable 20 percent rate of return. Suppose one is expected to earn 25 percent, the second 30 percent, and the third 35 percent. The selection process involves allocating cash to the proposal expected to earn the highest rate of return, 35 percent. Other things being equal, the proposal that yields the highest return is the best.

Corresponding to these two ways of applying net cash flow criteria are two different evaluation methods. One, the net present value method, takes the first approach of computing whether, at a specified rate of interest, the present value of a proposal's net cash flow is positive or negative. The second evaluation

Exhibit 11-2
Present Value of a Stream of Unequal Payments at 10% Interest

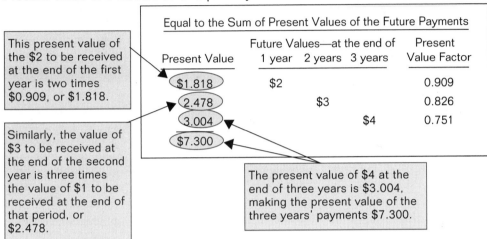

| | | Future Values—at the end of | | | Present |
This present value of the $2 to be received at the end of the first year is two times $0.909, or $1.818.	Present Value	1 year	2 years	3 years	Value Factor
	$1.818	$2			0.909
	2.478		$3		0.826
	3.004			$4	0.751
	$7.300				

Equal to the Sum of Present Values of the Future Payments

This present value of the $2 to be received at the end of the first year is two times $0.909, or $1.818.

Similarly, the value of $3 to be received at the end of the second year is three times the value of $1 to be received at the end of that period, or $2.478.

The present value of $4 at the end of three years is $3.004, making the present value of the three years' payments $7.300.

method, the time-adjusted rate of return method (also often called the "internal rate of return method") computes the interest rate at which the present value of a proposal's net cash flow is zero.

Two major conditions are necessary to successfully apply these evaluation methods to capital budgeting decisions. One is that the benefits and costs associated with a particular proposal must be measurable in monetary terms. The second, nonmonetary considerations are beyond the scope of these evaluation methods.

The second condition relates to unpredictability. Capital budgeting decisions involve investments that are expected to extend well into the future. Such long-term investment projects are subject to both speculative and pure risks. In most cases, the longer the expected life of a proposal, the less predictable is its rate of return. The discussion in this chapter assumes that present and future cash flows are known with certainty. Chapter 12 examines problems associated with making decisions when the future is, to some degree, unpredictable.

To evaluate capital investment proposals, one must know the following:

- The amount of initial investment
- The acceptable annual rate of return, expressed as a percentage of the initial investment
- The estimated useful life of the proposal, the number of years (or other periods) for which it will produce cash flows

- The amount of differential annual after-tax net cash flows associated with the proposal

Exhibit 11-3 illustrates the evaluation of a capital investment proposal using, first, the net present value method and, then, the time-adjusted rate of return method. The proposal involves acquiring an asset for $30,000 cash. The estimated useful life of the asset is three years, and the asset is expected to generate additional annual after-tax net cash inflows of $12,000, or a total of $36,000 over three years, with no salvage value.

Net Present Value Method

An asset or activity's **net present value** is the present value of future cash inflows minus the present value of future cash outflows. The **net present value method** can be used only when a minimum acceptable rate of return is predetermined. Typically, this minimum acceptable rate of return will be given to, not established by, a risk management professional. This given rate applies to the cash inflows and outflows from any proposal that the organization considers, including a proposed risk management technique.

Any proposal whose projected cash inflows have a present value greater than the present value of the required outflows is acceptable by this criterion. In Exhibit 11-3, for instance, the additional annual net cash inflows are a constant $12,000 each year, and the only required cash outflow is the $30,000 initial cost of the asset. The first step in using the net present value method is to calculate the present value of the additional annual after-tax net cash flows.

Appendix B indicates that the present value factor for $1 received annually at the end of each year for three years at 10 percent interest compounded annually is 2.487. Multiplying this present value factor by $12,000 yields the present value of the differential net cash inflows, $29,844. In other words, $29,844 is the amount that would have to be invested today at 10 percent interest compounded annually to receive $12,000 at the end of each year for a period of three years. The net present value of the proposal is the present value of the differential net cash inflows minus the investment's present value. The net present value of this proposal is a negative $156, computed by subtracting the $30,000 initial investment that the proposal requires from the $29,884 present value of the proposal's future cash inflows. This negative result shows that the proposal will not generate the minimum acceptable rate of return of 10 percent.

Time-Adjusted Rate of Return Method

Exhibit 11-3 also illustrates the same result, using the time-adjusted rate of return method. (The **time-adjusted rate of return**, also known as the internal

Exhibit 11-3
Evaluating a Capital Investment Proposal

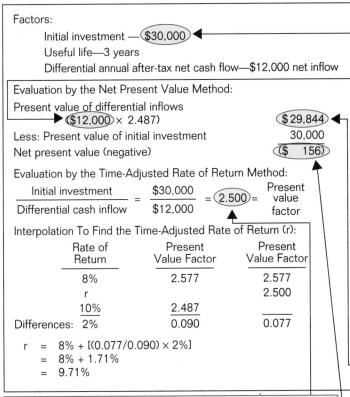

Factors:
 Initial investment — $30,000
 Useful life—3 years
 Differential annual after-tax net cash flow—$12,000 net inflow

Evaluation by the Net Present Value Method:

Present value of differential inflows
  ($12,000 × 2.487) $29,844
Less: Present value of initial investment   30,000
Net present value (negative)   ($ 156)

Evaluation by the Time-Adjusted Rate of Return Method:

$$\frac{\text{Initial investment}}{\text{Differential cash inflow}} = \frac{\$30,000}{\$12,000} = 2.500 = \text{Present value factor}$$

Interpolation To Find the Time-Adjusted Rate of Return (r):

Rate of Return	Present Value Factor	Present Value Factor
8%	2.577	2.577
r		2.500
10%	2.487	
Differences: 2%	0.090	0.077

 r = 8% + [(0.077/0.090) × 2%]
   = 8% + 1.71%
   = 9.71%

The proposal involves acquiring an asset for $30,000 cash.

The estimated useful life of the asset is three years, and the asset is expected to generate additional annual after-tax net cash inflows of $12,000.

Appendix B indicates that the present value factor for $1 received annually at the end of each year for three years at 10 percent interest compounded annually is 2.487. Multiplying this present value factor by $12,000 yields the present value of the differential net cash inflows, $29,844.

Because the asset's price is $30,000 and acquiring that asset is expected to generate $12,000 a year for three years, $30,000 is the present value of $12,000 received annually for a period of three years at some unspecified time-adjusted rate of return. Dividing $30,000 by $12,000 gives a present value factor for the proposal of 2,500. Therefore, 2,500 is the present value of $1 received annually for a three-year period at the yet undetermined time-adjusted rate of return for this proposal. One can determine this rate by finding the present value factor that comes closest to 2,500 in the three-year row of Appendix B. The factor of 2,500 lies between 2,577 for an 8 percent return and 2,487 for a 10 percent return over a three-year period. Therefore, the time-adjusted rate of return for this proposal is between 9 and 10 percent compounded annually.

The net present value of the proposal is the present value of the differential net cash inflows minus the investment's present value. The net present value of this proposal is a negative $156, computed by subtracting the $30,000 initial investment that the proposal requires from the $29,884 present value of the proposal's future cash inflows. This negative result shows that the proposal will not generate the minimum acceptable rate of return of 10 percent.

rate of return, is the interest or discount rate that equates the present value of the future cash inflows of an asset or activity with the present value of the future cash outflows that the asset or activity requires.) The **time-adjusted rate of return method** is a procedure for finding the interest or discount rate equating the present value of future cash inflows with the present value of present or future cash outflows. Because the asset's price in Exhibit 11-3 is $30,000 and acquiring that asset is expected to generate $12,000 a year for three years, $30,000 is the present value of $12,000 received annually for a period of three years at some unspecified time-adjusted rate of return. Dividing $30,000 by $12,000 gives a present value factor for the proposal of 2.500. Therefore, 2.500 is the present value of $1 received annually for a three-year period at the yet undetermined time-adjusted rate of return for this proposal. One can determine this rate by finding the present value factor that comes closest to 2.500 in the three-year row of Appendix B. The factor of 2.500 lies between 2.577 for an 8 percent return and 2.487 for a 10 percent return over a three-year period. Therefore, the time-adjusted rate of return for this proposal is between 8 and 10 percent, compounded annually.

When needing a more exact rate of return, estimate by interpolating—or splitting the differences—between known present value factors and the known rates of return associated with these factors. For example, a present value factor exactly halfway between the present value factors for a 10 percent time-adjusted rate of return and a 12 percent rate would be the present value factor for an 11 percent time-adjusted rate of return. A present value factor closer to, but still greater than, the present value factor for a 12 percent rate of return would indicate a rate of return between 11 and 12 percent a year.

For most risk management purposes, whereby the ranking of alternatives is typically the objective, it is enough to remember the following basic principle: For any given number of time periods, present value factors and rates of return are inversely related. This means that the lower the present value factor for a given number of years, the higher the projected time-adjusted rate of return, and vice versa for a higher present value factor.

For this course, students should be able to apply this principle to rank various investment and risk management alternatives; students need not interpolate to find exact rates of return. However, to make the text examples clear, many of them include interpolations of rather precise rates of return. All examples illustrate the same basic principle: For any given time interval, rates of return and present value factors are inversely related—that is, they move in opposite directions.

Had the cost of the asset been $27,000 instead of $30,000, and the other three factors remained unchanged, the net present value of the proposal would have been positive, as shown in Exhibit 11-4. The present value of the differential net cash flows would exceed the present value of the initial investment: $29,844 exceeds $27,000 by $2,844.

Exhibit 11-4

Evaluating an Alternative Capital Investment Project

Factors:

    Initial investment — $27,000

    Useful life—3 years

    Differential annual after-tax net cash flow—$12,000 net inflow

    Minimum acceptable rate of return—10% annually

Evaluation by the Net Present Value Method:

Present value of differential inflows ($12,000 × 2.487)	$29,844
Less: Present value of initial investment	27,000
Net present value	$ 2,844

Evaluation by the Time-Adjusted Rate of Return Method:

$$\frac{\text{Initial investment}}{\text{Differential cash inflow}} = \frac{\$27,000}{\$12,000} = 2.250 = \text{Present value factor}$$

Interpolation To Find the Time-Adjusted Rate of Return (r):

Rate of return	Present value factor	Present value factor
15%	2.283	2.283
r		2.250
16%	2.246	
Differences: 1%	0.037	0.033

$$
\begin{aligned}
r &= 15\% + [(0.033/0.037) \times 1\%] \\
&= 15\% + 0.89\% \\
&= 15.89\%
\end{aligned}
$$

In many cases, calculating the more precise rate of return by hand is unnecessary, since many calculators and computer programs can perform this calculation. Risk management professionals should know the procedures, however, including the interpolation technique, so that they can spot-check the reasonableness of the result obtained by other means.

Had the cost of the asset been $27,000 instead of $30,000, the present value of the differential net cash flows would exceed the present value of the initial investment: $29,844 exceeds $27,000 by $2,844.

To use the time-adjusted rate of return method, divide $27,000 by $12,000. The result is a present value factor of 2,250. Appendix B shows that 2,250 lies between the present value factors for 15 percent and 16 percent. Knowing that the rate of return is between 15 and 16 percent might be adequate for many purposes, certainly for showing that the rate exceeds the 10 percent minimum.

To use the time-adjusted rate of return method, divide $27,000 by $12,000. The result is a present value factor of 2.250. Appendix B shows that 2.250 lies between the present value factors for 15 percent and 16 percent. Knowing that the rate of return is between 15 percent and 16 percent might be adequate for many purposes, certainly for showing that the rate exceeds the 10 percent minimum. In many cases, calculating the more precise rate of return by hand is unnecessary, because many calculators and computer programs can perform this calculation. However, risk management professionals should know the procedure—including the interpolation technique, so that they can spot-check the reasonableness of the results obtained by other means.

Exhibit 11-5 illustrates the application of capital budgeting criteria to a proposal for which the estimated differential annual net after-tax cash flows are *not* uniform. The initial investment is $10,000, the estimated useful life is six years, and the differential annual after-tax net cash flows are as shown in Exhibit 11-6. The minimum acceptable rate of return is 16 percent. Because the annual net cash flows are not uniform, the present value of each year's differential net cash flows must be calculated separately, using the factors from Appendix A.

As shown in Exhibit 11-5, this present value equals $9,881, which is less than the $10,000 present value of the initial investment. The net present value of the proposal is therefore a negative $119. Using the time-adjusted rate of return method for evaluating this proposal requires calculating two present values— one each for two different rates of return (16 percent and 15 percent). The present value of the differential net cash flows at a 16 percent rate of return is calculated when evaluating the proposal by the net present value method. As also shown in Exhibit 11-5, at 15 percent, the present value of the net cash inflows is $10,220. By interpolation, the time-adjusted rate of return is 15.65 percent compounded annually, less than the specified minimum acceptable rate of 16 percent. The proposal should therefore be rejected.

Ranking Investment Proposals

Why do you rank investment proposals?
How do you rank them?

The discussion to this point has shown how both the net present value method and the time-adjusted rate of return method can be used to distinguish acceptable from unacceptable proposals. In addition, both methods can rank the order of preference of several acceptable proposals. Under the time-adjusted rate of return method, the best proposal is the one with the highest rate of return, the second best has the second highest rate, and so on. With the net present value method, any proposal that has a positive net present value is acceptable.

Exhibit 11-5

Evaluation of a Capital Investment Proposal—Unequal Cash Flow

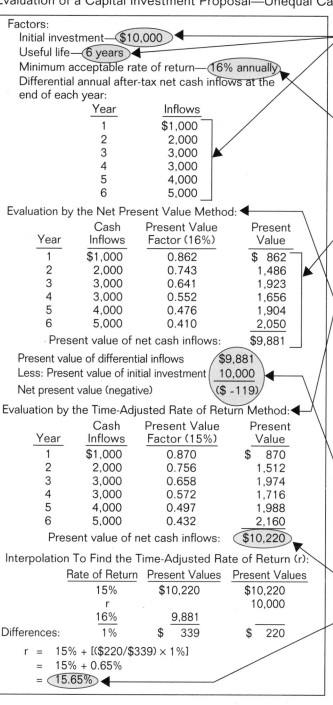

Factors:
Initial investment—$10,000
Useful life—6 years
Minimum acceptable rate of return—16% annually
Differential annual after-tax net cash inflows at the
end of each year:

Year	Inflows
1	$1,000
2	2,000
3	3,000
4	3,000
5	4,000
6	5,000

Evaluation by the Net Present Value Method:

Year	Cash Inflows	Present Value Factor (16%)	Present Value
1	$1,000	0.862	$ 862
2	2,000	0.743	1,486
3	3,000	0.641	1,923
4	3,000	0.552	1,656
5	4,000	0.476	1,904
6	5,000	0.410	2,050
Present value of net cash inflows:			$9,881

Present value of differential inflows $9,881
Less: Present value of initial investment   10,000
Net present value (negative)   ($ -119)

Evaluation by the Time-Adjusted Rate of Return Method:

Year	Cash Inflows	Present Value Factor (15%)	Present Value
1	$1,000	0.870	$ 870
2	2,000	0.756	1,512
3	3,000	0.658	1,974
4	3,000	0.572	1,716
5	4,000	0.497	1,988
6	5,000	0.432	2,160
Present value of net cash inflows:			$10,220

Interpolation To Find the Time-Adjusted Rate of Return (r):

	Rate of Return	Present Values	Present Values
	15%	$10,220	$10,220
	r		10,000
	16%	9,881	
Differences:	1%	$ 339	$ 220

r = 15% + [($220/$339) × 1%]
  = 15% + 0.65%
  = 15.65%

The initial investment is $10,000, the estimated useful life is six years, and the differential annual after-tax net cash flows are as shown.

The minimum acceptable rate of return is 16 percent.

Because the annual net cash flows are not uniform, the present value of each year's differential net cash flows must be calculated separately, using the factors from Appendix A.

Using the time-adjusted rate of return method for evaluating this proposal requires calculating two present values—one each for two different rates of return (16 percent and 15 percent). The present value of the differential net cash flows at a 16 percent rate of return is calculated when evaluating the proposal by the net present value method.

The present value equals $9,881, which is less than the $10,000 present value of the initial investment. The net present value of the proposal is therefore negative $119.

At 15 percent, the present value of the net cash inflows is $10,220. By interpolation, the time-adjusted rate of return is 15.65 percent compounded annually, less than the specified minimum acceptable rate of 16 percent. Therefore, the proposal should be rejected.

Ranking acceptable proposals by the net present value method requires computing a **profitability index**. This index is the ratio of the present value of the differential annual after-tax cash inflows expected from a proposal divided by the present value of the cash outflows that the proposal requires. (A **cash inflow** is a receipt of cash; a **cash outflow** is a payment of cash.) For most proposals, the present value of the required investment will equal the initial required cash outlay, undiscounted by any present value factors. The best proposal has the highest profitability index, and lower-ranking proposals have progressively lower profitability indices.

Notice that the profitability index of a proposal that just meets the minimum acceptable rate of return is 1.0—the present value of the expected net cash flows equals the present value of the required investment when both are discounted by the present value factor for the minimum acceptable rate of return. All acceptable proposals have a profitability index of at least 1.0. Therefore, any proposal with a profitability index of less than 1.0 is unacceptable when measured by specified minimum acceptable rates of return.

Computing Differential Annual After-Tax Net Cash Flows

> **What is a net cash flow (NCF)?**
>
> **How is an NCF calculated?**
>
> **How do non-cash expenses affect NCF?**

After-tax net cash flows, positive or negative, determine the rate of return on a proposal that involves investment of a specified amount of cash. However, the examples presented thus far have not explained how these differential after-tax net cash flows are calculated. In each case, the net cash flows have simply been stated as a "given." In practice, using capital budgeting techniques often requires computing net cash flows from more basic data on revenues and expenses. Some explanation of the computation of net cash flows is therefore in order.

The *net cash flow* (NCF) from a proposal in any year (or a sometimes shorter period) equals the cash inflows that adopting the proposal produces minus the cash outflows it requires. If inflows exceed outflows in any year, the net cash flow from that proposal is positive for that year. If outflows exceed inflows, net cash flow is negative. Thus, subject to the possible effect of income taxes, the net cash flow from a proposal in a given period equals the cash revenues it generates minus the cash outlays it requires during that period. The *differential* **annual after-tax net cash flow (NCF)** is the *change* in an organization's aggregate annual net cash flows resulting from adopting a proposal.

For profit-seeking organizations, income taxes, like other cash outlays, must be deducted from cash revenues in computing net cash flows. Taxes are treated like any other cash outlay and do not alter the basic procedure for computing net cash flows. A complication from income taxes arises because these taxes are computed as a percentage of *taxable income*, not as a percentage of net cash inflows. Taxable income recognizes some non-cash revenue and expense items. Therefore, in computing the cash outflow for income taxes, non-cash revenues and expenses must be considered. For organizations not subject to income taxes, these non-cash revenues and expenses can be ignored, thus simplifying cash flow calculations for public and other nonprofit entities.

In capital budgeting decisions, the main non-cash item affecting income tax is depreciation of long-lived assets. **Depreciation** is the periodic accounting expensing of the initial cost or acquisition price of an asset over the useful life of that asset. Depreciation is not a cash outflow in the period in which the expense is recognized. That outflow usually occurs when the asset is purchased. This expense merely recognizes the outlay in a way that spreads the cost of the asset over the years it produces revenue, thus matching expenses with revenues period by period. (Many organizations also have other substantial non-cash revenues and expenses that are properly recognized by their accrual accounting systems but that have no cash flow effects until they generate actual receipts or outlays. All such non-cash revenues and expenses are ignored in cash flow calculations until they result in an actual receipt or expenditure.)

The following illustrations compute depreciation expense by the **straight-line method** (expensing an asset's purchase price evenly over its life). **Salvage value**, the resale value of used property, is assumed to be zero unless otherwise specified. Thus, for example, if the initial investment in an asset with a seven-year useful life is $35,000, the annual depreciation expense is $5,000. Although not a cash outflow, depreciation should be added to other expenses when computing taxable income. For ease of calculation, income taxes, unless otherwise specified, are assumed to be 40 percent of taxable income.

Exhibit 11-6 illustrates the procedure for computing the differential annual after-tax net cash flow (NCF) from a proposal. The exhibit also evaluates the proposal by using both the net present value and the time-adjusted rate of return methods. The proposal involves an organization's proposed purchase of an automated accounting system that costs $35,000 and that has an expected useful life of seven years. Use of this system will add $500 annually to the organization's operating expenses and $100 a year to its property insurance outlay, both of which are cash expenses. Notice that maintenance and insurance expenses are *differential* expenses—the organization's *total* cash outlays for all maintenance and all insurance are far more than $500 and $100 a year, respectively. Under this proposal, the differential cash revenues to the organization, attributable to more prompt and accurate billing of customers, are

Exhibit 11-6
Calculation of Differential Annual After-Tax Net Cash Flow

<table>
<tr><td colspan="2">

Calculations of Differential Annual NCF

Differential cash revenues		$12,000
Less: Differential cash expenses (except income taxes):		
Maintenance expense	$ 500	
Insurance expense	100	600
Before-Tax NCF:		$11,400
Less: Differential income taxes:		
Before-tax NCF	$11,400	
Less differential depreciation		
expense ($35,000/7 years)	5,000	
Taxable income	$ 6,400	
Income taxes (40%)		2,560
After-Tax NCF:		$8,840

Evaluations of Differential Annual NCF

Factors:
    Initial investment—$35,000
    Useful life—7 years
    Differential annual after-tax NCF—$8,840
    Minimum acceptable rate of return—14% annually

Evaluation by the Net Present Value Method:

Present value of differential NCF	
($8,840 × 4.288)	$37,905.92
Less: Present value of initial investment	35,000.00
Net present value	$ 2,905.92

Evaluation by the Time-Adjusted Rate of Return Method:

$$\frac{\text{Initial investment}}{\text{Differential NCF}} = \frac{\$35,000}{\$8,840} = 3.959 = \text{Present value factor}$$

Interpolation To Find the Exact Time-Adjusted Rate of Return (r):

Rate of Return	Present Value Factor	Present Value Factor
16%	4.039	4.039
r		3.959
18%	3.812	
Differences: 2%	0.227	0.080

    r = 16% + [(0.080/0.227) × 2%]
      = 16% + 0.70%
      = 16.70%

</td>
<td>

Under this proposal, the differential cash revenues to the organization, attributable to more prompt and accurate billing of customers, are $12,000 a year.

Use of this system will add $500 annually to the organization's operating expenses and $100 a year to its property insurance outlay, both of which are cash expenses.

This calculation involves an organization's proposed purchase of an automated accounting system that costs $35,000 and that has an expected useful life of seven years.

Here, annual depreciation expense is $5,000 ($35,000/7 years), making taxable income $6,400 and differential income taxed $2,560. After the deduction of the cash outflow for taxes, this system's annual after-tax net cash flow ("after-tax NCF") becomes $8,840.

</td></tr>
</table>

$12,000 a year. (Again, this is a differential amount because the organization's total revenues from all operations greatly exceed $12,000.)

The procedure for computing differential annual after-tax net cash flows from this system starts by subtracting annual differential cash expenditures, other than income taxes, from differential cash revenues. The result is annual differential before-tax net cash flows ("before-tax NCF").

Although income taxes are like every other cash outflow in that they must be deducted from cash inflows to determine the net cash flow for any period, income taxes must be computed separately because they are a percentage of taxable income. Taxable income is equal to before-tax NCF minus depreciation expense for this accounting period. This cost, the original price of the asset, divided by the number of accounting periods in its expected life, is a non-cash expense. Here, annual depreciation expense is $5,000 ($35,000/7 years), making taxable income $6,400 and differential income taxes $2,560. After the deduction of the cash outflow for taxes, this system's annual after-tax net cash flow ("after-tax NCF") becomes $8,840.

For organizations not subject to income taxes, after-tax net cash flows are equal to before-tax net cash flows. Actual receipts and disbursements of cash have the same effects on public and other nonprofit organizations as they do on profit-seeking organizations, but income taxes are not an expense for nonprofit entities. Therefore, the non-cash expense of depreciation (which must be accounted for in computing income taxes) also has no effect on net cash flows of nonprofit organizations. For example, if the accounting system whose net cash flows are computed and evaluated in Exhibit 11-6 had been purchased by a public entity or other organization whose income is not taxable, the annual net cash flows to this tax-exempt organization from this system, either before or after taxes, would have been $11,400 (the result of the first subtraction at the top of Exhibit 11-6) rather than the $8,840 net cash flow to a taxable organization. The nontaxable organization would not have to pay $2,560 in income taxes each year. Thus, the nontaxable organization would have a higher time-adjusted rate of return on this accounting system than would a taxable one.

This $8,840 after-tax NCF for a profit-seeking organization is equivalent to "differential annual after-tax net cash flow" in previous exhibits in this chapter. Exhibit 11-6 shows how this $8,840 after-tax NCF can be evaluated by either the net present value method or the time-adjusted rate of return method. This evaluation reveals that this system surpasses the minimum acceptable rate of return of 14 percent compounded annually. Discounted at 14 percent, the net present value of the system is $2,905.92. The time-adjusted rate of return is 16.70 percent per year.

The present value of this $11,400 NCF to a nontaxable organization over seven years (assuming that this organization also required a 14 percent minimum annual rate of return) would be $48,883.20 ($11,400 × 4.288). For an organization not subject to income taxes, therefore, the net present value of this investment would be $13,883.20 ($48,883.20 − $35,000). With respect to the time-adjusted rate of return, the present value factor for this accounting system to a nontaxable organization would be approximately 3.070 ($35,000/$11,400), in contrast to the 3.959 present value factor for a taxable organization. Therefore, for a nontaxable organization, the time-adjusted rate of return for this accounting system, computed by the same procedure illustrated at the bottom of Exhibit 11-6, would be 26.18 percent.

Regardless of whether the organization must consider the effect of income taxes, this procedure for computing net cash flow and determining the net present value or the time-adjusted rate of return provides a basis for evaluating all risk management investments.

Summary

Maximizing the present value of net cash flows is the decision guideline that best enhances the organization's ability to apply resources to fulfill its basic objectives. Using cash flow analysis to select risk management techniques puts risk management decisions on the same level as most other decisions in well-managed organizations.

Through its net cash flow during any period, an organization can command resources to pursue its organizational objectives. Projecting net cash flows likely to be generated by alternative assets or activities gives management a valid criterion for choosing those assets or activities that promise the most benefit to the organization.

The net cash flow of an organization determines how much that organization can afford to do. Its net cash flow serves as a barometer of an organization's strength and a measure of its short-range capabilities and its long-range value to its owners and to those whom it serves. Using present values of net cash flows as a decision criterion also promotes other organizational objectives that guide an organization's decisions.

When selecting assets or activities to which to commit an organization's resources, senior management should give priority to those alternatives that promise the net cash flows having the greatest present value. Capital budgeting is the decision-making process involving the evaluation of various alternative capital investment proposals in terms of the cash outlays that they require and the present values of the cash inflows that they are likely to generate.

Capital budgeting techniques recognize that money has a time value because investing money over time in a project or in a financial investment generates more money. The additional amount of money earned by a given dollar over a given time period is the time value of that dollar over that period. Computing the present value of a sum of money to be received in the future incorporates its time value.

A dollar immediately available has a greater time value than a dollar to be received in the future because the dollar in hand can be invested immediately. The two factors that determine the present value of a particular sum are the appropriate interest rate and the length of time before that sum becomes available for use.

The chapter explained how to determine the present value of a present payment, a single future payment, a series of equal future payments, or a series of unequal future payments.

Capital budgeting decisions apply cash flow criteria in one of two ways. One way involves determining whether a particular investment proposal is expected to meet some predetermined minimum acceptable level of performance. The other way involves selecting the most promising proposal by computing the rate of return that each proposal promises to earn on the investment that it requires.

The net present value method can be used only when a minimum acceptable rate of return is predetermined.

Under the time-adjusted rate of return method, the best proposal is the one with the highest rate of return.

With the time-adjusted rate of return method, the best proposal has the highest rate of return, the second best has the next highest, and so on. Ranking proposals by the net present value method requires computing a profitability index. This index is the ratio of the present value of the differential annual after-tax cash inflows expected from a proposal divided by the present value of the cash outflows that the proposal requires.

After-tax net cash flows, positive or negative, determine the rate of return on a proposal that involves investing a specified amount of cash. The net cash flow from a proposal in any year equals the cash inflows it produces minus the cash outflows it requires. If inflows exceed outflows in any year, the net cash flow from that proposal is positive for that year. If outflows exceed inflows, net cash flow is negative. So, subject to the possible effect of income taxes, the net cash flow from a proposal in a given period equals the cash revenues that it generates, minus the cash outlays it requires during that period. For profit-seeking organizations, income taxes, like other cash outlays, must be deducted from cash revenues in computing net cash flows. Taxes are treated like any other cash outlay and do not alter the basic procedure for computing net cash flows.

Appendices

Present Value Tables

Appendix A
Present Value of $1 Received at the End of Period

Years Hence	1%	2%	4%	6%	8%	10%	12%	14%	15%	16%
1	0.990	0.980	0.962	0.943	0.926	0.909	0.893	0.877	0.870	0.862
2	0.980	0.961	0.925	0.890	0.857	0.826	0.797	0.769	0.756	0.743
3	0.971	0.942	0.889	0.840	0.794	0.751	0.712	0.675	0.658	0.641
4	0.961	0.924	0.855	0.792	0.735	0.683	0.636	0.592	0.572	0.552
5	0.951	0.906	0.822	0.747	0.681	0.621	0.567	0.519	0.497	0.476
6	0.942	0.888	0.790	0.705	0.630	0.564	0.507	0.456	0.432	0.410
7	0.933	0.871	0.760	0.665	0.583	0.513	0.452	0.400	0.376	0.354
8	0.923	0.853	0.731	0.627	0.540	0.467	0.404	0.351	0.327	0.305
9	0.914	0.837	0.703	0.592	0.500	0.424	0.361	0.308	0.284	0.263
10	0.905	0.820	0.676	0.558	0.463	0.386	0.322	0.270	0.247	0.227
11	0.896	0.804	0.650	0.527	0.429	0.350	0.287	0.237	0.215	0.195
12	0.887	0.788	0.625	0.497	0.397	0.319	0.257	0.208	0.187	0.168
13	0.879	0.773	0.601	0.469	0.368	0.290	0.229	0.182	0.163	0.145
14	0.870	0.758	0.577	0.442	0.340	0.263	0.205	0.160	0.141	0.125
15	0.861	0.743	0.555	0.417	0.315	0.239	0.183	0.140	0.123	0.108
16	0.853	0.728	0.534	0.394	0.292	0.218	0.163	0.123	0.107	0.093
17	0.844	0.714	0.513	0.371	0.270	0.198	0.146	0.108	0.093	0.080
18	0.836	0.700	0.494	0.350	0.250	0.180	0.130	0.095	0.081	0.069
19	0.828	0.686	0.475	0.331	0.232	0.164	0.116	0.083	0.070	0.060
20	0.820	0.673	0.456	0.312	0.215	0.149	0.104	0.073	0.061	0.051
21	0.811	0.660	0.439	0.294	0.199	0.135	0.093	0.064	0.053	0.044
22	0.803	0.647	0.422	0.278	0.184	0.123	0.083	0.056	0.046	0.038
23	0.795	0.634	0.406	0.262	0.170	0.112	0.074	0.049	0.040	0.033
24	0.788	0.622	0.390	0.247	0.158	0.102	0.066	0.043	0.035	0.028
25	0.780	0.610	0.375	0.233	0.146	0.092	0.059	0.038	0.030	0.024
26	0.772	0.598	0.361	0.220	0.135	0.084	0.053	0.033	0.026	0.021
27	0.764	0.586	0.347	0.207	0.125	0.076	0.047	0.029	0.023	0.018
28	0.757	0.574	0.333	0.196	0.116	0.069	0.042	0.026	0.020	0.016
29	0.749	0.563	0.321	0.185	0.107	0.063	0.037	0.022	0.017	0.014
30	0.742	0.552	0.308	0.174	0.099	0.057	0.033	0.020	0.015	0.012
40	0.672	0.453	0.208	0.097	0.046	0.022	0.011	0.005	0.004	0.003
50	0.608	0.372	0.141	0.054	0.021	0.009	0.003	0.001	0.001	0.001

18%	20%	22%	24%	25%	26%	28%	30%	35%	40%	45%	50%
0.847	0.833	0.820	0.806	0.800	0.794	0.781	0.769	0.741	0.714	0.690	0.667
0.718	0.694	0.672	0.650	0.640	0.630	0.610	0.592	0.549	0.510	0.476	0.444
0.609	0.579	0.551	0.524	0.512	0.500	0.477	0.455	0.406	0.364	0.328	0.296
0.516	0.482	0.451	0.423	0.410	0.397	0.373	0.350	0.301	0.260	0.226	0.198
0.437	0.402	0.370	0.341	0.328	0.315	0.291	0.269	0.223	0.186	0.156	0.132
0.370	0.335	0.303	0.275	0.262	0.250	0.227	0.207	0.165	0.133	0.108	0.088
0.314	0.279	0.249	0.222	0.210	0.198	0.178	0.159	0.122	0.095	0.074	0.059
0.266	0.233	0.204	0.179	0.168	0.157	0.139	0.123	0.091	0.068	0.051	0.039
0.225	0.194	0.167	0.144	0.134	0.125	0.108	0.094	0.067	0.048	0.035	0.026
0.191	0.162	0.137	0.116	0.107	0.099	0.085	0.073	0.050	0.035	0.024	0.017
0.162	0.135	0.112	0.094	0.086	0.079	0.066	0.056	0.037	0.025	0.017	0.012
0.137	0.112	0.092	0.076	0.069	0.062	0.052	0.043	0.027	0.018	0.012	0.008
0.116	0.093	0.075	0.061	0.055	0.050	0.040	0.033	0.020	0.013	0.008	0.005
0.099	0.078	0.062	0.049	0.044	0.039	0.032	0.025	0.015	0.009	0.006	0.003
0.084	0.065	0.051	0.040	0.035	0.031	0.025	0.020	0.011	0.006	0.004	0.002
0.071	0.054	0.042	0.032	0.028	0.025	0.019	0.015	0.008	0.005	0.003	0.002
0.060	0.045	0.034	0.026	0.023	0.020	0.015	0.012	0.006	0.003	0.002	0.001
0.051	0.038	0.028	0.021	0.018	0.016	0.012	0.009	0.005	0.002	0.001	0.001
0.043	0.031	0.023	0.017	0.014	0.012	0.009	0.007	0.003	0.002	0.001	
0.037	0.026	0.019	0.014	0.012	0.010	0.007	0.005	0.002	0.001	0.001	
0.031	0.022	0.015	0.011	0.009	0.008	0.006	0.004	0.002	0.001		
0.026	0.018	0.013	0.009	0.007	0.006	0.004	0.003	0.001	0.001		
0.022	0.015	0.010	0.007	0.006	0.005	0.003	0.002	0.001			
0.019	0.013	0.008	0.006	0.005	0.004	0.003	0.002	0.001			
0.016	0.010	0.007	0.005	0.004	0.003	0.002	0.001	0.001			
0.014	0.009	0.006	0.004	0.003	0.002	0.002	0.001				
0.011	0.007	0.005	0.003	0.002	0.002	0.001	0.001				
0.010	0.006	0.004	0.002	0.002	0.002	0.001	0.001				
0.008	0.005	0.003	0.002	0.002	0.001	0.001	0.001				
0.007	0.004	0.003	0.002	0.001	0.001	0.001					
0.001	0.001										

Appendix B

Present Value of $1 Received Annually at the End of Each Period
for N Periods

Years (N)	1%	2%	4%	6%	8%	10%	12%	14%	15%	16%
1	0.990	0.980	0.962	0.943	0.926	0.909	0.893	0.877	0.870	0.862
2	1.970	1.942	1.886	1.833	1.783	1.736	1.690	1.647	1.626	1.605
3	2.941	2.884	2.775	2.673	2.577	2.487	2.402	2.322	2.283	2.246
4	3.902	3.808	3.630	3.465	3.312	3.170	3.037	2.914	2.855	2.798
5	4.853	4.713	4.452	4.212	3.993	3.791	3.605	3.433	3.352	3.274
6	5.795	5.601	5.242	4.917	4.623	4.355	4.111	3.889	3.784	3.685
7	6.728	6.472	6.002	5.582	5.206	4.868	4.564	4.288	4.160	4.039
8	7.652	7.325	6.733	6.210	5.747	5.335	4.968	4.639	4.487	4.344
9	8.566	8.162	7.435	6.802	6.247	5.759	5.328	4.946	4.772	4.607
10	9.471	8.983	8.111	7.360	6.710	6.145	5.650	5.216	5.019	4.833
11	10.368	9.787	8.760	7.887	7.139	6.495	5.988	5.453	5.234	5.029
12	11.255	10.575	9.385	8.384	7.536	6.814	6.194	5.660	5.421	5.197
13	12.134	11.343	9.986	8.853	7.904	7.103	6.424	5.842	5.583	5.342
14	13.004	12.106	10.563	9.295	8.244	7.367	6.628	6.002	5.724	5.468
15	13.865	12.849	11.118	9.712	8.559	7.606	6.811	6.142	5.847	5.575
16	14.718	13.578	11.652	10.106	8.851	7.824	6.974	6.265	5.954	5.669
17	15.562	14.292	12.166	10.477	9.122	8.022	7.120	6.373	6.047	5.749
18	16.398	14.992	12.659	10.828	9.372	8.201	7.250	6.467	6.128	5.818
19	17.226	15.678	13.134	11.158	9.604	8.365	7.366	6.550	6.198	5.877
20	18.046	16.351	13.590	11.470	9.818	8.514	7.469	6.623	6.259	5.929
21	18.857	17.011	14.029	11.764	10.017	8.649	7.562	6.687	6.312	5.973
22	19.660	17.658	14.451	12.042	10.201	8.772	7.645	6.743	6.359	6.011
23	20.456	18.292	14.857	12.303	10.371	8.883	7.718	6.792	6.390	6.044
24	21.243	18.914	15.247	12.550	10.529	8.985	7.784	6.835	6.434	6.073
25	22.023	19.523	15.622	12.783	10.675	9.077	7.843	6.873	6.464	6.097
26	22.795	20.121	15.983	13.003	10.810	9.161	7.896	6.906	6.491	6.118
27	23.560	20.707	16.330	13.211	10.935	9.237	7.943	6.935	6.514	6.136
28	24.316	21.281	16.663	13.406	11.051	9.307	7.984	6.961	6.534	6.152
29	25.066	21.844	16.984	13.591	11.158	9.370	8.022	6.983	6.551	6.166
30	25.808	22.396	17.292	13.765	11.258	9.427	8.055	7.003	6.566	6.177
40	32.835	27.355	19.793	15.046	11.925	9.779	8.244	7.105	6.642	6.234
50	39.196	31.424	21.482	15.762	12.234	9.915	8.304	7.133	6.661	6.246

18%	20%	22%	24%	25%	26%	28%	30%	35%	40%	45%	50%
0.847	0.833	0.820	0.806	0.800	0.794	0.781	0.769	0.741	0.714	0.690	0.667
1.566	1.528	1.492	1.457	1.440	1.424	1.392	1.361	1.289	1.224	1.165	1.111
2.174	2.106	2.042	1.981	1.952	1.923	1.868	1.816	1.696	1.589	1.493	1.407
2.690	2.589	2.494	2.404	2.362	2.320	2.241	2.166	1.997	1.849	1.720	1.605
3.127	2.991	2.864	2.745	2.689	2.635	2.532	2.436	2.220	2.035	1.876	1.737
3.498	3.326	3.167	3.020	2.951	2.885	2.759	2.643	2.385	2.168	1.983	1.824
3.812	3.605	3.416	3.242	3.161	3.083	2.937	2.802	2.508	2.263	2.057	1.883
4.078	3.837	3.619	3.421	3.329	3.241	3.076	2.925	2.598	2.331	2.108	1.922
4.303	4.031	3.786	3.566	3.463	3.366	3.184	3.019	2.665	2.379	2.144	1.948
4.494	4.192	3.923	3.682	3.571	3.465	3.269	3.092	2.715	2.414	2.168	1.965
4.656	4.327	4.035	3.776	3.656	3.544	3.335	3.147	2.752	2.438	2.185	1.977
4.793	4.439	4.127	3.851	3.725	3.606	3.387	3.190	2.779	2.456	2.196	1.985
4.910	4.533	4.203	3.912	3.780	3.656	3.427	3.223	2.799	2.468	2.204	1.990
5.008	4.611	4.265	3.962	3.824	3.695	3.459	3.249	2.814	2.477	2.210	1.993
5.092	4.675	4.315	4.001	3.859	3.726	3.483	3.268	2.825	2.484	2.214	1.995
5.162	4.730	4.357	4.003	3.887	3.751	3.503	3.283	2.834	2.489	2.216	1.997
5.222	4.775	4.391	4.059	3.910	3.771	3.518	3.295	2.840	2.492	2.218	1.998
5.273	4.812	4.419	4.080	3.928	3.786	3.529	3.304	2.844	2.494	2.219	1.999
5.316	4.844	4.442	4.097	3.942	3.799	3.539	3.311	2.848	2.496	2.220	1.999
5.353	4.870	4.460	4.110	3.954	3.808	3.546	3.316	2.850	2.497	2.221	1.999
5.384	4.891	4.476	4.121	3.963	3.816	3.551	3.320	2.852	2.498	2.221	2.000
5.410	4.909	4.488	4.130	3.970	3.822	3.556	3.323	2.853	2.498	2.222	2.000
5.432	4.925	4.499	4.137	3.976	3.827	3.559	3.325	2.854	2.499	2.222	2.000
5.451	4.937	4.507	4.143	3.981	3.831	3.562	3.327	2.855	2.499	2.222	2.000
5.467	4.948	4.514	4.147	3.985	3.834	3.564	3.329	2.856	2.499	2.222	2.000
5.480	4.956	4.520	4.151	3.988	3.837	3.566	3.330	2.856	2.500	2.222	2.000
5.492	4.964	4.524	4.154	3.990	3.839	3.567	3.331	2.856	2.500	2.222	2.000
5.502	4.970	4.528	4.157	3.992	3.840	3.568	3.331	2.857	2.500	2.222	2.000
5.510	4.975	4.531	4.159	3.994	3.841	3.569	3.332	2.857	2.500	2.222	2.000
5.517	4.979	4.534	4.160	3.995	3.842	3.569	3.332	2.857	2.500	2.222	2.000
5.548	4.997	4.544	4.166	3.999	3.846	3.571	3.333	2.857	2.500	2.222	2.000
5.554	4.999	4.545	4.167	4.000	3.846	3.571	3.333	2.857	2.500	2.222	2.000

Chapter 12

Making Risk Management Decisions Through Cash Flow Analysis

Educational Objectives

1. Apply the financial management concepts learned in Assignment 11 to make recommendations of specific risk management techniques to use in given situations.

   In support of the above educational objective, you should be able to do the following:

   a. Explain how the possibilities of accidental losses and the use of various risk management techniques to cope with these losses affect the net investment in, and the differential after-tax net cash flows from, a capital investment proposal.

   b. Illustrate how risk management investments can generate negative initial cash flows but positive cash flows in subsequent periods.

Outline

Cash Flow Analysis of Risk Management Techniques

Recognizing Risk Management Concerns

Applying Risk Control Techniques

Applying Risk Financing Techniques

Combining Risk Management Techniques

Cash Flow Analysis as a Selector of Risk Management Techniques

Advantages and Disadvantages of Cash Flow Analysis for Risk Management Decisions

Adapting Cash Flow Analysis for Uncertainty

Adapting Cash Flow Analysis for Business Risks

Summary

    c. Compute a series of time-adjusted rates of return on a capital investment proposal, each rate reflecting the use of a different risk management technique to cope with the risks of accidental loss to that investment.

    d. Select the risk management technique that, on the basis of the assumptions of the capital budgeting framework (discussed in Chapter 11 and Assignment 12 of the course guide), offers the highest time-adjusted rate of return on a given capital investment.

    e. Explain and apply the worry method of recognizing the cost of the unpredictability involved in risk management decisions.

2. Identify the possible advantages and disadvantages of using a capital budgeting framework to select risk management techniques.

3. Define or describe each of the Key Words and Phrases for this assignment.

Making Risk Management Decisions Through Cash Flow Analysis

This chapter shows how to select the best risk management technique by combining the forecasts developed in Chapters 9 and 10 with the cash flow analysis developed in Chapter 11 to formulate a risk management decision rule. This **decision rule** can guide an organization in making the most cost-effective allocations of its risk management resources to meet the demands that accidental losses place on that organization. Given a loss exposure and the feasible alternative risk management techniques, the rule developed in this chapter answers the question "Which techniques should be used?" For example, should the exposure be avoided or insured, or should both insurance and loss prevention be used?

This chapter describes how the traditional cash flow decision framework incorporates risk management considerations, catalogs the effects that various risk management techniques are likely to have on an organization's cash flows and rates of return, and explains the advantages and disadvantages of cash flow analysis for selecting risk management techniques.

The chapter uses illustrations to show how each risk control and risk financing technique could be applied to a specific exposure facing Sheltering Arms Hospital: fire damage to a building on the hospital's grounds. Analysis of that exposure highlights the differing effects that alternative risk management techniques are likely to have on the hospital's cash flows, uses of cash, and therefore profitability or operating efficiency. The illustrations presented are specific, but the types of cash flows that they illustrate tend to be universal.

Illustration (or technique) 2, recognizing (but doing nothing to manage) expected losses, is the most basic illustration, the one against which the cash flow and rate of return effects of each of the other risk control and risk financing techniques should be compared. Illustrations 3 through 15 should be examined separately and contrasted with "doing nothing," which is Illustration 1. These illustrations are not cumulative. Their sequence allows each risk management technique to be analyzed on its own merits for its own contribution to an organization's net cash flows. However, the techniques can also be used to analyze the combined cash flow effects of several risk management techniques, particularly combinations of risk financing and risk control techniques, in other situations.

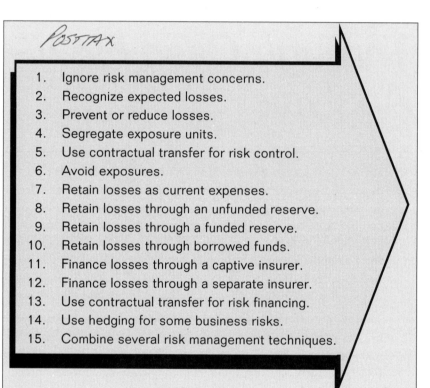

POSTTAX

The illustrations that follow demonstrate how actions taken based on these risk management techniques change cash flows and resulting profitability or operating efficiency.

1. Ignore risk management concerns.
2. Recognize expected losses.
3. Prevent or reduce losses.
4. Segregate exposure units.
5. Use contractual transfer for risk control.
6. Avoid exposures.
7. Retain losses as current expenses.
8. Retain losses through an unfunded reserve.
9. Retain losses through a funded reserve.
10. Retain losses through borrowed funds.
11. Finance losses through a captive insurer.
12. Finance losses through a separate insurer.
13. Use contractual transfer for risk financing.
14. Use hedging for some business risks.
15. Combine several risk management techniques.

Cash Flow Analysis of Risk Management Techniques

What types of cash flow effects do the various risk management techniques have?

How do these effects help in making risk management decisions?

Traditional cash flow analysis omits any mention of risk management considerations. The annual differential after-tax net cash flows (NCFs) that an asset or activity is projected to generate are typically presumed to be highly predictable. Except perhaps in the most hazardous of situations, little consideration is given to the possibility that, for example, an investment that is projected to have a ten-year useful life will be destroyed by fire three years after the investment has been made.

Similarly, most cash flow analyses do not explicitly recognize that the *one-time* costs of implementing risk management techniques should often be *added* to the initial investment in a proposal, while other *continuing* risk management expenses should be *deducted* from its projected annual NCFs. Some more sophisticated analyses recognize that NCF might be represented only as a probability distribution rather than as a fixed stream, but even these analyses might assume that variations in NCF by year arise from speculative risks (such as changes in market conditions) rather than from pure risks of accidental losses, liability claims, or other mishaps.

This chapter deals with risk management considerations within the traditional flow analysis framework. Cash flow analysis is one tool, although not a perfect one, for selecting the most appropriate risk management technique (or combination of techniques) to cope with exposures to accidental loss. The chapter considers how various risk management techniques might change the net present value or time-adjusted rate of return for a proposed asset or activity. The chapter then explores the extent to which the net present value or time-adjusted rate of return can be used to select the most cost-effective risk management techniques.

Although each of the following illustrations features the cash flow effects of only one risk control or risk financing technique, tracing the cash flows of the risk control techniques requires assuming how any remaining risks are to be financed. Unless otherwise specified, these risk control illustrations take into account that any losses are fully retained and paid as current expenses and that each risk financing technique is used without any other risk financing or risk control measure.

Recognizing Risk Management Concerns

The techniques shown in the following illustrations could be applied to most loss exposures that confront any organization. To better understand how those techniques are widely applicable, consider situations involving the Ames Research Center (ARC), located in a three-story building owned by Sheltering Arms Hospital, one of the organizations involved in the tire fire case. The center was established four years ago when the hospital succeeded in attracting Dr. Ames, renowned for his research to develop innovative surgical procedures. Subject to the terms of a ten-year contract, Dr. Ames agreed to conduct his research under Sheltering Arms's auspices with the understanding that all revenue generated by this research would go to the hospital. The hospital projected that this revenue would average $60,000 annually. In exchange, Sheltering Arms provided Dr. Ames with a $200,000 grant to help establish the research facility and obtain necessary equipment. The hospital retained ownership of the building itself.

Over the past four years, fire losses to the building structure have averaged $16,000 annually in repair costs. The hospital is not responsible for fire damage to the building's contents, furnishings, and fixtures, all of which belong to Dr. Ames. The doctor had also agreed to hold the hospital harmless for any liability claims that might arise out of his use of the building. Sheltering Arms's risk management professional is satisfied that Dr. Ames has purchased adequate insurance to meet his obligations under this agreement. In short, the hospital's only significant loss exposure attributable to ARC is physical damage to the building itself, principally because of fire. This commitment, made four years ago, has six years to run.

Illustration 1: Ignoring risk management concerns

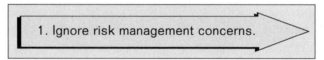

Because the fire hazard is extreme, Sheltering Arms's risk management professional has been exploring various risk management techniques for dealing with this fire exposure, hoping to find a technique (or combination of techniques) that will effectively manage this exposure. The risk management professional has begun his work by developing the figures presented in Exhibit 12-1.

Notice that the figures in this exhibit, and in this chapter's subsequent exhibits, reflect the fact that Sheltering Arms is a private hospital and, as such, must pay income taxes. If Sheltering Arms were a public, tax-exempt entity, the computations for differential income taxes would have been unnecessary. The entry for income taxes would have been zero (instead of $20,000), and the after-tax NCF would have been the same as the before-tax NCF ($60,000). The evaluation of this tax-exempt NCF would have followed the process that is shown in the bottom portion of Exhibit 12-1, substituting $60,000 for $44,000. If Sheltering Arms were a tax-exempt hospital (or any other type of tax-exempt organization), comparable changes would be made in other exhibits throughout this chapter.

Exhibit 12-1 calculates the differential annual after-tax NCF from Dr. Ames's research activity and evaluates this cash flow by both the net present value and the time-adjusted rate of return methods. The $60,000 differential cash revenue in this and related exhibits is the added revenue that the hospital expects to collect from patients and other sources because of Sheltering Arms's association with Dr. Ames. Depreciation (amortization) of the $200,000 grant is taken on a straight-line basis, income taxes are at a 40 percent rate, and Sheltering Arms's minimum acceptable rate of return is 12 percent per year. This exhibit does *not*

Exhibit 12-1
Differential Annual After-Tax Cash Flow—Risk Management
Considerations Ignored

Calculations of NCF		
Differential Cash Revenue		$60,000
Less: Differential cash expenses (except income taxes)		none
Before-Tax NCF:		$60,000
Less: Differential income taxes:		
• Before-tax NCF	$60,000	
• Less differential depreciation expense ($200,000/10 years)	20,000	
• Taxable income	$40,000	
• Income taxes (40%)		$16,000
After-Tax NCF:		$44,000

The $60,000 "differential cash revenue" represents the revenue the hospital expects to collect from patients and other sources because of Sheltering Arms's association with Dr. Ames.

Depreciation of the $200,000 grant is taken on a straight-line basis.

Evaluations of This NCF

Factors:
- Initial investment—$200,000
- Life of project—10 years
- Differential annual after-tax NCF—$44,000
- Minimum acceptable rate of return—12% annually

Evaluation by Net Present Value Method:
- Present value of differential NCF
  ($44,000 × 5.650) $248,600
- Less: Present value of initial investment   200,000
- Net present value $ 48,600

Evaluation by the Time-Adjusted Rate of Return Method:

$$\frac{\text{Initial investment}}{\text{Differential NCF}} = \frac{\$200,000}{\$44,000} = 4.545 = \text{Present value factor}$$

Interpolation To Find the Time-Adjusted Rate of Return (r):

Rate of Return	Present Value Factor	Present Value Factor
16%	4.833	4.833
r		4.545
18%	4.494	
Differences: 2%	0.339	0.288

r = 16% + [(0.288/0.339) × 2%]
= 16% + 1.70%
= 17.70%

Notice in this and the following exhibits that Sheltering Arms is a private hospital and must pay taxes (based on a 40% rate). If Sheltering Arms were a public tax-exempt entity, computations for differential income taxes would be unnecessary (and the entry for income taxes would be zero). The NCF would be $60,000 and would then be substituted throughout the evaluation.

reflect any risk management considerations. Ignoring the possibility that the ARC building could be damaged accidentally, the net present value of the investment at 12 percent interest compounded annually is $48,600, and the time-adjusted rate of return is 17.70 percent annually, making the investment appear to be profitable.

Illustration 2: Recognizing expected losses

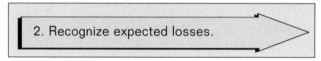

Accurate cash flow analysis should consider cash outlays for accidental losses and related risk management expenses in the same way that the analysis reflects other cash outlays. The choice of risk management techniques, by affecting NCF, can change the rate of return on capital investment proposals and, ultimately, the choices of assets and activities to which an organization should devote its resources.

To stress to Sheltering Arms's senior administrators the effect of fire losses to the ARC building, the risk management professional has drawn on the past four years' experience to project a probability distribution of fire losses to the building. This probability distribution follows:

Probability	Annual Fire Damage	Expected Value
0.80	$ 0	$ 0
0.10	30,000	3,000
0.07	100,000	7,000
0.03	200,000	6,000
1.00		$16,000 = Annual expected value

The annual expected value of this damage is $16,000. This average annual loss—considered the incremental annual after-tax NCF—and rates of return from the ARC building are shown in Exhibit 12-2.

If Sheltering Arms considers the cost of retaining the expected annual fire losses to the ARC building, the resulting net present value, a negative $5,640, fails to meet the minimum acceptable 12 percent return, and the rate of return falls to 11.34 percent. Those calculations recognize only the expected value of fire losses, not the effects that any risk management technique (other than the assumed retention through current expensing) might have on those losses and on the resulting NCF.

Exhibit 12-2
Differential Annual After-Tax Cash Flow—Retention Through Current
Expensing of Losses

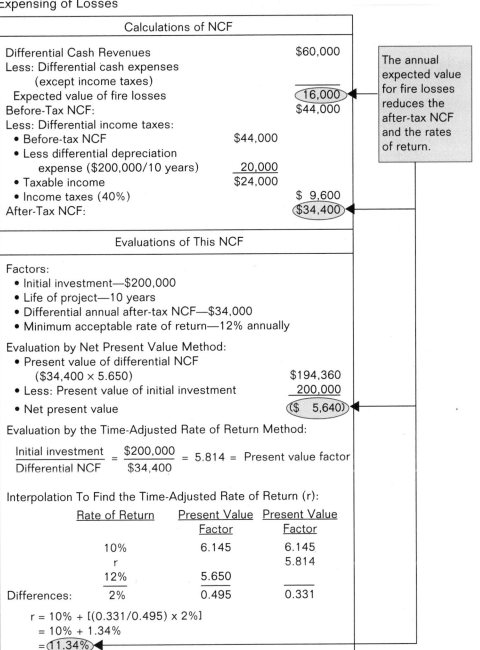

Calculations of NCF	
Differential Cash Revenues	$60,000
Less: Differential cash expenses	
(except income taxes)	
Expected value of fire losses	16,000
Before-Tax NCF:	$44,000
Less: Differential income taxes:	
• Before-tax NCF	$44,000
• Less differential depreciation	
expense ($200,000/10 years)	20,000
• Taxable income	$24,000
• Income taxes (40%)	$ 9,600
After-Tax NCF:	$34,400

> The annual expected value for fire losses reduces the after-tax NCF and the rates of return.

Evaluations of This NCF

Factors:
• Initial investment—$200,000
• Life of project—10 years
• Differential annual after-tax NCF—$34,000
• Minimum acceptable rate of return—12% annually

Evaluation by Net Present Value Method:
• Present value of differential NCF
   ($34,400 × 5.650) $194,360
• Less: Present value of initial investment   200,000
• Net present value   ($ 5,640)

Evaluation by the Time-Adjusted Rate of Return Method:

$$\frac{\text{Initial investment}}{\text{Differential NCF}} = \frac{\$200,000}{\$34,400} = 5.814 = \text{Present value factor}$$

Interpolation To Find the Time-Adjusted Rate of Return (r):

Rate of Return	Present Value Factor	Present Value Factor
10%	6.145	6.145
r		5.814
12%	5.650	
Differences: 2%	0.495	0.331

   r = 10% + [(0.331/0.495) × 2%]
   = 10% + 1.34%
   = 11.34%

Three assumptions underlie the 11.34 percent time-adjusted rate of return. First, the substantial difference between the rates of return in Exhibits 12-1 and 12-2 is due mainly to the expected value of fire losses—$16,000 before taxes each year on the $200,000 investment. However, the relatively large value of expected losses only emphasizes the importance of risk management considerations. It does not distort the logic of the principles involved or of the methods for accounting for these losses and how they are managed.

Similarly, the sizes of the different rates of return to be developed later in the chapter by using other risk management techniques depend on the particular numbers assumed in the basic statement of facts. Thus, the specific sizes of the rates of return and the particular ranking of risk management techniques by rates of return in the following examples are not important, but the methods and underlying logic are crucial because they, unlike any specific numerical results, can be applied to any risk management decision.

A second important assumption of these calculations is that the after-tax expected value of fire losses represents the true cost of retention. This is a simplifying assumption because losses are highly unpredictable and are therefore likely to vary by year. Only an organization with a large number of exposure units could reasonably expect its actual fire damage losses to conform to this $16,000 average in a particular year. Unpredictability of losses is perhaps the most difficult problem in risk management. This problem requires that probability and trend analyses be used in conjunction with capital budgeting to select appropriate risk management techniques.

A third assumption underlying the 11.34 percent time-adjusted rate of return is that fire damage to the ARC building is the only exposure being considered. Physical damage from perils other than fire, such as net income, personnel, and liability losses that may arise from the ARC activity, are not considered here. This assumption avoids unnecessarily complicating the principles being illustrated.

Applying Risk Control Techniques

Several risk control techniques are available to Sheltering Arms. Other than exposure avoidance (here, closing down), the techniques include loss prevention to cut loss frequency, loss reduction to cut loss severity, segregation of exposures to make losses more predictable in the aggregate, and contractual transfer for loss control to shift all responsibility for any losses to a third party.

Illustration 3: Preventing or reducing losses

3. Prevent or reduce losses.

Knowing that Sheltering Arms's senior administrators are not content to tolerate the projected $16,000 annual loss, the hospital's risk management professional has developed the following probability distribution of annual fire losses if a $10,000 sprinkler system had been installed when the hospital entered into its contract with Dr. Ames and had depreciated over the then ten-year life of the agreement. The system would have had a $400 annual cash maintenance expense and would have had no salvage value at the end of the ten years. The risk management professional has estimated that the system would have reduced the severity of fire losses so that the annual fire damage would have been as shown in the following probability distribution:

Probability	Annual Fire Damage	Expected Value
0.80	$ 0	$ 0
0.10	5,000	500
0.07	10,000	700
0.03	100,000	3,000
1.00		$4,200

The before-tax expected value of annual fire losses decreases to $4,200 in this case. Illustration Three, which would call for the ARC building with a sprinkler system, implies the following changes from Illustration Two, retention through current expensing of losses (to the ARC building without sprinklers):

- The sprinkler reduces the expected value of fire losses that the hospital will retain.
- The sprinkler's cost is added to the initial investment.
- The depreciation and maintenance expenses on the sprinkler system are considered in the computing of taxable income.

The differential annual after-tax NCF from the ARC building with a sprinkler system is calculated in the upper portion of Exhibit 12-3. The lower portion shows the evaluation of this cash flow by the net present value method for a required minimum 14 percent annual return and by the time-adjusted rate of return method. The key changes from Exhibit 12-2 involve the preceding three bulleted items.

As Exhibit 12-3 indicates, installing a sprinkler system would have raised the initial investment to $210,000 and the time-adjusted rate of return on the ARC to 14.88 percent annually, giving it a $25,266 net present value when discounted at 12 percent. Providing the building with a sprinkler system makes the

Exhibit 12-3
Differential Annual After-Tax Cash Flow—Loss Reduction Prevention Device

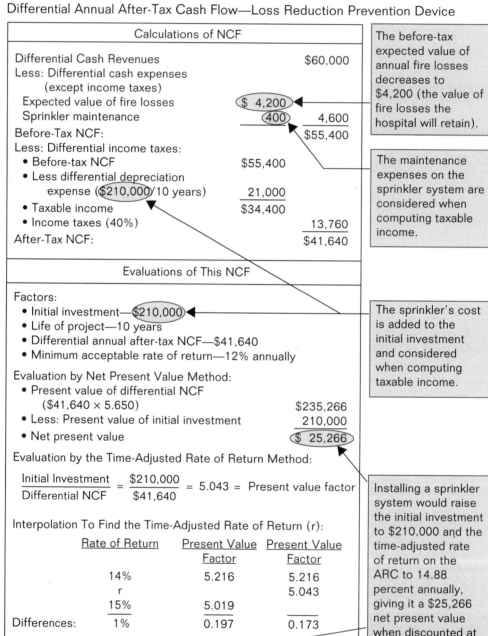

Calculations of NCF		
Differential Cash Revenues		$60,000
Less: Differential cash expenses (except income taxes)		
Expected value of fire losses	$ 4,200	
Sprinkler maintenance	400	4,600
Before-Tax NCF:		$55,400
Less: Differential income taxes:		
• Before-tax NCF	$55,400	
• Less differential depreciation expense ($210,000/10 years)	21,000	
• Taxable income	$34,400	
• Income taxes (40%)		13,760
After-Tax NCF:		$41,640

The before-tax expected value of annual fire losses decreases to $4,200 (the value of fire losses the hospital will retain).

The maintenance expenses on the sprinkler system are considered when computing taxable income.

Evaluations of This NCF

Factors:
• Initial investment—$210,000
• Life of project—10 years
• Differential annual after-tax NCF—$41,640
• Minimum acceptable rate of return—12% annually

The sprinkler's cost is added to the initial investment and considered when computing taxable income.

Evaluation by Net Present Value Method:
• Present value of differential NCF
   ($41,640 × 5.650) $235,266
• Less: Present value of initial investment   210,000
• Net present value $ 25,266

Evaluation by the Time-Adjusted Rate of Return Method:

$$\frac{\text{Initial Investment}}{\text{Differential NCF}} = \frac{\$210,000}{\$41,640} = 5.043 = \text{Present value factor}$$

Interpolation To Find the Time-Adjusted Rate of Return (r):

Rate of Return	Present Value Factor	Present Value Factor
14%	5.216	5.216
r		5.043
15%	5.019	
Differences: 1%	0.197	0.173

r = 14% + [(0.173/0.197) × 1%]
  = 14% + 0.88%
  = 14.88%

Installing a sprinkler system would raise the initial investment to $210,000 and the time-adjusted rate of return on the ARC to 14.88 percent annually, giving it a $25,266 net present value when discounted at 12 percent.

hospital's investment in Dr. Ames's research acceptable when the possibility of accidental fire losses and the costs of coping with them are considered. As Exhibit 12-2 reveals, if the building does not have a sprinkler system, the investment would not have generated the required 12 percent annual rate of return. The fact that loss reduction increased the time-adjusted rate of return is a result of the particular details of this case. Not all loss prevention or reduction techniques improve profitability.

Illustration 4: Segregating exposure units

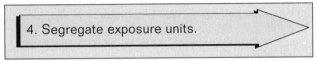

4. Segregate exposure units.

Segregation of exposure units can be achieved either through *separation* (dividing one unit into two or more independent units, each normally used in daily operations) or by *duplication* (creating standby units that are used only when a regular unit has been lost). For example, dividing an inventory equally between two warehouses is separation; having duplicate records or spare parts for key machines is duplication.

In either case, segregation involves increasing the number of exposure units. Segregation makes these losses more predictable by reducing the variation in the total amount of these losses to a percentage of their expected value. With inventory in two geographically separated warehouses, for example, the maximum possible loss from any one occurrence is reduced to one half what it was in the single warehouse. This separation reduces the variation in the amount of individual losses and in the annual totals of loss.

By the law of large numbers, an organization that has a larger number of independent loss exposures can more accurately project its aggregate losses. In terms of net investment and NCF, this more accurate projection of losses reduces the size of any **contingency fund** (funded reserve) needed to pay retained accidental losses. As the number of exposed units increases, any contingency fund that an organization establishes to absorb retained losses can be reduced. This contingency fund reduction allows more of an organization's assets to be devoted to its normal productive activities, which generally yield a higher rate of return than do funds earmarked to pay accidental losses. Having a greater portion of its funds more productively invested increases an organization's overall rate of return.

To see how separation can reduce the amount of funded reserve needed to absorb retained losses, compare Exhibits 12-4 and 12-5. Exhibit 12-4 shows the cash flow implications if Sheltering Arms established a funded fire loss reserve equal to the full value of its initial $200,000 investment. Sheltering Arms's adminis-

Exhibit 12-4

Differential Annual After-Tax Cash Flow—Investment and $200,000
Funded Reserve

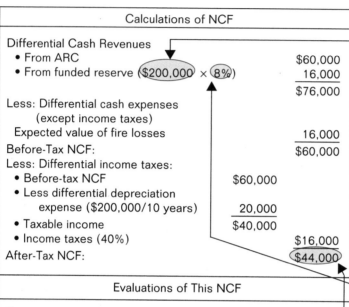

Calculations of NCF		
Differential Cash Revenues		
• From ARC		$60,000
• From funded reserve ($200,000 × 8%)		16,000
		$76,000
Less: Differential cash expenses (except income taxes)		
Expected value of fire losses		16,000
Before-Tax NCF:		$60,000
Less: Differential income taxes:		
• Before-tax NCF	$60,000	
• Less differential depreciation expense ($200,000/10 years)	20,000	
• Taxable income	$40,000	
• Income taxes (40%)		$16,000
After-Tax NCF:		$44,000

Sheltering Arms established a funded fire loss reserve equal to the full value of its initial $200,000 investment. Sheltering Arms's administrators might have judged such a fund necessary to restore any of Dr. Ames's property that might be irreplaceably damaged by a fire.

Evaluations of This NCF

Factors:
- Initial investment—$400,000
- Life of project—10 years
- Differential annual after-tax NCF—$44,000
- Minimum acceptable rate of return—12% annually

Evaluation by Net Present Value Method:
- Present value of differential NCF
  ($44,000 × 5.650) $248,600
- Less: Present value of initial investment 400,000
- Net present value (negative) .... ($151,400)

If the funded reserve can earn an 8 percent annual rate of return, then the resulting cash flows equal $16,000 of revenue each year before taxes.

Evaluation by the Time-Adjusted Rate of Return Method:

$$\frac{\text{Initial investment}}{\text{Differential NCF}} = \frac{\$400,000}{\$44,000} = 9.091 = \text{Present value factor}$$

Interpolation To Find the Time-Adjusted Rate of Return (r):

Rate of Return	Present Value Factor	Present Value Factor
1%	9.471	9.471
r		9.091
2%	8.983	
Differences: 1%	0.488	0.380

$$r = 1\% + [(0.380/0.488) \times 1\%]$$
$$= 1\% + 0.78\%$$
$$= 1.78\%$$

Using the funded reserve yields an annual after-tax NCF of $44,000. However, because establishing a funded reserve equal to the initial grant doubles that investment, the resulting annual after-tax NCF yields a highly negative net present value and does not approach the 12 percent after-tax return that the hospital requires.

trators might have judged such a fund necessary to restore any of Dr. Ames's property that might be irreplaceably damaged by a fire. If this fund can earn an 8 percent annual rate of return, then the resulting cash flows are as shown in Exhibit 12-4. The fund generates $16,000 of revenue each year before taxes. Using such a fund means that this investment yields an annual after-tax NCF of $44,000. However, because establishing a funded reserve equal to the initial grant doubles that investment, the resulting annual after-tax NCF yields a highly negative net present value and does not approach the 12 percent after-tax return that the hospital requires.

(Some might want to analyze the cash flows in this funded reserve example as merely a substitution between two rates of return: an 8 percent return on the $200,000 reserve replaces the 12 percent return that the hospital requires on its assets as a whole. By this analysis, such a substitution imposes on the funded reserve an additional cash cost of 4 percent—12 percent minus 8 percent—of $200,000, or an $8,000 cash outflow for the funded reserve. Although this analysis would be correct if a 12 percent after-tax return could be guaranteed to the hospital, there is no such guarantee—actual returns might be greater or smaller. Throughout these illustrations, 12 percent is used only as a discount rate for the minimum *acceptable* rate of return, not as the assumed *actual* rate. In contrast, the figures in Exhibit 12-4 deal only with forecast actual results.)

If, instead of a single grant to Dr. Ames, Sheltering Arms had invested its $200,000 in ten separate research areas dispersed throughout the hospital, the predictability of any resulting fire losses would have improved, and their maximum likely size reduced. Assume that such segregation reduced aggregate expected losses to $15,000. Assume further that the standard deviation of this aggregate is such that the hospital could have been 99 percent certain that annual losses to the ten separate areas would not have exceeded $25,000. If the funded reserve, earning 8 percent each year, had been only $25,000, the resulting after-tax NCF would have been as shown in Exhibit 12-5.

Although the amount of the annual after-tax NCF is smaller with segregation ($36,200 rather than the $44,000 in Exhibit 12-4), reducing the required investment from $400,000 to $225,000 means that the NCF resulting from segregation more nearly approaches the hospital's minimum requirement. Segregation raises the net present value of the research facilities to a negative $20,470 (in contrast to the negative $151,400 in Exhibit 12-4) and generates a 9.75 percent annual time-adjusted rate of return.

Three of the conditions in this illustration might appear to limit its validity, but they do not. First, actual losses are assumed to equal expected losses. This is a more reasonable assumption with ten separate areas than with one research facility. Notice, however, that if actual losses to the ARC building exceed their

Exhibit 12-5
Differential Annual After-Tax Cash Flow—Segregation With $25,000
Funded Reserve

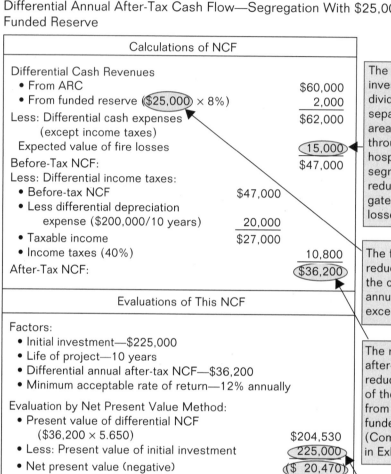

Calculations of NCF	
Differential Cash Revenues	
• From ARC	$60,000
• From funded reserve ($25,000 × 8%)	2,000
Less: Differential cash expenses	$62,000
(except income taxes)	
Expected value of fire losses	15,000
Before-Tax NCF:	$47,000
Less: Differential income taxes:	
• Before-tax NCF	$47,000
• Less differential depreciation	
expense ($200,000/10 years)	20,000
• Taxable income	$27,000
• Income taxes (40%)	10,800
After-Tax NCF:	$36,200

The $200,000 investment has been divided into ten separate research areas dispersed throughout the hospital. This segregation has reduced the aggregate expected losses.

The funded reserve is reduced because of the certainty that annual losses will not exceed this figure.

Evaluations of This NCF

Factors:
- Initial investment—$225,000
- Life of project—10 years
- Differential annual after-tax NCF—$36,200
- Minimum acceptable rate of return—12% annually

Evaluation by Net Present Value Method:
- Present value of differential NCF
  ($36,200 × 5.650) $204,530
- Less: Present value of initial investment   225,000
- Net present value (negative)   ($ 20,470)

The resulting after-tax NCF is reduced as a result of the reduced income from the smaller funded reserve. (Compare to $44,000 in Exhibit 12-4.)

Evaluation by the Time-Adjusted Rate of Return Method:

$$\frac{\text{Initial investment}}{\text{Differential NCF}} = \frac{\$225,000}{\$36,200} = 6.215 = \text{Present value factor}$$

Interpolation To Find the Time-Adjusted Rate of Return (r):

Rate of Return	Present Value Factor	Present Value Factor
8%	6.710	6.710
r		6.215
10%	6.145	
Differences: 2%	0.565	0.495

r = 8% + [(0.495/0.565) × 2%]
= 8% + 1.75%
= 9.75%

The required investment is reduced to $225,000 (compared to $400,000 in Exhibit 12-4). Segregation raises the net present value of the research facilities (in contrast to the negative $151,000 in Exhibit 12-4) and generates a higher time-adjusted rate of return.

$16,000 expected value, these losses would decrease the time-adjusted rate of return in that illustration, making segregation even more attractive in terms of predictability and profitability.

Second, establishing ten separate areas instead of one might be an extreme example of segregation, but a large number of separate units is not essential to the improved NCF that comes from reducing a funded reserve as potential loss severity is reduced. Establishing as few as three research areas within the hospital instead of one might have reduced the funded reserve to $100,000. Under these conditions, $100,000 would be liberated to earn at least the 12 percent rate of return that the hospital requires of funds invested in its own operations instead of 8 percent in the loss reserve, a difference of at least $4,000 in before-tax earnings. Thus, adjusting the number of exposure units can greatly narrow the range of predictable loss severity even though the predictability of loss frequency might not be greatly enhanced.

Third, at the end of the useful life of any investment, the amount of a funded reserve presumably would be released back into the stream of an organization's cash flows—in essence, a cash inflow attributable to the recouping of the funded reserve. For an entire funded reserve to be recouped, any such fund must have been periodically restored to its original amount whenever a loss has been paid out of it. Additional computations to account for final recovery of the funded reserve would not alter the basic thrust of this example. Segregation of exposure units reduces the commitment of resources that must provide assurance that losses can be restored from available funds.

Illustration 5: Using contractual transfer for risk control

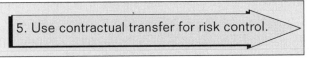

5. Use contractual transfer for risk control.

Two risk management techniques involve contractual transfer: *contractual transfer for risk control*, in which an entire activity and all its related exposures are transferred to another, and *contractual transfer for risk financing*, in which an organization enters into a contract under which another—not an insurance company—agrees to pay for specified losses to that organization. In both cases, the organization being protected is the transferor, and the other, protecting entity is the transferee.

Contractual transfer for risk control involves shifting a loss exposure through a change in the control of property, involves the subcontracting of an activity, or the transfer of a legal responsibility to another party. For example, Sheltering Arms could have transferred the exposure of fire damage to the ARC building by leasing appropriate research space for Dr. Ames to use for ten years for a $100,000 lump-sum lease payment when the lease began. The results of such an arrangement are shown in Exhibit 12-6. Added to the $200,000 grant, this lease payment would have raised the hospital's total investment in Dr. Ames's research to $300,000 but would have shifted the exposure of fire damage to the leased building to the landlord. Income tax regulations would have allowed Sheltering Arms, a private hospital, to write off $30,000 as a deductible expense in each of the ten years, a write-off similar to straight-line depreciation. The differential annual after-tax NCF to Sheltering Arms is computed and evaluated by the net present value and the time-adjusted rate of return methods in Exhibit 12-6.

The relatively low net present value and time-adjusted rate of return on this leasing arrangement are due to the higher investment required without any increase in annual revenues. This example does not show that leasing is a necessarily unprofitable way of coping with a loss exposure, nor can the procedure demonstrated here be applied to all contractual transfers. The terms of each transfer agreement must be examined to trace their effects on net investment and after-tax NCF. In fact, most contractual transfers are more complex than the example presented here.

Illustration 6: Avoiding exposures

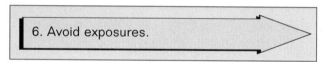

6. Avoid exposures.

When an organization chooses to avoid a loss exposure by refraining from some hazardous activity, it forgoes the benefit that the activity would generate. By choosing exposure avoidance, the organization implicitly or explicitly concludes that the potential benefits from the avoided activity are not worth the exposure to loss. More precisely, the net present value or time-adjusted rate of return from an avoided activity, after one deducts the cost of coping with the exposures to accidental loss by the best risk management techniques other than exposure avoidance, is less than the net present value or time-adjusted rate of return from some other proposal.

With regard to fire damage to a facility (owned or leased) in which Sheltering Arms might have housed the Ames Research Center, exposure avoidance would have denied any grant to Dr. Ames and, with it, deprived the hospital of the prestige and anticipated revenue derived from being associated with his research. As long as Sheltering Arms's senior administrators considered it essential to provide facilities for Dr. Ames's research, exposure avoidance would have been an unlikely feasible risk management alternative for dealing with the fire damage exposure.

Exhibit 12-6
Differential Annual After-Tax Net Cash Flow—Leased Building

Calculations of NCF	
Differential Cash Revenues	$60,000
Less: Differential cash expenses (except income taxes)	none
Before-Tax NCF:	$60,000

Research space was leased to Dr. Ames for ten years for a $100,000 lump-sum lease payment when the lease began.

Less: Differential income taxes:

• Before-tax NCF		$60,000
• Less: Amortization		
of lease ($100,000/10 years)	10,000	
of grant ($200,000/10 years)	20,000	
• Taxable income		$30,000
• Income taxes (40%)		12,000
After-Tax NCF:		$48,000

Income tax regulation would allow Sheltering Arms, a private hospital, to write off $30,000 as a deductible expense in each of the ten years (a write-off similar to a straight-line depreciation).

Evaluations of This NCF

Factors:
- Initial investment—$300,000
- Life of project—10 years
- Differential annual after-tax NCF—$48,000
- Minimum acceptable rate of return—12% annually

Evaluation by Net Present Value Method:
- Present value of differential NCF
  ($48,000 × 5.650) $271,200
- Less: Present value of initial investment ... 300,000
- Net present value (negative) ...... ($ 28,800)

Evaluation by the Time-Adjusted Rate of Return Method:

$$\frac{\text{Initial Investment}}{\text{Differential NCF}} = \frac{\$300,000}{\$48,000} = 6.250 = \text{Present value factor}$$

The $200,000 initial investment plus the lease payment increased the hospital's total investment in Dr. Ames's research to $300,000 but shifted the exposure of fire damage to the landlord.

Interpolation To Find the Time-Adjusted Rate of Return (r):

Rate of Return	Present Value Factor	Present Value Factor
8%	6.710	6.710
r		6.250
10%	6.145	
Differences: 2%	0.565	0.460

$$r = 8\% + [(0.460/0.565) \times 2\%]$$
$$= 8\% + 1.63\%$$
$$= 9.63\%$$

In allowing Dr. Ames to occupy the ARC building it owns, Sheltering Arms is foregoing the benefits it might gain from devoting that building to some other purpose. Doing without these benefits from some alternative use imposes an **opportunity cost** on the hospital. If Sheltering Arms had some other highly productive use of this building, and if the cost of finding other space for Dr. Ames also was very high, the hospital—practicing exposure avoidance—might have chosen not to grant Dr. Ames the $200,000 for research.

Applying Risk Financing Techniques

Unless otherwise specified, the following discussion of risk financing techniques assumes that the full amount of potential losses is to be treated by the one risk financing technique featured in that particular illustration, without considering any risk control measures. In practice, some form of risk control is usually combined with some form of risk financing.

Illustration 7: Retaining losses as current expenses

> 7. Retain losses as current expenses.

Exhibit 12-2 illustrated the most basic form of retention: treating losses as current expenses. An organization that pays losses as they occur treats these losses like any other business expense. Expenditures made to investigate or document a loss or to negotiate with third parties about legal claims are included in these losses.

Such **loss adjustment and settlement costs** are only one example of several additional expenses, beyond the amounts of losses or claims, that an organization practicing any form of retention must be prepared to pay. Other costs include many administrative expenditures that an organization might have to pay if it does not transfer to an insurer or other transferee the financial burden of paying for and settling losses.

These additional cash expenditures are recognized in Exhibit 12-7, which portrays and evaluates Sheltering Arms's expected NCF if it treats the expected value of fire damage to the ARC building as current expenses. To allow Dr. Ames to resume his research as quickly as possible following fire losses, the hospital anticipates paying an average of $2,000 per year in special expediting expenses for building repairs. Because of these additional cash outlays for expediting expenses, the rate of return and net present value of the ARC building are lower in Exhibit 12-7 than in Exhibit 12-2, which merely recognized expected losses without directly controlling or financing recovery from these losses.

Exhibit 12-7

Differential Annual After-Tax Cash Flow—Retention Through Current Expensing of Losses and Administrative Expenses

Calculations of NCF		
Differential Cash Revenues		$60,000
Less: Differential cash expenses (except income taxes)		
• Expected value of fire losses	$16,000	
• Administrative expenses	2,000	18,000
Before-Tax NCF:		$42,000
Less: Differential income taxes:		
• Before-tax NCF	$42,000	
• Less differential depreciation expense ($200,000/10 years)	20,000	
• Taxable income	$22,000	
• Income taxes (40%)		8,800
After-Tax NCF:		$33,200

To allow Dr. Ames to resume his research as quickly as possible following fire losses, the hospital anticipates paying an average of $2,000 per year in special expediting expenses for building repairs.

Evaluations of This NCF

Factors:
- Initial investment—$200,000
- Life of project—10 years
- Differential annual after-tax NCF—$33,200
- Minimum acceptable rate of return—12% annually

Evaluation by Net Present Value Method:
- Present value of differential NCF
  ($33,200 × 5.650) $187,580
- Less: Present value of initial investment   200,000
- Net present value (negative)   ($ 12,420)

Evaluation by the Time-Adjusted Rate of Return Method:

$$\frac{\text{Initial Investment}}{\text{Differential NCF}} = \frac{\$200,000}{\$33,200} = 6.024 = \text{Present value factor}$$

Interpolation To Find the Time-Adjusted Rate of Return (r):

Rate of Return	Present Value Factor	Present Value Factor
10%	6.145	6.145
r		6.024
12%	5.630	
Differences: 2%	0.495	0.121

$r = 10\% + [(0.121/0.495) \times 2\%]$
$= 10\% + 0.49\%$
$= 10.49\%$

Because of these additional cash outlays for expediting expenses, the rate of return and net present value of the ARC building are lower than in Exhibit 12-2, which merely recognized losses without directly controlling or financing recovery from these losses.

Because current expensing of losses is the least formal method of risk financing, it tends to be the least expensive method, *provided* the following are true:

- Actual losses do not exceed levels that the organization can comfortably absorb as current expenses.
- The organization does not need, or can efficiently perform itself, the administrative and risk control tasks typically performed by an insurer or other transferee.

Those are significant provisos. Although current expensing of losses often appears attractive in principle before losses occur, actual experience might prove that some other risk financing technique (alone or in combination with current-expense retention) would have been less costly.

Illustration 8: Retaining losses through an unfunded reserve

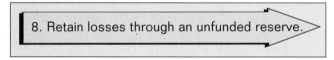

8. Retain losses through an unfunded reserve.

Except for some possible extra administrative costs, the cash flow effects of an unfunded reserve are identical to the cash flow effects of retaining losses as current expenses. An unfunded reserve represents no formal commitment or source of funds. It is merely an accounting recognition of an anticipated expenditure designed to more nearly match the timing of expenses and revenues among accounting periods.

Illustration 9: Retaining losses through a funded reserve

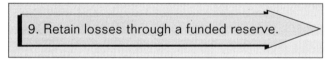

9. Retain losses through a funded reserve.

The funded reserve was previously discussed in Illustration 4: Segregating Exposure Units. Completely apart from segregation of exposure units, the basic purpose of such a reserve—pre-funding of losses—is to smooth over time the highly fluctuating demands that retaining unpredictable losses would otherwise place on an organization's cash flows. Without a formal reserve, an organization's management might be highly uncertain of whether the organization will have access to the cash needed to finance recovery from a loss at the time that a particularly substantial loss occurs.

Establishing a funded reserve to pay losses increases the initial investment in the asset or activity whose losses are to be restored from the fund. The amount of the fund must be added to the cost of the asset or activity as part of the initial investment. Beyond that large initial investment, however, using a funded reserve does not change the cash *outflows* that would otherwise arise from paying losses as current expenses. A funded reserve does create one significant cash *inflow* not present with other forms of retention: earnings on the fund held in the reserve. The reserve funds are normally invested in highly liquid securities, that is, securities that can be quickly sold at a predictable price.

For example, the cash flows to Sheltering Arms from a funded reserve earning 8 percent and used to pay the $16,000 expected value of fire losses to the ARC building would be as computed and evaluated in Exhibit 12-4. (Although one of the purposes of using a funded reserve is to cushion the effect of losses of varying size, the assumption that each year's losses equal their $16,000 expected value does not change the logic of this analysis.) Because establishing and maintaining a funded reserve requires a higher initial investment, retaining losses in this way reduces the rate of return (compared with other forms of retention) whenever the funds placed in the reserve earn less than the funds employed in the organization's normal productive activities.

Illustration 10: Retaining losses through borrowed funds

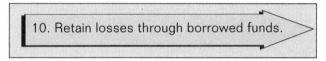

10. Retain losses through borrowed funds.

An organization may borrow funds as needed to pay its accidental losses to keep its own funds productively employed within its normal operations. If an organization can earn more by investing funds in its operations than it costs that organization to borrow these funds (whether to pay losses or for any other purpose), borrowing will improve cash flows. The precise nature of the cash flows associated with borrowing depends on the loan's conditions.

Because of the diversity of possible borrowing arrangements, the cash flows arising from a loan to finance recovery from accidental losses cannot be fully generalized but must be specified in each particular instance. Consequently, an organization's risk management professional will want to work especially closely with its financial officers, analyzing the various forms of short-term and long-term borrowing and the various terms on which borrowed funds might be available to pay for accidental losses. Despite this diversity, one generalization—important to borrowing and to insurance and other contractual transfers—is that funds an organization receives to pay losses should not be considered a cash inflow. Any funds received to pay for accidental losses are disbursed immediately (or at least within the same accounting period) to finance recovery from these losses. Cash received and promptly paid out is merely a "wash transaction," a simultaneous receipt and disbursement of cash, not a net addition to the organization's usable NCF.

The key purpose for borrowing funds to finance recovery from accidental losses is to keep funds working in the organization, earning a higher after-tax rate of return than the after-tax rate of interest that the organization pays for using the borrowed funds. Assume that Sheltering Arms borrows $16,000 on January 1 from its bank for one year at an annual effective before-tax interest rate of 16.67 percent. On December 31 of this same year, Sheltering Arms has to pay the bank $18,667 (the $16,000 return of principal and $2,667 interest). Meanwhile, the hospital plans to use these borrowed funds to pay for expected losses to the ARC building whenever they occur throughout the year, and more important, to keep invested—earning 20 percent before taxes in its operations—the $16,000 of its own funds that would otherwise have been expended during the year to restore these losses.

At the end of the year, the $16,000 principal can be repaid to the bank. The repayment is made using the same $16,000 of the hospital's own money that, at the beginning of the year, it would have had to earmark for retaining the annual expected value of fire losses to the ARC building. The $16,000 principal borrowed and repaid is a wash transaction. However, the difference between the net cash inflow that the hospital can generate by leaving $16,000 at work within the hospital's operation is greater than its cost of borrowing $16,000. Borrowing under these circumstances benefits the hospital because, before income taxes, the $2,667 of interest paid on the loan is less than the $3,200 before-tax earnings on the $16,000 of its own funds that the hospital can keep by borrowing.

Exhibit 12-8 details these results of borrowing at a lower after-tax cost than the ARC earns on its normal operations. The total cost of repaying the loan is $18,667, with the resulting before-tax net cash flow on the ARC as a whole being $44,533. After depreciation (still $20,000 because borrowing does not change the amount of the overall investment) and income taxes of $9,813 on income of $24,533 reflecting the cost of borrowing, this NCF becomes $34,720 after taxes. Discounted at 12 percent in the lower portion of Exhibit 12-8, the net present value of this net cash flow is a negative $3,832, because the time-adjusted rate of return is projected to be only 11.56 percent.

An organization whose internal operations do not generate such a high rate of return (or an organization that faces higher costs of borrowing) is not likely to plan on using borrowed funds to pay losses except under emergency conditions. Relatively few organizations normally find themselves in the favorable hypothetical position that Exhibit 12-8 portrays for Sheltering Arms. Instead, most organizations find their position reversed. The after-tax cost of borrowed funds is typically higher than the after-tax rate of earnings foregone by using internal funds to pay losses. However, the depletion of cash from a particularly severe single loss or a series of small losses that aggregates to a substantial total might necessitate borrowing.

Exhibit 12-8

Differential Annual After-Tax Cash Flow—Retention Through Borrowed Funds

Calculations of NCF		
Differential Cash Revenues		
• From ARC	$60,000	
• From $16,000 used in operations		
($16,000 × 0.20)	3,200	
Total revenues:		$63,200
Less: Differential cash expenses		
(except income taxes)		
• Repayment of loan (1.1667 × $16,000)		18,667
Before-Tax NCF:		$44,533
Less: Differential income taxes:		
• Before-tax NCF	$44,533	
• Less differential depreciation		
expense ($200,000/10 years)	20,000	
• Taxable income	$24,533	
• Income taxes (40%)	9,813	
After-Tax NCF:		$34,720

Sheltering Arms borrows $16,000 on January 1 from its bank for one year at an annual effective before-tax interest rate of 16.67 percent. On December 31 of this same year, Sheltering Arms has to pay the bank $18,667 (the $16,000 return of principal and $2,667 interest).

The total cost of repaying the loan is $18,667, with the resulting before-tax net cash flow on the ARC, as a whole, being $44,533. After depreciation (still $20,000 because borrowing does not change the amount of the overall investment) and income taxes of $9,813 on the income of $24,533 reflecting the cost of borrowing, this NCF becomes $34,720 after taxes.

Evaluations of This NCF		
Factors:		
• Initial investment—$200,000		
• Life of project—10 years		
• Differential annual after-tax NCF—$34,720		
• Minimum acceptable rate of return—12% annually		
Evaluation by Net Present Value Method:		
• Present value of differential NCF		
($34,720 × 5.650)	$196,168	
• Less: Present value of initial investment	200,000	
• Net present value (negative)	($ 3,832)	

Evaluation by the Time-Adjusted Rate of Return Method:

$$\frac{\text{Initial investment}}{\text{Differential NCF}} = \frac{\$200,000}{\$34,720} = 5.760 = \text{Present value factor}$$

Interpolation To Find the Time-Adjusted Rate of Return (r):

Rate of Return	Present Value Factor	Present Value Factor
10%	6.145	6.145
r		5.760
12%	5.650	
Differences: 2%	0.495	0.385

r = 10% + [(0.385/0.495) × 2%]
= 10% + 1.56%
= 11.56%

Discounted at 12 percent in the lower portion of Exhibit 12-8, the net present value of this net cash flow is a negative $3,832 because the time-adjusted rate of return is projected to be only 11.56.

Relatively few organizations normally find themselves in the favorable hypothetical position that Exhibit 12-8 portrays for Sheltering Arms. Instead, most organizations find their position reversed. The after-tax cost of borrowed funds is typically higher than the after-tax rate of earnings forgone by using internal funds to pay losses. However, the depletion of cash from a particularly severe single loss or a series of small losses that aggregates to a substantial total might necessitate borrowing.

The illustration portrayed in Exhibit 12-8, retaining losses through borrowed funds, makes two simplifying assumptions that lessen the complications that could arise from complex financing arrangements. First is the assumption that Sheltering Arms repays the entire loan in one payment at the end of the year rather than through, for instance, monthly or quarterly payments. Second, the example also assumes that the only fee levied by the bank for this loan is the interest charged. Ignoring these or other banking intricacies, as well as other accounting and finance considerations, clarifies the cash flow analysis of borrowing as a risk management technique.

This analysis also suggests why borrowing should be considered retention rather than transfer. Transfer has been previously defined in this text as using outside funds to pay losses, while retention has been defined as using internal funds to pay losses. Why, then, is borrowing outside funds not considered transfer? There are at least two reasons. First, borrowing reduces an organization's resources because credit is an important asset. An organization that borrows to pay its losses draws on its own resources because it cannot borrow these same funds for other purposes.

A second reason for considering borrowing to be retention is that, unlike transfer to an insurer or a noninsurer, borrowing involves no transfer of risk, no shifting of uncertainty to an insurer or other transferee, arising out of the loss exposure originally facing the transferor. For example, Sheltering Arms's borrowing funds to pay for fire losses to the ARC building transfers none of this fire exposure to the lender. When funds are borrowed to pay particular losses (reducing an organization's otherwise available credit), the amount and terms of the loan are known. Except possibly for uncertainty regarding the borrower's ability or willingness to repay, the lender takes on no additional loss exposures. With borrowing, the exposure to accidental losses remains with the borrower.

Illustration 11: Financing losses through a captive insurer

11. Finance losses through a captive insurer.

An organization may establish an insurance subsidiary, or "captive," through which it insures some or all of its loss exposures. The captive can be owned solely by this one parent organization or by a number of parents whose exposures the captive insures. The captive can also insure some loss exposures of organizations that are not owners of the captive.

Principally because of tax and regulatory issues, considerable controversy exists over whether using a captive insurer constitutes retention or transfer for the parent organization. The present discussion of the cash flow effects of premiums paid by the parent to a captive briefly examines both perspectives: retention and transfer.

If the captive arrangement is considered to be retention, the premiums paid to the captive are not tax-deductible, and the cash flows to the parent would be similar to those shown in Exhibit 12-1, which ignores risk management considerations. The resulting annual after-tax NCF would be $44,000 minus whatever annual premium was paid to the captive.

If the captive arrangement is considered to be a transfer, the cash flow of the premium paid to the captive would be identical to those in the following discussion of financing losses through a separate insurer.

Illustration 12: Financing losses through a separate insurer

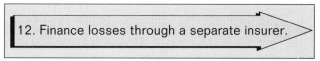

Rather than using internal funds to finance losses through some form of retention, an organization can use transfer, using funds originating in an outside organization to pay for losses. The most frequent form of transfer is to an insurer that agrees, in exchange for a premium, to pay to or on behalf of the insured any losses or claims that fall within the scope of the insurance contract. Under such an arrangement, the premium for the insurance replaces the expected value of retained losses as a cash expense to the insured in the year in which the insurance premium is actually paid. In other respects, the computation of net present value and time-adjusted rate of return for insurance parallels those in previous illustrations.

Much depends on the size of the insurance premium, which could exceed the expected value of the losses that the insurance covers because the premium is designed to provide for the insurer's overhead (including profit). An example is provided in Exhibit 12-9. Sheltering Arms purchases $200,000 of fire insurance on the ARC building. Under the insurance market conditions existing at that time, Sheltering Arms's fire insurer designed its premiums so that 60 percent of the gross premium was allocated to paying insured losses, expected to average

Exhibit 12-9

Differential Annual After-Tax Cash Flow—Full Insurance

Calculations of NCF		
Differential Cash Revenues		$60,000
Less: Differential cash expenses (except income taxes):		
Insurance expense		26,667
Before-Tax NCF:		$33,333
Less: Differential income taxes:		
• Before-tax NCF	$33,333	
• Less differential depreciation expense ($200,000/10 years)	20,000	
• Taxable income	$13,333	
• Income taxes (40%)		5,333
After-Tax NCF:		$28,000

Evaluations of This NCF

Factors:
• Initial investment—$200,000
• Life of project—10 years
• Differential annual after-tax NCF—$28,000
• Minimum acceptable rate of return—12% annually

Evaluation by Net Present Value Method:
• Present value of differential NCF
   ($28,000 × 5.650) $158,200
• Less: Present value of initial investment   200,000
• Net present value (negative)   ($ 41,800)

Evaluation by the Time-Adjusted Rate of Return Method:

$$\frac{\text{Initial investment}}{\text{Differential NCF}} = \frac{\$200,000}{\$28,000} = 7.143 = \text{Present value factor}$$

Interpolation To Find the Time-Adjusted Rate of Return (r):

Rate of Return	Present Value Factor	Present Value Factor
6%	7.360	7.360
r		7.143
8%	6.710	
Differences: 2%	0.650	0.217

$$r = 6\% + [(0.217/0.650) \times 2\%]$$
$$= 6\% + 0.67\%$$
$$= 6.67\%$$

Sheltering Arms purchases $200,000 of fire insurance on the ARC building. Under the insurance market conditions existing at that time, Sheltering Arms's fire insurer designed its premiums so that 60 percent of the gross premium was allocated to pay insured losses, expected to average $16,000 with 40 percent devoted to the insurer's overhead. The total annual premium for fire insurance on the ARC building, P, can be computed as follows:

60% of P = $16,000

$$P = \frac{\$16,000}{0.60}$$

P = $26,667

Note that the premium is a tax-deductible expense. The differential annual after-tax NCF is computed and evaluated from insuring the ARC building for a $26,667 annual premium.

At a 12 percent annual rate of return, fully insuring the ARC building for this premium gives the investment in the building a net present value of negative $41,800. The time-adjusted rate of return is 6.67 percent per year. Contrast this return with that from retaining all losses, either with a sprinkler system (14.88 percent) or without one (11.34 percent).

$16,000 with 40 percent devoted to the insurer's overhead. The total annual premium for fire insurance on the ARC building, P, can be computed as follows:

$$60\% \text{ of } P = \$16,000$$

$$P = \frac{\$16,000}{0.60}$$

$$P = \$26,667$$

Note that the premium is a tax-deductible expense. The differential annual after-tax NCF is computed and evaluated from insuring the ARC building for a $26,667 annual premium. At a 12 percent annual rate of return, fully insuring the ARC building for this premium gives the investment in the building a net present value of negative $41,800. The time-adjusted rate of return is 6.67 percent per year. Contrast this return with that from retaining all losses, either with a sprinkler system (14.88 percent) or without one (11.34 percent).

As long as the expected value of accidental losses is considered the only cost of retention, insurance usually produces a lower net present value or time-adjusted rate of return than retention. This is because an insurance premium typically is larger than the expected value of the insured losses. How much lower the rate of return with insurance is depends on the following:

- The size of the insurer's premium "loading" for its expenses and any profit (40 percent in this case).

- The additional costs of retention to an organization, such as the expenses of performing the safety, loss settlement, and other services that otherwise would be provided by the insurer.

- The intangible burden of the uncertainty of knowing that retained losses can fluctuate greatly by year around their long-term expected value. Many organizations purchase insurance mainly to remove this uncertainty despite the lower net present value and time-adjusted rate of return on insurance when compared with retention.

Illustration 13: Using contractual transfer for risk financing

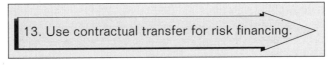

13. Use contractual transfer for risk financing.

Another possible risk management technique is contractual transfer for risk financing, often associated with a hold harmless agreement. Under such an agreement, the transferor's protection can be broad or limited, strong or insecure, depending on (1) the scope—both amount and types—of losses for which the transferee agrees to pay and (2) the financial responsibility—both ability and willingness—of the transferee to pay for those losses that fall within the contractual transfer. Thus, effective use of contractual transfer for risk financing requires that (1) the transfer agreement clearly specify the transferor's losses for which the transferee agrees to be financially responsible and that (2) the transferee have adequate financial resources to meet its obligations under the contractual transfer.

From the transferor's standpoint, contractual transfer for risk financing generally has the following cash flow characteristics:

- The losses paid by the transferee are no longer expenses of the transferor.

- The transferor may, depending on the terms of the transfer agreement, pay some compensation to the transferee for entering into the agreement.

- The transferor may incur some administrative expenses enforcing the transfer agreement, such as in collecting indemnity payments from the transferee.

Although contractual transfers for risk financing are typified by hold harmless agreements for shifting liability exposures, such transfers can also shift property exposures. An example is provided in Exhibit 12-10. To give Dr. Ames an added incentive for fire safety, suppose Sheltering Arms required Dr. Ames to sign a contract whereby he agrees to reimburse the hospital for the first $100 of each fire loss to the ARC building. Because eight fires are expected to occur each year due to the hazards inherent in the research activity, the hospital has projected an $800 annual reimbursement from Dr. Ames and $160 in additional administrative costs to the hospital. Here, the expected $800 indemnity payments from Dr. Ames are treated as a source of incremental revenues, and the $160 administrative costs are incremental expenses. The net present value resulting from this use of contractual transfer for risk financing is a negative $3,470, and the rate of return is 11.15 percent.

Illustration 14: Using hedging for some business risks

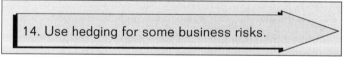

14. Use hedging for some business risks.

Unforeseen changes in the prices at which an organization purchases supplies, raw materials, or product components—as well as changes in the prices it receives for the goods or services it sells—are major sources of speculative risk that can greatly affect the organization's operating efficiency or profits. Increases in the prices it pays for inputs and decreases in the prices it receives for its outputs bring net income losses to the organization; conversely, decreases in an organization's input costs and increases in its selling prices bring the organization unexpectedly large net revenues. The managements of many organizations

Exhibit 12-10
Differential Annual After-Tax Cash Flow—Contractual Transfer Through
Risk Financing

Calculations of NCF		
Differential Cash Revenues		
• From ARC	$60,000	
• From Dr. Ames for fire losses	(800) ◄	
Total cash revenues:		$60,800
Less: Differential cash expenses (except income taxes)		
• Expected value of fire losses	$16,000	
• Administrative expenses	(160) ◄	
Total cash expenses (except income taxes):		$16,160
Before-Tax NCF:		$44,640
Less: Differential income taxes:		
• Before-tax NCF	$44,640	
• Less differential depreciation expense ($200,000/10 years)	20,000	
• Taxable income	$24,640	
• Income taxes (40%)		9,856
After-Tax NCF:		$34,784

To give Dr. Ames an added incentive for fire safety, Sheltering Arms has required Dr. Ames to sign a contract whereby he agrees to reimburse the hospital for the first $100 of each fire loss to the ARC building. Because eight fires are expected to occur each year due to the hazards inherent in the research activity, the hospital has projected an $800 annual reimbursement from Dr. Ames and $160 in additional administrative costs to the hospital. Here, the expected an $800 indemnity payments from Dr. Ames are treated as a source of incremental revenues, and the $160 administrative costs are incremental expenses.

Evaluations of This NCF

Factors:
- Initial investment—$200,000
- Life of project—10 years
- Differential annual after-tax NCF—$34,784
- Minimum acceptable rate of return—12% annually

Evaluation by Net Present Value Method:
- Present value of differential NCF
  ($34,784 × 5.650) $196,529.60
- Less: Present value of initial investment   200,000.00
- Net present value (negative)   ($ 3,470.40)

Evaluation by the Time-Adjusted Rate of Return Method:

$$\frac{\text{Initial investment}}{\text{Differential NCF}} = \frac{\$200,000}{\$34,784} = 5.750 = \text{Present value factor}$$

Interpolation To Find the Time-Adjusted Rate of Return (r):

Rate of Return	Present Value Factor	Present Value Factor
10%	6.145	6.145
r		5.750
12%	5.650	
Differences: 2%	0.495	0.395

r = 10% + [(0.395/0.495) × 2%]
  = 10% + 1.5%
  = (11.6%) ◄

The net present value resulting from this use of contractual transfer for risk financing is a negative $3,470.40, and the rate of return is 11.6 percent.

know with virtual certainty that their input and output prices will change during the next year or other accounting period, but they cannot reliably predict the direction or size of these price changes.

Organizations unwilling or unable to tolerate such fluctuations in their operating results from one time period to another can often turn to hedging as a risk financing technique to stabilize their net incomes. For hedging to function effectively, the preconditions for hedging specified in Chapter 8 must also exist for the goods or services whose price fluctuations destabilize the organization's operating results. Furthermore, the organization's management must be willing to forego potential gains in net revenues from favorable price changes in order to achieve protection against net income losses from adverse price changes. By sacrificing through hedging possible speculative gains, an organization's management secures protection against possible speculative losses. That sacrifice enables the organization to more nearly reach its projected operating results despite unpredictable price changes.

The activities of the Ames Research Center would offer few opportunities for hedging, largely because the ARC does not rely heavily on any commodity for which both a spot and futures market exist. However, Aunt Melinda's Cookie Company (one of the firms involved in the tire fire case introduced in Chapter 1) would have opportunities for managing business risks through hedging. For example, the profitability of Aunt Melinda's depends heavily on the often-fluctuating prices it must pay for the ingredients of its cookies. Aunt Melinda's is constantly buying fresh supplies of wheat flour, needing an average of 10,000 units of flour each month. The price of this flour changes, moving in the same direction (and roughly by the same magnitude) as the price of the wheat from which this flour is made. If Aunt Melinda's must pay $3.00 per unit of flour, then—as shown in Aunt Melinda's simplified "normal" monthly income statement presented in Exhibit 12-11—the company's anticipated profit would be $11,000. This would be the monthly net profit result without any hedging against fluctuations in the flour prices that Aunt Melinda's pays.

If, again without any hedging, Aunt Melinda's had to pay $4.00 for each unit of flour, its monthly net profit would be only $1,000 (shown in Exhibit 12-12). But, if, in contrast, flour prices fell so that Aunt Melinda's could get flour for $2.50 per unit, then the company's monthly net profit would rise to $16,000 (shown in Exhibit 12-13).

Assume that Aunt Melinda herself is uncomfortable with this potential $15,000 swing (from as little as $1,000 to as much as $16,000) in her company's monthly profits as a result of just a $1.00 (or even a $0.50) shift in what Aunt Melinda considers the "normal" $3.00 price of a unit of flour. To smooth these likely but largely unpredictable fluctuations in flour prices and, therefore, in monthly oper-

Exhibit 12-11
Aunt Melinda's Cookie Company
"Normal" Anticipated Monthly Income Statement, No Hedging

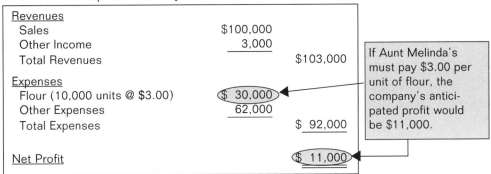

Revenues		
Sales	$100,000	
Other Income	3,000	
Total Revenues		$103,000
Expenses		
Flour (10,000 units @ $3.00)	$ 30,000	
Other Expenses	62,000	
Total Expenses		$ 92,000
Net Profit		$ 11,000

If Aunt Melinda's must pay $3.00 per unit of flour, the company's anticipated profit would be $11,000.

Exhibit 12-12
Aunt Melinda's Cookie Company
Monthly Income Statement—Rising Flour Prices, No Hedging

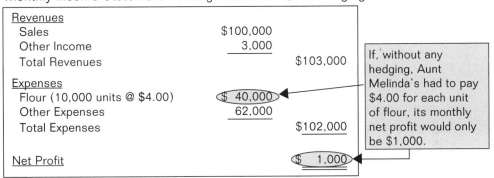

Revenues		
Sales	$100,000	
Other Income	3,000	
Total Revenues		$103,000
Expenses		
Flour (10,000 units @ $4.00)	$ 40,000	
Other Expenses	62,000	
Total Expenses		$102,000
Net Profit		$ 1,000

If, without any hedging, Aunt Melinda's had to pay $4.00 for each unit of flour, its monthly net profit would only be $1,000.

Exhibit 12-13
Aunt Melinda's Cookie Company
Monthly Income Statement—Falling Flour Prices, No Hedging

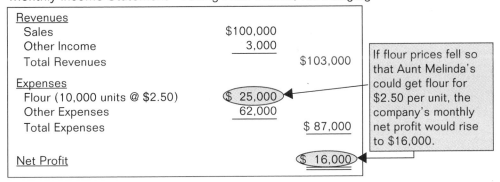

Revenues		
Sales	$100,000	
Other Income	3,000	
Total Revenues		$103,000
Expenses		
Flour (10,000 units @ $2.50)	$ 25,000	
Other Expenses	62,000	
Total Expenses		$ 87,000
Net Profit		$ 16,000

If flour prices fell so that Aunt Melinda's could get flour for $2.50 per unit, the company's monthly net profit would rise to $16,000.

ating results, Aunt Melinda's could hedge against this business risk, giving up potential profits from falling flour prices in order to obtain protection against business losses from rising flour prices. This would give Aunt Melinda greater assurance that her company's normal $11,000 monthly profit would actually materialize despite any increase or decrease in Aunt Melinda's cost of flour.

To make this hedge, Aunt Melinda's would purchase the type of wheat future that is known as a "call." A wheat call is an option that Aunt Melinda's could exercise to purchase a specified quantity of wheat at a given price at any time before a specified expiration date of the call option. Call futures (as well as "put" futures, which are options to sell a specified money of a commodity such as wheat at a given price at any time before a specified date) have their own "futures" or "options" markets, where these rights to buy and sell commodities are themselves bought and sold. A call option has value only if the current market price of actual wheat (known as the "spot price of wheat") is greater than the call price, because only then does the call give its holder the ability to obtain wheat at a lower price than the spot market currently offers. The value of such a wheat call future rises as the current market price of wheat continues to increase above the call price. If the current spot market price falls below the call price, the call option has little current value as an option because buying wheat in the spot market is, at such a time, cheaper than obtaining wheat by exercising the call option. However, a call may regain value if the spot market price rises above the price specified in the call.

For any commodity for which futures are traded in an organized market, the price of a call future and the spot price of the commodity tend to move up or down proportionally. Therefore, for Aunt Melinda's, buying a wheat future call option gives it an asset whose market value will increase as the price of wheat increases or will decrease as the price of wheat decreases. (The current spot price of wheat is the major, but not the only, determinant of the price of wheat flour.) Hence, as flour prices increase, raising Aunt Melinda's cost of producing cookies and lowering the company's operating profit, Aunt Melinda's opportunities for selling its wheat call option for more than the company paid for it increase. The profit from selling the wheat call option can at least partially balance the loss of profit from rising flour prices. Conversely, as flour prices fall and Aunt Melinda's cookie-producing profit rises above normal, some of these extra profits offset the loss that Aunt Melinda's suffers from the falling price of its wheat call option in the wheat futures market.

Exhibits 12-14 and 12-15, involving call option hedges for rising and falling flour prices, depict the "cushioning" effects of hedging. Those effects tend to be approximate, bringing Aunt Melinda's net profits back to near their $11,000

Exhibit 12-14

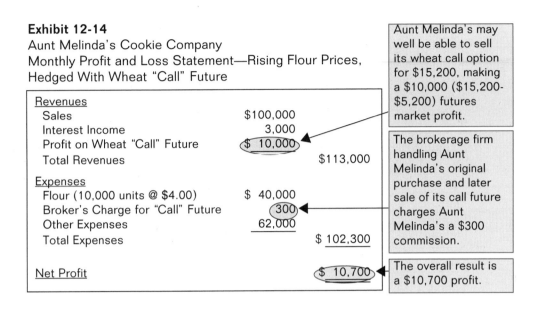

Aunt Melinda's Cookie Company
Monthly Profit and Loss Statement—Rising Flour Prices,
Hedged With Wheat "Call" Future

Revenues		
Sales	$100,000	
Interest Income	3,000	
Profit on Wheat "Call" Future	$ 10,000	
Total Revenues		$113,000
Expenses		
Flour (10,000 units @ $4.00)	$ 40,000	
Broker's Charge for "Call" Future	300	
Other Expenses	62,000	
Total Expenses		$ 102,300
Net Profit		$ 10,700

Aunt Melinda's may well be able to sell its wheat call option for $15,200, making a $10,000 ($15,200-$5,200) futures market profit.

The brokerage firm handling Aunt Melinda's original purchase and later sale of its call future charges Aunt Melinda's a $300 commission.

The overall result is a $10,700 profit.

Exhibit 12-15

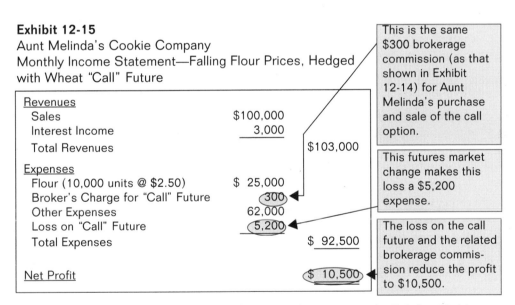

Aunt Melinda's Cookie Company
Monthly Income Statement—Falling Flour Prices, Hedged
with Wheat "Call" Future

Revenues		
Sales	$100,000	
Interest Income	3,000	
Total Revenues		$103,000
Expenses		
Flour (10,000 units @ $2.50)	$ 25,000	
Broker's Charge for "Call" Future	300	
Other Expenses	62,000	
Loss on "Call" Future	5,200	
Total Expenses		$ 92,500
Net Profit		$ 10,500

This is the same $300 brokerage commission (as that shown in Exhibit 12-14) for Aunt Melinda's purchase and sale of the call option.

This futures market change makes this loss a $5,200 expense.

The loss on the call future and the related brokerage commission reduce the profit to $10,500.

normal level, but not necessarily achieving this exact result. Exhibit 12-14 gives a simplified general example of rising flour prices, falling operating profit on cookies, and opportunities for profiting from the rising price of wheat futures call options. Assume that, in a particular month, Aunt Melinda's purchases for $5,200 a call option for enough units of wheat to produce the 10, 000 units of wheat flour that the company plans to use during the month. As the price of wheat rises during the month (as Exhibit 12-14 assumes), Aunt Melinda's may well be able to sell this wheat call option for $15,200, making a $10,000 ($15,200-$5,200) futures market profit. The brokerage firm handling Aunt Melinda's original purchase and later sale of its call future charges Aunt Melinda's a $300 commission. The overall result, shown at the bottom of Exhibit 12-14, is a $10,700 profit, close to the $11,000 "normal" profit that Aunt Melinda's would have earned had the price of flour been $3.00. Aunt Melinda's only real cost in this particular example was the $300 brokerage commission; without it, the company would again have made its anticipated $11,000 profit.

Exhibit 12-15 shows the opposite case whereby falling wheat prices enable Aunt Melinda's to make a greater profit producing cookies but force the company to lose money on its wheat call option. Assume here that the spot market price of wheat falls below the price specified in the wheat call option that Aunt Melinda's purchased for $5,200, reducing the value of this option to virtually zero. This futures market change makes this loss a $5,200 expense, shown in the bottom portion of the Exhibit. Exhibit 12-14 also shows as an expense the $300 brokerage commission for Aunt Melinda's purchase and sale of the call option. The loss on the call future and the related brokerage commission reduce to $10,500 the greater profit of $16,000 that Aunt Melinda's would have earned because of falling flour prices had it purchased no call option futures protection (see Exhibit 12-13). Again, however, this $10,500 profit is close to the $11,000 normal monthly profit.

These profit-normalizing or leveling effects of call options for Aunt Melinda's result from market forces, not from exact cash flow computations or other mathematical calculations. Markets reflect the expectations and attitudes of those who buy and sell these options and the balancing of the supply and demand of a particular type of option (such as a thirty-day wheat call future in the above example) at the moment that an organization like Aunt Melinda's wishes to buy or sell an option. Therefore, the cash flow effects of futures market transactions are not as precise as other calculations presented in the chapter, nor do they typically extend over several accounting periods. Therefore, this particular use of hedging as a risk financing device for short-term business risks does not require present value computations.

Combining Risk Management Techniques

Each of the preceding examples of how risk management techniques affect an organization's net cash flows and operating efficiency has focused on a single risk control or risk financing technique. In practice, however, it is usually best to apply several risk management techniques, typically at least one risk control technique with at least one risk financing technique, to each significant loss exposure that an organization faces. Several techniques together, used in varying degrees, usually reduce an organization's cost of risk from an exposure to accidental loss more than does any single risk management technique.

Illustration 15: Combining several risk management techniques

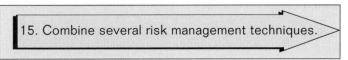

15. Combine several risk management techniques.

The possibilities for combining one or more techniques to manage one loss exposure, and for applying a given technique to a greater or lesser degree (such as a large, complex firefighting sprinkler system rather than a small, basic one or retention through a small insurance deductible rather than a large one) are virtually infinite. Each possibility has its own projected levels of initial investment and annual net cash flows. To illustrate one possibility for the Ames Research Center's exposure to fire losses, Exhibit 12-16 analyzes the projected cash flow implications of investing in a sprinkler system (using figures drawn from Exhibit 12-3), using borrowed funds to finance recovery from the reduced expected level of fire losses (drawing from figures in Exhibit 12-8) and assuming the $2,000 of administrative expenses (assumed in Exhibit 12-7). Other organizations in other situations are likely to have different amounts—even different types—of net cash flow effects from this combination of risk control and risk financing techniques.

This combination of risk control and risk financing techniques should generate the annual net cash flows computed and evaluated in Exhibit 12-16. The notable accounting and cash flow consequences of this exhibit include (1) reduced fire losses, (2) maintenance expenses for the sprinkler system, (3) an initial depreciable investment that includes $10,000 for the sprinklers, (4) annual cash outlays to repay funds borrowed to finance recovery from expected fire losses, and (5) significant cash outlays ($2,000) for administrative expenses. This sprinklers-with-borrowing combination offers a higher projected rate of return than either the loss-controlling sprinklers alone or borrowing funds alone for the following reasons:

- The sprinklers lower the fire losses expected each year.
- Typically, less money must be removed from normal productive operation to pay for losses.

The resulting anticipated $18,486 net present value and 14.12 percent time-adjusted rate of return compare favorably with other single-technique alternatives examined previously in this chapter. This result is consistent with the principle that combining good risk control with proper risk financing is usually more efficient than either sound risk control or sound risk financing. But this is

Exhibit 12-16

Differential Annual After-Tax Cash Flow—Combining Loss Prevention/Reduction
With Borrowed Funds

Calculations of NCF		
Differential Cash Revenues		$60,000
• From $4200 used in operation		
(0.20 × $4,200)		840
Total Revenues		$60,840
Less: Differential cash expenses		
• Repayment of loan (1.20 × $4,200)	$5,040	
• Administrative costs	2,000	
• Sprinkler maintenance	400	7,440
Before-Tax NCF:		$53,400
Less: Differential income taxes:		
• Before-tax NCF	$53,400	
• Less differential depreciation		
expense ($210,000/10 years)	21,000	
• Taxable income	$32,400	
• Income taxes (40%)		12,960
After-Tax NCF:		$40,440

Invest in a sprinkler system (using figures drawn from Exhibit 12-3), using $4,200 borrowed funds to finance recovery from the reduced expected level of fire losses (drawing from figures in Exhibit 12-8), and assuming the $2,000 of administrative expenses (assumed in Exhibit 12-7).

Evaluations of This NCF

Factors:
- Initial investment—$210,000
- Life of project—10 years
- Differential annual after-tax NCF—$40,440
- Minimum acceptable rate of return—12% annually

Evaluation by Net Present Value Method:
- Present value of differential NCF
  ($40,440 × 5.650) $228,486
- Less: Present value of initial investment   210,000
- Net present value $ 18,486

Evaluation by the Time-Adjusted Rate of Return Method:

$$\frac{\text{Initial investment}}{\text{Differential NCF}} = \frac{\$210,000}{\$40,440} = 5.193 = \text{Present value factor}$$

Interpolation To Find the Time-Adjusted Rate of Return (r):

Rate of Return	Present Value Factor	Present Value Factor
14%	5.216	5.216
15%	5.019	5.193
Differences: 1%	01.97	0.023

$r = 14\% + [(0.023/0.197) \times 1\%]$
$= 14\% + 0.12\%$
$= 14.12\%$

The resulting anticipated $18,486 present value and 14.12 percent time-adjusted rate of return compare favorably with other single technique alternatives examined previously in this chapter.

not always the case. Everything depends on the types, amounts, and timing of the cash flows, and these will all differ by organization. The logic of the process for computing and evaluating net cash flows, not the specific dollar amounts of these or any other particular examples, is significant.

Cash Flow Analysis as a Selector of Risk Management Techniques

What are the advantages/ disadvantages of this cash flow analysis?

How can this analysis take account of uncertainty?

How can this analysis encompass business risks?

Cash flow analysis has two alternative methods, the net present value method and the time-adjusted rate of return method, for most profitably allocating an organization's financial resources. The present value method applies the rule that an organization should accept only those proposals that have a positive net present value when both the differential after-tax NCF and the initial investment are discounted at a minimum acceptable rate of return. When evaluating proposals using the net present value method, an organization should give first preference to the proposal offering the highest profit.

Alternatively, the time-adjusted rate of return method applies the equally valid decision rule that an organization should rank alternative proposals in terms of the time-adjusted rate of return that each promises. Foregoing sections of this chapter have demonstrated how the net present value or the time-adjusted rate of return from a proposal are affected by the costs of possible accidental losses and by the costs of risk management techniques to cope with these losses.

These decision rules should also be used to select risk management techniques. For this purpose, the net present value rule can be restated as follows: An organization should give first preference to that risk management technique that promises the highest net present value for the proposal to which that technique is applied. Similarly, the time-adjusted rate of return decision rule becomes the following: An organization should select the risk management technique that promises the highest time-adjusted rate of return on the proposal to which that technique is applied.

To select the technique giving the highest net present value or time-adjusted rate of return, however, a risk management professional must consider an exhaustive list of all possibilities. This can be done by evaluating each proposal (such as the ARC building in the previous examples) not as a proposal alone but as a proposal coupled with a risk management technique. Such a list of possibilities might resemble the following:

ARC Building With

Risk Control	Risk Financing
Through prevention/reduction	Through retaining losses as
Through segregation of exposure	current expenses
units	Through an unfunded reserve
	Through a funded reserve
Through contractual transfer	Through borrowed funds
Through exposure avoidance	Through a captive insurer
	Through a separate insurer
	Through contractual transfer
	Through hedging

Through combining risk management techniques

If one ignores the possibility of using two or more risk management techniques simultaneously, the above listing regarding the ARC building is complete because it (1) allows for "doing nothing" about risk management (a phrase that usually signifies planned or unplanned retention), (2) includes the major types of risk management techniques, and (3) allows the ARC building to be compared with all other proposals. If another proposal yields a higher net present value or time-adjusted rate of return than this ARC building can generate with any risk management technique other than exposure avoidance, the exposures associated with the ARC building should be avoided by investing in that other proposal.

Thus, expanding the final item in the above list makes the list into a complete enumeration of all possible proposals, each coupled with all possible risk management techniques. The list of alternatives is then much longer than a list of traditional alternative capital investment proposals, which usually ignore risk management considerations. The rule for maximizing profit remains essentially the same: Invest first in the proposal having the risk management technique yielding the highest net present value or time-adjusted rate of return, and give progressively lower rankings to alternatives with lower net present values or time-adjusted rates of return.

Advantages and Disadvantages of Cash Flow Analysis For Risk Management Decisions

The major advantages of using the above adaptation of cash flow analysis for selecting risk management techniques is that this adaptation puts risk management decisions on the same footing as any other profit-maximizing decisions.

The net present value and time-adjusted rate of return tests theoretically are proper for the organization that seeks to increase profits. They also are best for the nonprofit organization striving to increase its operating efficiency. By using cash flow analysis, the risk management professional is "speaking the language of management," justifying his or her actions and supporting his or her proposals on a basis that all managers should use and understand.

The disadvantages of cash flow analysis are the weaknesses of the assumptions that must be made to employ this analysis conveniently. First, in the above examples, each risk management technique is handled individually, ignoring all the combinations of techniques that could have been used. In practice, at least one risk control technique and one risk financing technique should be applied to every significant loss exposure. Risk control must be backed by risk financing for those risks that cannot be eliminated completely. Risk financing becomes much less expensive when supported by effective risk control.

Another assumption is that there are no degrees to which a particular technique can be used. For example, the ARC building was either sprinklered or unsprinklered (without any comparison of different sizes or types of sprinklers). That assumption leads to oversimplified yes/no decisions rather than a more thorough analysis. A third assumption is that damage by fire is the only loss involved while, in fact, many property, personnel, liability, and net income losses could result from a single event.

Fourth, the expected value of losses is a measure of the losses that actually occur regardless of the unpredictability of the future. Fifth, and in some respects most important, cash flow analysis assumes that the only goal of the organization is to maximize profits. Humanitarian and social values are irrelevant. For example, this approach attaches no explicit value to human life saved by preventing an industrial accident or to a river kept clean by an organization's avoiding pollution.

The flaws inherent in those assumptions can be at least partially overcome. More lengthy net present value or time-adjusted rate of return computations, incorporating combinations of risk management techniques used in varying degrees to cope with several types of losses, can be performed, especially if a computer is available. Values can be assigned to humanitarian and social factors to include them in the computations.

The problem of unpredictability can be handled in several ways, one of the most straightforward being the worry factor method described below.

Adapting Cash Flow Analysis for Uncertainty

The procedures just discussed for making risk management decisions on the basis of net present values and time-adjusted rates of return assume, unrealistically, that accidental losses equal their expected value each year. Because accidental losses are not this predictable, using a risk management technique that exposes the organization to massive unanticipated losses naturally creates uncertainty about whether the implemented risk management technique is, indeed, the one that contributes most to the organization's profitability or operating efficiency. Some degree of uncertainty is unavoidable with every risk management technique. The cost of this uncertainty must be considered when evaluating risk management alternatives.

The worry factor method assigns a "price tag" to this uncertainty. The **worry factor** is an implicit after-tax cost that, once identified, can be treated like any other cost, or cash outflow, in a cash flow analysis of any risk management technique. In applying the **worry factor method**, the first step is to assign (somewhat arbitrarily) a cost of worry to each alternative risk management technique. This cost should reflect the uncertainty to be suffered by the people who must endure the uncertainty associated with each risk management decision. These people would include primarily senior management or the owners of the organization, since top management or the owners often stand to lose the most from an unwise or unlucky risk management decision. The attitudes of these top managers or owners are often communicated to the risk management professional who assumes these worries as his or her own. The worry factor generally increases with the size of potential losses to be absorbed. Therefore, full insurance often has little of a worry factor associated with it on the assumption that insurance will pay all losses.

Applying the worry factor to risk management decisions requires the following two-step process:

1. Determine the amount of the worry factor (for example, the cost of worry for each risk management technique for a given loss exposure).

2. Deduct this cost from the net cash inflow (or add it to the net cash outflow) for each period in which that technique would be used for that exposure.

The first step can be accomplished by asking the appropriate manager how much he or she would be willing to pay each year (or other period) to know exactly what that year's accidental losses will be. Once these losses are known, risk management decisions become comparable to other management decisions.

To complete the second step, subtract the value of the worry factor from the annual *after-tax* net cash inflow (or add it to the annual *after-tax* net cash outflow) from each risk management technique. The worry factor is deducted from the after-tax NCF because the worry factor is only an implicit expense, not a tax-deductible expenditure. Once the "after-worry" after-tax annual net cash flow is determined, it can be inserted into the net present value and time-adjusted rate of return evaluation computations and be evaluated just like the "before-worry" after-tax NCF.

To further describe the worry-factor method, Exhibit 12-3 computes and evaluates the annual after-tax NCF of the ARC building on which Sheltering Arms retains fire losses but installs a sprinkler system as a loss reduction measure. The after-tax net cash flow (computed without reference to the cost of worry) is $41,640, which, given the other facts in that example, yields a net present value, discounted at 12 percent, of $25,266 and a time-adjusted rate of return of 14.88 percent.

In this case, assume that the hospital's senior administrators are very disturbed by the uncertainties associated with retaining the losses on the ARC building and are willing to pay another $5,000 per year to ensure that fire losses to the building actually equal the projected $4,200 value. As shown in Exhibit 12-17, deducting this $5,000 worry factor from the previously calculated annual after-tax NCF of $41,640 gives an NCF of $36,640. The present value of this adjusted NCF, discounted at 12 percent, is $207,016, giving a net present value of a negative $2,984.

In terms of the time-adjusted rate of return method, the ARC building's present value factor adjusted for the cost of worry is 5.731, which is equivalent to an 11.67 percent annual time-adjusted rate of return. Contrast this 11.67 percent return with the 6.67 percent time-adjusted rate of return on the ARC building if fully insured (Exhibit 12-10). If no worry factor is associated with a fully insured ARC building, the gap in present value factors (and rates of return) between insurance and retention narrows. However, the projected rate of return for retention still remains higher than for insurance. In fact, had the worry factor associated with retention been $9,000, for example, the worry-adjusted after-tax NCF on the sprinklered ARC building would have been so low that fully insuring an unsprinklered ARC building would have been more profitable than retaining losses on a sprinklered one.

The worry factor method provides a fairly easy and understandable method for adapting cash flow analysis to the uncertain environment in which many risk management decisions must be made. This method makes the cost of uncertainty explicit and adjustable to the attitudes of senior management. Although necessarily somewhat arbitrary, this method is sufficiently straightforward to appeal to the senior management of many organizations. In an organization in which other, more complex methods of adjusting for the lack of certainty are used, the risk management professional should seriously consider adopting that organization's methods of analysis.

Exhibit 12-17

Differential Annual After-Tax Cash Flow—Recognition of the Worry Factor

Calculations of NCF		
Differential Cash Revenues		$60,000
Less: Differential cash expenses (except income taxes):		
• Expected value of fire losses	$4,200	
• Sprinkler maintenance	400	4,600
Before-Tax NCF:		$55,400
Less: Differential income taxes:		
• Before-tax NCF	$55,400	
• Less differential depreciation expense ($210,000/10 years)	21,000	
• Taxable income	$34,400	
• Income taxes (40%)		$13,760
After-Tax NCF:		$41,640
Less worry factor		5,000
After-Worry NCF:		$36,640

Deducting this $5,000 worry factor from the previously calculated annual after-tax NCF of $41,640 gives an NCF of $36,640.

Evaluations of This NCF

Factors:
- Initial investment—$210,000
- Life of project—10 years
- Differential annual after-tax NCF—$36,640
- Minimum acceptable rate of return—12% annually

Evaluation by Net Present Value Method:
- Present value of differential NCF ($36,640 × 5.650) — $207,016
- Less: Present value of initial investment — 210,000
- Net present value (negative) — ($ 2,984)

The present value of this adjusted NCF, discounted at 12 percent, is $207,016, giving a net present value of a negative $2,984.

Evaluation by the Time-Adjusted Rate of Return Method:

$$\frac{\text{Initial investment}}{\text{Differential NCF}} = \frac{\$210,000}{\$36,640} = 5.731 = \text{Present value factor}$$

Interpolation To Find the Time-Adjusted Rate of Return (r):

Rate of Return	Present Value Factor	Present Value Factor
10%	6.145	6.145
r		5.731
12%	5.650	
Differences: 2%	0.495	0.414

The ARC building's present value factor adjusted for the cost of worry is 5.731, which is equivalent to an 11.67 percent annual time-adjusted rate of return.

$r = 10\% + [(0.414/0.495) \times 2\%]$
$= 10\% + 1.67\%$
$= 11.67\%$

Adapting Cash Flow Analysis for Business Risks

The accidental losses on which this text mainly focuses are almost always linked to business risks. Unlike exposures to accidents, business risks offer opportunities for gain as well as loss. Except when truly major accidents strike an organization, as when the tire fire struck Wheeler's Tire Disposal and many of its riverfront neighbors, the business risks that organizations willingly undertake for profit or to meet other objectives usually affect their net cash flows much more substantially than do accidental losses. For example, a significant upward or downward change in the prices at which Wheeler's can sell its recycled rubber (or in the level of the wages it must pay its employees) almost always changes its net cash flows much more than do most of the employee injuries, vehicle collisions, and resignations of key personnel that inflict accidental losses on Wheeler's.

In all organizations, effective risk management deals with risks of accidental losses in the context of business risks. In many of today's best-managed organizations, effective risk management equally considers both types of risk, accidental losses and business risks to (1) increase the amount of an organization's net cash flows, (2) speed its cash inflows and slow its cash outflows, and (3) smooth fluctuations in its cash flows, regardless of whether the fluctuations arise from accidents or from adverse business developments. That third, stabilizing effect on net cash flows is a particularly important result of good risk management because, given any two streams of future net cash flows that have the same present value, the stream that is the more predictable is the more highly valued by investors, owners, creditors, and customers who are risk-averse (that is, who prefer greater certainty to less certainty). Thus, when done well, truly strategic risk management increases an organization's operating efficiency/profitability, its value to the organization's owners, and its appeal to risk-averse creditors, customers, employees, neighbors, and other constituencies.

Like all good managers, risk management professionals try to increase as much as possible their time-adjusted rates of return or the present value of their organizations' net cash flows (and, hence, their operating efficiency/profitability) without increasing the risk associated with those cash flows beyond the owners' and managers' tolerance for uncertainty. Business executives generally measure risk by the standard deviation or the coefficient of variation of an organization's year-to-year or month-to-month net cash flows. A fact of most business activities is that achieving greater profitability or operating efficiency requires taking greater risks. Thus, higher time-adjusted rates of return or net present values of net cash flows typically come only with greater standard deviations or coefficients of variation in those net cash flows. This persisting relationship is often presented as a risk-return function or curve, such as that portrayed by line A in

Exhibit 12-18. For an organization whose risk-return possibilities are indicated by curve A, the points along the curve form a "frontier" of the greatest rates of return that this organization can expect to generate at a given level of variability in its net cash flows. Alternatively, the curve shows the least risk (cash flow variability) that its owners and managers can expect to tolerate to achieve a given rate of return.

Well-managed organizations operate along highest risk-return frontiers that they can reach. Not-so-well-managed organizations fall somewhere below their attainable frontier. Thus, of two organizations that could each potentially operate along risk-return frontier B in Exhibit 12-18, the organization whose position is shown by the star is somewhere along its frontier and is well-managed. The organization positioned at the X in the exhibit has relatively inferior management.

By making decisions that move an organization up or down risk-return curve A, an organization's managers can increase its rate of return by tolerating greater uncertainty or can gain more certain returns by sacrificing some profits or operating efficiency. Moving from point 1 down to point 2 on curve A lowers the organization's expected rate of return to achieve greater predictability of that return. Conversely, moving from point 2 up to point 1 raises the expected profitability or operating efficiency, but at the cost of greater risk that these profits or efficiencies will not materialize.

For instance, for accidental fire losses, an organization can take less risk, smooth out its period-to-period net cash flows, and typically lower its profitability. In effect, the organization moves from point 1 to point 2 on curve A in Exhibit 12-18 by purchasing more fire insurance and retaining fewer destabilizing fire damage losses. On the other hand, the organization can move from point 2 to point 1 by taking more risk, and striving for greater profits if it is lucky, by buying less fire insurance and retaining more potential fire damage. An organization's business risk decisions also can move it along a risk return curve. Buying raw materials at lower prices from less reliable suppliers increases the buying organization's risk, tending to move it upward along curve A from point 2 to point 1. Buying its own source of these raw materials, reducing the organization's risks from depending on any outside suppliers, pushes its risk-return position down curve A toward point 2.

Organizations in different industries often operate along different risk-return curves. For example, airplane manufacturing often is viewed as a high-risk/high-return industry. Such a manufacturer's executives probably make decisions along the risk-return frontier shown as curve C in Exhibit 12-18. In contrast, the executives in relatively low-risk/low-return industries like retailing groceries or mortuaries are likely to make decisions along curve B in the exhibit.

Exhibit 12-18
Typical Risk Return Curves

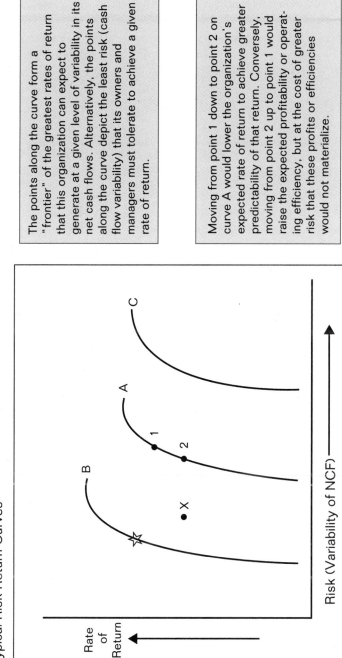

The points along the curve form a "frontier" of the greatest rates of return that this organization can expect to generate at a given level of variability in its net cash flows. Alternatively, the points along the curve depict the least risk (cash flow variability) that its owners and managers must tolerate to achieve a given rate of return.

Moving from point 1 down to point 2 on curve A would lower the organization's expected rate of return to achieve greater predictability of that return. Conversely, moving from point 2 up to point 1 would raise the expected profitability or operating efficiency, but at the cost of greater risk that these profits or efficiencies would not materialize.

In the context of this exhibit, good strategic management of both accidental and business risks can move an organization from the inferior position shown by the X to the frontier of its capabilities symbolized by the star.

The risk-return curves in Exhibit 12-18 have some significant implications for managing an organization's exposures to accidental losses. First, the amount of uncertainty that an organization can tolerate in its management of exposures to either business reversals or accidental losses is limited by the risk-return frontier appropriate for its industry. Second, within that frontier, the organization's capacity to absorb fluctuations in its cash flows because of good or bad luck with exposures to accidental losses depends on the cash flow fluctuations stemming from its business risks. The more stable the business, other things being equal, the greater the chances that the organization might be able to retain exposures to accidental losses. However, if business risks (and resulting cash flow fluctuations) increase, a more conservative, usually more costly, approach to preventing and paying for accidental losses usually becomes more appropriate. Third, because different teams of managers and owners for different organizations have different tolerance levels for risk, any two organizations have different risk-return frontiers, or one organization's frontier might shift over time as its leadership changes. Fourth, and perhaps most important, an organization that is not well managed (is not now at its risk-return frontier) can, in principle, become more profitable and more productive, without assuming greater overall risk, if its executives become more skilled in applying risk management techniques to either the organization's exposures to accidental losses or its business risks. In the context of Exhibit 12-18, good strategic management of both accidental and business risks can move an organization from the inferior position shown by the X to the frontier of its capabilities symbolized by the star.

Summary

The selection of risk management techniques (the third step in the risk management decision process) uses the net present value and time-adjusted rate of return decision criteria. Those techniques—discussed in Chapter 11—help select, from among the risk management techniques cataloged in Chapter 8, those techniques that promise to most cost-effectively counter the adverse effects of accidental losses forecast by the statistical techniques discussed in Chapters 9 and 10. Cash flow analysis provides decision criteria for dealing with these adverse effects in ways that enhance the present value of an organization's NCF and internal rates of return.

Those decision criteria require, first, identifying the effects that exposures to accidental losses can be expected to have on an organization's NCF if these exposures are not managed. Second, they require tracing the cash flow effects of each of the separate risk control and risk financing techniques that could be applied to each exposure. Third, they require selecting the technique that is most cost-effective in promising to generate the highest net present value or time-adjusted rate of return.

Chapter 13

Risk Management Information Systems

2. Describe the characteristics and potential advantages and disadvantages of each of the principal alternatives among which an organization may choose in acquiring (a) hardware, (b) software, and (c) personnel for a computer-based risk management information system.

3. Describe the potential advantages and disadvantages to an organization of establishing and relying on a computer-based risk management information system.

4. Explain the importance of, the kinds of information needed for, and the actions that should be taken in
   a. conducting a needs analysis for a proposed computer-based risk management information system.
   b. identifying the information flows required for a proposed computer-based risk management information system.
   c. determining the feasibility of a proposed computer-based risk management information system.
   d. deciding whether to build, buy, or lease the hardware, software, and personnel needed for a proposed computer-based risk management information system.

5. Describe, and explain how to overcome, the (a) data problems and (b) system problems frequently encountered in managing a computer-based risk management information system.

6. Describe, and explain how to manage, loss exposures arising out of a risk management information system.

7. Define or describe each of the Key Words and Phrases for this assignment.

Risk Management Information Systems

All managers, probably all people, possess a management information system in the broadest sense. Such a system is a set of procedures (physical or mental) for gathering facts (data) about one's environment, generating information (useful statements about the present or expected future condition of that environment), and reaching and implementing decisions about how to deal with that environment. In that generic sense, perhaps every creature able to manipulate or respond to its environment has some sort of management information system for protecting its own well-being. It follows that every organization, even those without a designated risk manager or risk management department, also has some sort of a risk management information system (or RMIS) for protecting the organization against the adverse effects of accidental losses by recognizing and coping with actual or potential accidental losses.

This chapter examines how a risk management information system, whether manual or computerized, can be designed, implemented, and protected from accidental losses in ways that enhance the effectiveness of an organization's overall risk management program. Any management information system is a tool for achieving a particular managerial and organizational goal. A **risk management information system (RMIS)** is a tool for better protecting an organization against the adverse effects of actual and potential accidental losses, thereby lowering the organization's overall cost of risk. As a tool tailored to each organization's loss exposures and mission, a risk management information system can be useful in any or all steps of the risk management decision process for any or all of an organization's operations.

Many perfectly good risk management information systems can be entirely manual, operating on the basis of traditional paper records and communications. Others demand computer-based facilities because of (1) the volume of exposure and loss data involved; (2) the number and locations of persons (inside or outside the organization) who must have access to exposure, loss, or other risk management data; or (3) the complexity of the risk control or risk financing decisions to be made on the basis of information derived from these data. Although manual risk management information systems are valid in many settings, this chapter focuses on computerized systems by explaining the following:

- The fundamental concepts underlying all proper management information systems

- The conditions under which a computerized, rather than a manual, risk management information system is appropriate

- The steps in, and the decisions required for, designing a computerized risk management information system

- The implementation and the management of a risk management information system, including managing the loss exposures that the system generates

- The applications of a risk management information system throughout the risk management decision process

- The exposures to accidental loss that a risk management information system creates or intensifies, and how these exposures should be manage

Information Systems—Fundamental Concepts[1]

What is information management?

For risk management, what is management information?

As managers throughout an organization use computer technology to deal more effectively with the quantitative aspects of their work and to improve their own performance, risk management professionals will want, or will feel pressured, to do the same. Like many activities and decisions throughout an organization, risk management also lends itself to a management information system and, more specifically, to a risk management information system. To understand the purposes and components of an RMIS, students should begin with some fundamental concepts underlying all management information systems: (1) the distinction between information management and management information, (2) the distinction between operating data and management information, and (3) the costs and values of information and its management.

Information Management and Management Information

Information management and management information, while related, have significantly distinct meanings. **Information management** is the process by which management information is extracted from all the available data and manipulated so that it is available in the proper form to the managers who need it. **Management information** is that portion of all of an organization's available information that its managers need to know to make sound decisions.

Information Management

Information management is the process of managing information within an organization. It refers to any manager's concern with the creation, flow, and use of information in fulfilling his or her responsibilities. Indeed, some managers refer to their "responsibility to manage the organization's information system." Although a computer is not essential for information management—both information and its management existed long before computers existed—many managers consider the computer an essential tool of information management.

Management Information

Management information refers to a particular type of information: information used by managers for particular purposes. For example, an organization's general management information system may contain information on many kinds of expenses; some of these costs (such as for workers compensation claims) will be of direct risk management concern. Some of this workers compensation and other costs of risk information will be useful for the organization's general financial management.

Other information, such as the workers compensation benefits paid to a particular employee for a specific disability or information about the causes of several work-related injuries and illnesses, will be useful to the risk management department. The department might use such information to monitor a particular employee's recovery and return to work or to identify frequent causes of work injuries toward which preventive efforts should be directed. Depending on the purpose—general financial management, claim monitoring, or loss prevention—all of these data are potential management information. Management information is information—extracted from the mass of information on an organization's operations—that is needed by managers to fulfill specific responsibilities.

Management Information System (MIS)

A management information system (MIS) is a particular kind of system. As usually defined, a system is a set of components that interact with one another from some purpose. A **management information system (MIS)** is a group of people, a set of procedures, and (usually) data processing equipment that select, store, process, and retrieve data to reduce the uncertainty in decision making by yielding information for managers

Thus, the ultimate purpose of any MIS is to reduce uncertainty—a most important goal given the unpredictability of accidental losses. Notice, however, that the uncertainty to be reduced for an RMIS is not that which arises from the unpredictability of losses but, rather, the uncertainty associated with making decisions. An MIS, and particularly an RMIS, should be designed to give a manager the maximum confidence that, given the information available, a particular decision is the best one that can be made at that time.

An MIS reduces uncertainty in decision making by providing as much management information, in the most understandable and most useful form, as the decision requires. To do this, an MIS takes raw data about an organization's operations and generates useful management information from them.

Operating Data and Management Information

When discussing an MIS or an RMIS, one must distinguish between data and information. *Data* are isolated facts not placed in any meaningful context that would permit inferences or conclusions to be drawn. For example, a chronological listing of work injuries (perhaps showing the names of injured employees, the nature of the injuries, and the estimated ultimate dollar values of the claims) would be data. Arranged simply by the dates of injury, these data would not easily yield meaningful conclusions about the causes, costs, or control of work injury exposures.

In contrast, *information* is data organized in ways that identify certain variables or conditions helpful in making decisions, that is, data put into a context for decision making. Within an organization, information about its operations guides its management

The distinction between data and information suggests a potential defect in many MIS and RMIS. Those systems might be filled with data that do not provide adequate management information. For example, historical "loss runs" giving the date, the location, the perils, the coded category of cause, and the amount for individual losses provide an organization's risk management professional with much data, but the "loss runs" often go unread because the unorganized, isolated facts yield little information. However, once these data are organized and perhaps summarized by location, cause, date, time of day, or dollar size category, the risk management professional can begin to glean information useful in cost-effectively preventing or paying for these individual losses. A well-designed RMIS can structure data properly, yielding true information and improving risk management performance.

Information: Costs and Values

Gathering raw data can be costly. Deciding how to organize raw data into useful information and then producing the information itself can be even more expensive. Generally, any organization should seek to gather only those data and generate only that information whose values are greater than their costs. That principle underlies much of the cost-benefit analysis for deciding among types of RMIS. Even before considering specific types of systems, however, the risk management professional should have in mind the types of costs and the values of information inherent in a computerized RMIS.

Costs of Information

The cost of obtaining, or capturing, information can be divided into the following six general categories:

1. Cost of Hardware. Because the cost of the hardware is the price actually paid to purchase or lease equipment, this cost probably is the easiest to determine.

2. Cost of Additional Software or Modified Software. The RMIS could require special computer software that the organization's overall MIS does not need.

3. Cost of Systems Analysis, Design, and Implementation. This includes all program development costs, from the design phase through the implementation phase.

4. Cost for Space and Environment Control Factors. This includes floor space, preparation, special temperature and humidity controls, and power control units. With large-scale computers, these costs can be significant.

5. Cost of Conversion. This includes both the one-time cost associated with conversion from a manual procedure to a computerized procedure and the cost of upgrading or converting from one computer system to another. The conversion cost is often considerably higher than the total costs of hardware, installation, and program development.

6. Cost of Operation. This includes the personnel, supplies, space, utilities, and other costs associated with maintaining and operating the information management function.

Value of Information

Unlike the costs of information, the value of the information is extremely difficult to quantify and must be approached almost exclusively from a conceptual point of view. The value of information is based on the following ten considerations:

1. Accessibility. How easily and quickly can the information be accessed? It might be a matter of seconds through a **cathode-ray tube (CRT)** (that resembles a television screen) or a matter of hours through some batch method.

2. Comprehensiveness. Not how voluminous, but how comprehensive is the information in question? Does it convey meaning in its own right or only in relation to some other information?

3. Accuracy. To what degree is the information free from error? (Because no human information is infallible, an error rate—however small—is inevitable.)

4. Appropriateness. Is the information relevant to the user's request or need and presented in a way that the user can apply?

5. Timeliness. How much time elapses from the transaction or event until the output is available to the user? Is information available when needed for activities and decisions?

6. Clarity. How is the information presented? Can the inexperienced or occasional user understand it without aid?

7. Flexibility. How flexibly can the information be used? Can it be used for more than one decision or by more than one decision maker?

8. Verifiability. Can the information be easily verified?

9. Freedom From Bias. Has the information been free from any attempt to alter or modify it to support a preconceived conclusion? (If the information has been "screened," its objectivity—and hence its value—has been reduced.)

10. Quantifiability. To what extent is the raw data numerical and susceptible to the kinds of mathematical manipulation for which computers are designed? (The more quantifiable the data, the more information a computer can generate from it and the greater the merit of investing in computer equipment and programs.)

Risk Management Information Systems

How is the RMIS evolving?

What are the components of an RMIS?

What are the likely benefits and limitations of an RMIS?

A risk management information system, whether simple or complex, is a process for gathering, analyzing, and reporting data and information relevant to an organization's risk management program. Those data, and the meaningful information derived from them for making risk control or risk financing decisions, may (1) encompass the entire scope of an organization's risk management program (including all loss exposures that the organization's senior management perceives as falling within the scope of "risk management" and all the risk control and risk financing tools for dealing with these exposures) or (2) focus on a particular type of loss exposure (products liability, for example, for a firm facing many such claims) or on a particular risk management technique (such as prevention of employee injuries). The scope of any RMIS is unessential to the definition of the system. Also unessential to the definition is the particular use of any RMIS, which may range from transaction processing and standard risk management reporting to affording random access to a database and providing quantitative analysis to support risk management decisions. The essence of the definition is the gathering, analysis, and reporting of data and information in carefully specified ways that ensure the greatest accuracy and cost-effectiveness of the information generated and the decisions reached.

This discussion considers the historical development of risk management information systems, the components of an RMIS, and some potential benefits and limitations of such a system.

Evolution of Risk Management Information Systems

In the late 1950s and early 1960s, the only risk management information systems were manual procedures followed by the participants in insurance transactions: insurance buyers, insurers, brokers, and some outside claim administrators and consultants. During the mid-1960s, computers began to perform more of the repetitive tasks involved in insurance buying and selling. As computer technology advanced, continuing cycles of innovation gave rise to four recognizable stages in the development of an RMIS: (1) transaction processing, (2) standard risk management reporting, (3) random data access, and (4) risk management decision support.

Not every RMIS in use today has progressed through these four stages. Some systems have bypassed the earlier phases to focus on risk management decision support, while others have been developed specifically for—and continue to perform most appropriately and cost-effectively—transaction processing, preparation of standard reports, or random access to data.

Stage 1: Transaction Processing

The earliest risk management applications of computerized insured loss and premium record keeping, beginning in the late 1960s, were developed by a few insurers to help selected insureds keep records on their insured losses and target risk control efforts on specific causes of frequent accidents. Shortly thereafter, comparable computer programs were marketed by independent vendors to all organizations wanting them.

These early transaction-processing systems were perceived as suffering from two significant defects. First, centered on insurance transactions, these Stage 1 systems were seen as not giving enough attention to an organization's overall cost of risk (made up of insurance premiums, retained losses, risk control costs, and risk management administrative expenses) and thus were not fully effective in communicating risk management concerns and achievements to senior management. Second, these early systems suffered from the apparent inability to capture credible data on a timely basis. Inaccurate, out-of-date information was not fully usable in making current risk management decisions and did not project to senior management a favorable impression of the risk management department.

Stage 2: Standard Risk Management Reporting

Stage 2 of RMIS development began in the early 1970s when the cost-of-risk concept became widely recognized and risk management professionals increasingly turned to independent vendors for computerized assistance in calculating and controlling their organizations' overall costs of risk. In addition, Stage 2 systems made significant progress on strengthening communication in risk management matters not only with senior executives but also with managers throughout an organization.

Stage 2 provided risk management professionals with a consistent basis for gathering, analyzing, and displaying cost-of-risk data from each of an organization's major departments. Stage 2 systems eliminated the time-consuming practice of manually compiling tables of losses and premiums as well as other elements of the cost of risk and provided a format suitable for producing monthly, quarterly, or annual reports for an organization's board of directors, auditors, and owners.

Although Stage 2 systems enabled risk management professionals to gather more data more quickly, much of the basic data continued to come from insurers rather than from within the organization. Moreover, vendors' ability to prepare a great variety of reports sometimes generated the criticism that their risk management clients were "buried in reams of computer paper"—much data, but little management information.

Stage 3: Random Data Access

In response to these criticisms, a number of independent vendors, brokerage organizations, and insurers began in the mid-1970s to offer their risk management clients more flexible risk management information systems. Clients could not only design their own reports but could also have *random access* to their own risk management data. Random, or direct, access to computerized data gives the computer user the ability to refer to a particular data item in a file or in a portion of a report without having to read the entire file or reproduce the entire report.

In contrast, sequential access requires reading the entire file or reproducing the entire report from the beginning until the desired portion is reached.

For example, when rereading a familiar novel, a reader can have random access to particular passages by quickly finding the appropriate page. In contrast, when the novel is made into a movie, the viewer has only *sequential access* to a favorite portion by waiting for it to appear on the movie screen.

Random access to a database—to an organized collection of related computerized files that contain data relevant to a particular operation such as risk management—gave risk management professionals the ability to tailor their own reports and to respond quickly to requests for information from senior executives and other managers. This ability to extract data in any format on demand made at least three important contributions to effective risk management.

First, awareness of the risk management function increased through interaction with the risk management database, particularly among line management. After witnessing a successful application of the system, managers grew more interested in analyzing accidental losses and the cost they generate and became sophisticated users of the RMIS.

Second, support of the risk management function typically improved as a direct result of satisfying line and staff management's information needs. Not recognizing the assistance that can be provided from the risk management department is often a major reason for limited support of the risk management function within organizations.

Third, communications dealing with risk management within an organization were improved with the risk management professional's ability to monitor and control costs, thereby increasing his or her ability to respond quickly to other managers' questions and problems.

Stage 4: Risk Management Decision Support

The focus of Stage 1 through Stage 3 was to store and display efficiently and accurately data useful in reviewing losses, insurance premiums, and other internal indicators of risk management performance. As more data were added to system databases, and as random access gave the risk management professional more opportunity to interact with the RMIS, the possibility of computers actually making risk management decisions became more realistic.

The key to interactive risk management decision support is the ability of the computer to respond to "what if" inquiries by using the data in its database to project the likely consequences of various alternative actions that the risk management professional might recommend. Such forecasting has required developing various analytical modules for loss forecasting, allocation of the costs of risk, and macroeconomic (economy-wide) projections. Once having verified the assumptions underlying these forecasting and decision support capabilities, a risk management professional with a Stage 4 RMIS can use it in many ways, including the following:

- Projecting the costs and benefits of the specific risk management measures being considered
- Forecasting changes in the organization's overall cost of risk and in each of the components of that cost
- Selecting cost-effective per-loss and annual aggregate retention levels
- Correlating actual safety practices (such as machine guards or safety training programs) with records of changes in accident frequency and severity rates
- Testing the adequacy of reserves for retained workers compensation or other losses

Access to broad databases can enhance the value of an RMIS as decision support. Such access increases the reliability of the data on which these decisions are based and broadens the types of decisions with which the computer can help. Of particular use are the broad databases accessed through telephone (modem) interconnections of an organization's internal computers with external sources of data on financial markets, levels of economic activity, and regulatory developments (A **modem**—MOdulator + DEModulator—is a device that converts data to a form that can be transmitted, as by a telephone, to data processing equipment, where a similar device reconverts it.)

Future RMIS developments are likely to result in the following, perhaps in additional stages:

- Much wider availability of mini- and microcomputers that will be as accessible, familiar, and open to as wide a range of information as is the telephone today
- Use of RMIS communication capabilities among organizations—especially insurers and other providers of risk control and risk financing services—to negotiate the terms of purchase for insurance or other risk financing or risk controls
- Integration of an organization's risk management decision process with its other financial decision processes, all rooted in an MIS that coordinates all of the organization's most crucial managerial decisions

Such integration and coordination through a Stage 4 RMIS facilitates two-way exchanges between an organization's risk management department and others within and outside the organization, as shown in Exhibit 13-1.

Exhibit 13-1
Data and Information Flows With a Stage 4 RMIS

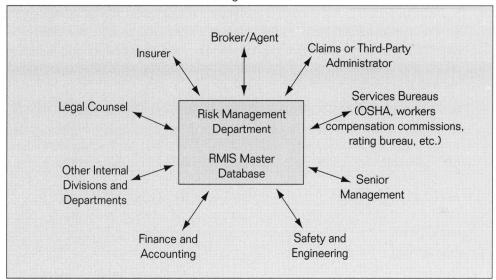

Components of an RMIS

An RMIS has the same following four basic components as all management information systems:

1. Relevant data
2. Procedures for gathering and manipulating the data to produce information
3. Computer equipment
4. Personnel to operate the RMIS

In computer terminology, the data are often labeled the "database"; the computer programs, which involve the procedures for managing the data, are known as "software"; and the computer equipment itself is known as "hardware."

Database

The **database** is the core of any RMIS, the "memory" in which is stored the basic information on which the analytical software components of the RMIS operate. The following are the critical activities in database construction:

- Selecting the types of data to be included and the quantity of each kind of data that the organization considers adequate to support reliable decisions
- Determining the format, types of summarizing, and random access capabilities required to perform the functions expected of the RMIS

- Updating and periodically verifying the factual data that are the raw material for this system

Any RMIS based on a mainframe possesses a nearly inexhaustible limit of data storage; systems based on a micro- or minicomputer, although less expensive than mainframes, necessarily have more limited storage capacity and require a user to give more thought to the types and volumes of information to be stored in them.

In a computerized RMIS, data are stored (usually as magnetic charges) in files. As displayed on a computer screen, a file—as the one in Exhibit 13-2—appears containing data records like the rows shown across the exhibit and data items like the vertical columns in the exhibit. The file segment in the exhibit, containing data on liability claims against an organization, consists of any number of records (like the first for claimant Smith, and the second for claimant Jones), with each record consisting of five data items (also known as "attributes" or "data fields") within a given record.

Exhibit 13-2
Examples of RMIS File Display

Claims Data

Claimant	Acct Date	Cause of Loss	Location	Loss Amount
Smith, S.	900116	007	B1234	10027.20
Jones, M.	900315	208	AA007	75.00
Brown, R.	890212	201	B9303	2830.00
Schultz, D.	900720	999	C0200	65.00
Abbot, B.	880511	100	SAA01	250.00
Baker, D.	819088	033	J0940	
Carth,				

Every proper RMIS must be built on a body of data that is complete, accurate, consistent, relevant, and timely. Otherwise, the inevitable results are described by the tested computer maxim, "garbage in, garbage out," or GIGO. The types of data commonly recorded in an **RMIS database** (that is, quantitative information for risk management purposes that is organized and stored in a computer) can be classified as loss data, exposure data, legal data, financial data, administrative data, risk control data, and risk financing data. Some of these types of data are shown in Exhibit 13-3.

Exhibit 13-3

Frequent Database Components

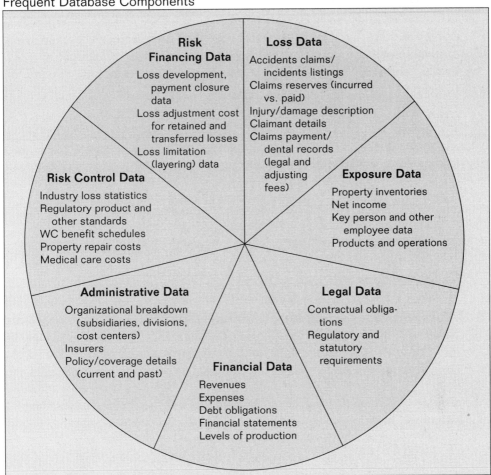

Risk Financing Data
Loss development, payment closure data
Loss adjustment cost for retained and transferred losses
Loss limitation (layering) data

Loss Data
Accidents claims/ incidents listings
Claims reserves (incurred vs. paid)
Injury/damage description
Claimant details
Claims payment/ dental records (legal and adjusting fees)

Risk Control Data
Industry loss statistics
Regulatory product and other standards
WC benefit schedules
Property repair costs
Medical care costs

Exposure Data
Property inventories
Net income
Key person and other employee data
Products and operations

Administrative Data
Organizational breakdown (subsidiaries, divisions, cost centers)
Insurers
Policy/coverage details (current and past)

Legal Data
Contractual obliga-tions
Regulatory and statutory requirements

Financial Data
Revenues
Expenses
Debt obligations
Financial statements
Levels of production

Loss Data

Details of an organization's past losses usually occupy the largest segment of its risk management database. From loss data, risk management professionals, brokers and agents, and insurers can develop information on the frequency, severity, causes, and final settlement of past losses and can project reasonable reserves for current and future losses. Most risk management decisions require forecasts, such as forecasts of future losses and of the effects that various risk control and risk financing techniques can have on the costs of those losses. The loss portion of a well-constructed RMIS database provides much of the foundation needed for such forecasts. For loss prevention and loss reduction, extensive details on the precise circumstances of each loss can be most helpful in tailoring cost-effective controls of loss frequency and loss severity.

Exposure Data

These type of data, quite extensive and diverse, are important to risk management professionals and to insurers' representatives in staying abreast of potential losses. Exposure data often deal with the general characteristics of an organization, its property, its operating relationships with major suppliers and customers, and its personnel.

Regarding property, the database should identify the organization's assets by type, location, historical and current values, and ownership status (owned, leased, or held in bailment). Property data also frequently include construction details for real property and vendor information for personal property as well as estimates of the maximum potential loss to which each item of property is subject.

If the RMIS is designed to include analysis for employee benefit plans, employee data (name, sex, age, occupation, and the like) from the personnel department might be part of the database. Information such as a Social Security number, past medical conditions, and any other pertinent items can be included in this database.

Legal Data

The legal information in this portion of the database should include sufficient details for identifying, locating, and summarizing the major features of the organization's contractual obligations. In addition, if its operations expose it to civil or criminal liability under federal or state statutes, then the database should provide references and perhaps brief summaries of the pertinent legislation. Finally, if an organization's alleged breaches of its common-law or statutory duties have led to specific legal claims against it, then the database should provide information to identify and track the status of these claims.

Financial Data

The financial section of many risk management information systems provides current data on and forecasts for revenues and expenses, cash flows, debt obligations and borrowing plans, levels of production, and other sources and uses for funds. This financial data pertains to the organization's general financial conditions and management, not to its risk financing of accidental losses.

Administrative Data

If a firm's organizational structure is diverse, perhaps involving multiple departments, several subsidiaries, or widespread locations constituting different cost centers, the database should be constructed to reflect this hierarchy and to segregate risk management data to reflect this diversity. So structured, the database can greatly simplify risk management cost allocation, even if the organization is restructured.

To use the RMIS to analyze the losses that the organization will retain, those losses covered by insurance, and the cost of that insurance coverage, the database must include information about coverage limits, deductibles, expiration dates, annual premiums, rating information, insurers, underwriters, and brokers/agents for each insurance policy protecting the organization. Comparable data on previous policies should also be retained within the RMIS because the data on them are likely to provide valuable trending information as well as perhaps valuable insurance coverage for claims arising out of the organization's past conduct.

Risk Control Data

To supplement the data in the other segments of the RMIS database, the risk control segment should include other data to help assess the quality of the organization's loss prevention efforts and to estimate the financial savings that they generate. For such assessment, the database is likely to include industry-wide statistics on the frequency and severity of various types of accidents and claims. The database will also include the standards applicable to work safety, product safety, and environmental protection that have been promulgated by federal and state regulatory agencies as well as by the relevant industry and trade groups. To estimate the financial benefits of risk control, the database should include relevant workers compensation benefit schedules, costs of real property and automobile repair, and indexes of medical care costs. Those costs can be used to demonstrate the value of preventing accidents and claims.

Risk Financing Data

This section of an RMIS database should hold information about the organization's activities and costs for financing recovery of its accidental losses. Those are losses that are recorded in the "Loss Data" portion of the database. This risk financing data encompasses such items as loss adjustment expenses for both retained and insured (or otherwise transferred) losses; loss development, payout, and closure patterns from past losses that should be helpful in forecasting equivalent patterns for comparable future losses; commissions or fees paid to risk financing intermediaries; and other data pertaining to risk financing activities. Many RIMS databases also house dollar amounts of past losses, adjusted for price level changes and organized in layers so that the organization's risk management professional evaluating insurance proposals can estimate the costs of adopting alternative retention levels.

Software

Software comprises the instructions that direct the computer to perform a given set of tasks. Without software, a computer does virtually nothing except hum softly and perhaps flash a few lights to indicate that it has been turned on. Software, or programs, may be permanently stored in the mainframe, mini-, or microcomputer or may be loaded into the computer from magnetic tapes, floppy disks, or other sources when needed for a particular project. In addition, programs stored in a mainframe or other computer may be transferred, or downloaded, into a smaller computer (or uploaded into a larger one). The kinds of software required for most RMIS applications include the following:

- Database management programs for adding to, updating, or restructuring data in the database

- Analysis software that performs statistical and financial procedures (for example, forecasting future losses based on actual or adjusted past loss data, computing regression equations that relate the organization's loss experience to operational changes such as new levels of production or the use of new safety equipment, and computing cash flows and rates of return based on projected loss experience as affected by different risk management techniques)

- Communications programs for transmitting database information or software programs among computers within or outside the organization

The most common types of software include word processing programs; accounting and other reporting spreadsheets; database management systems; graphics packages; and special-purpose programs, such as for payroll administration or an RMIS, which could use several of these more generalized software programs. Software is becoming faster, more powerful, and more expensive (both in actual cost and in space).

An RMIS having somewhat limited built-in data storage capacity, or "memory," typically relies on "batch" programs. "Batching" refers to how changes are made to the database. In a batch system, all of the data are entered into the computer at one session. Various processing programs then can be applied to that data, but the data cannot be changed while the processing program is operating.

In contrast, an RMIS with larger memory capacity often has what is known as "interactive" or **on-line capabilities** through which particular items in the database can be changed while a processing program is operating. Such a system is described as interactive because the risk management professional or other computer user can direct specific "What if . . . ?" questions to the computer by changing the data or other assumptions with which the program is operating. The user is on-line with the computer, able to conduct a "conversation" with it rather than having to wait for the entire program to be completed under a batch system. In time, with sufficient recycling of the programs, a batch system can deal with all of the same questions as an interactive system. However, if the amount of data is great or the program is complex, a batch system operates at a much slower speed and consumes a great deal more costly computer time.

In selecting ready-made software programs for an RMIS—or in calling on others within the organization or outside vendors or consultants to develop customized software programs—a risk management professional should ask several questions about the desirable features of such software. Some of these features and some corresponding questions follow:

- *Reliability*—How dependable is the RMIS and what is the potential down-time associated with this product? Are there any discernible "bugs" within the software? What kind of guarantees does the vendor provide if problems develop?

- *User-Friendliness*—How easy-to-use is this system? Does it require extensive operator training? Are there "help" screens or English language prompts?

- *Flexibility*—What types of analyses or functions can it perform? Is the software adaptable enough to analyze many risk control and risk financing options under differing scenarios? Does the software have the capability to tap into different databases within different hardware environments? Is there flexible reporting capability? Can reports be instantaneously generated on site, or do they need to be prepared elsewhere?

- *Degree of Integration*—Can the RMIS link with other existing company database files (such as those from the finance department) or with external organizations (such as insurers, brokers, or governmental agencies)?

- *Accuracy*—Are there enough proven editing capabilities and constraints to prevent inadvertent errors or intentional tampering? (Could February 32 be added as an acceptable date, for example?)

- *Expandability*—Can the system grow along with the user's needs without requiring a complete overhaul every two or three years as needs grow or the organization changes?

- *Analytical Power*—What types of analytical capabilities are provided by the system? Is it simply a word processing/tracking system, or can it provide cash flow analyses, modeling of different funding options, cost-of-risk allocation, or loss forecasting?

- *Security*—What types of security features are built into the software to prevent tampering or unauthorized access to different levels of sensitive data?

Hardware

Hardware is the physical equipment to which most people point when they speak of "the computer." It is the machinery that runs the software. The essential hardware components of any computer system are its central processing unit

(CPU), an input device (such as a keyboard, mouse, or touch-sensitive screen, an output or display device (such as a printer or a visual monitor in the form of a cathode-ray tube or CRT), and a storage medium (such as computer tapes or disk drives). Most hardware systems are also equipped with a communication device like a modem for linking computers and exchanging data and programs through telephone wires.

Computer hardware has chronologically evolved from mainframes (in the past, they were often room-sized assemblages of components), through minicomputers (now considered mid-sized, perhaps filling the space of a desk), to personal computers (or PCs, the size of a portable television or microwave oven), to the current laptops (which often fit into a normal briefcase.) Any of those devices can be interconnected to exchange information or to draw on the data or software residing in a mainframe or minicomputer.

Hardware and software are the tools that risk management professionals can use to turn good data into good information that supports better decisions. Decision support is not the same as decision making; intelligent and informed humans are essential for knowing what kinds of information to gather and analyze and for the actual choices that are the heart of risk management and other decision making. Data analysis and decision support are often highly repetitive tasks involving the management of large amounts of data—tasks for which the appropriate hardware and software greatly assist the decision-maker. Because computers can do many tasks with much data very rapidly, they provide excellent decision support.

The type of computer equipment that should be used depends on the user's needs. Size is a major factor. The larger the database required, the more powerful should be the computer. As an example, for historical claims databases including five years' records of frequent losses and related information, a mainframe computer would provide the required storage capacity and speed. A 50,000-claim database would take seconds for a mainframe to sort, analyze, and generate a report; the same task could take much longer on a small computer. The number of work stations also governs the choice of computer equipment. Although sharing a computer terminal once was common, it is now quite likely that each user has an individual terminal.

Two important characteristics of any good hardware are reliability and expandability. Any system should be dependable and supported by readily available service facilities. The hardware itself should not create significant business interruption or downtime exposures. Backup computers—extra minis or micros—or access to others' mainframes that can operate compatibly with the organization's own computers and have adequate available processing time are essential. If the organization already has a general management information system, careful consideration should be given to using this system's hardware for the RMIS so that the RMIS and the MIS can be readily integrated.

Personnel

Of all the components of any management information system, and especially RMIS, people are the most important. People supply and interpret the data; design, build, install, and service the hardware; conceive and write the software; train and support those internal staff members who work with the RMIS; and use RMIS information for refining and supporting their decisions. It is also the people component of an effective RMIS whose cost—mainly consisting of salaries and fringe benefits—probably is rising the fastest.

The number of people required to operate an RMIS depends on the system's size and requirements. Some RMIS require a team of experts including computer programmers, analysts, and hardware/software professionals. Other systems— particularly those relying on ready-made programs and one or two terminals attached to the general MIS—may require only one or two support personnel.

The needs and levels of expertise of the end users of the system—the organization's risk management professional, broker or agent, insurance underwriter, and claim administrator, for example—also affect personnel needs. If those individuals are computer literate, the need for additional personnel is reduced.

The personnel to operate an RMIS need not all come from within the organization. Persons with information systems expertise are often available on a part-time, consulting, or "loan" basis from insurers, brokerage organizations, hardware/software vendors, outside claim administration organizations, and consulting firms.

Potential Benefits and Limitations of an RMIS

Although a risk management information system can be useful in many ways, it also has limitations. Thus, the decision to establish such a system should consider both the benefits and the limitations at the outset.

Potential Benefits

A well-designed RMIS can perform many clerical, computational, communication, and decision activities more quickly and accurately than can people. Consequently, an RMIS can increase the efficiency of a risk management program, reduce costs, improve communication, improve credibility for risk management, and enhance the quality of information for decisions.

Increased Efficiency

Eliminating or reducing paperwork increases the risk management professional's time for analytical decision making. A well-designed database management system within an RMIS can store, categorize, analyze, and extract needed data within seconds and reduce the chances of error, thus increasing the efficiency and the quality of decisions. For example, calls from varied sources to produce a loss forecast, a cost of risk allocation, or a summary of all claims over $50,000 at Location 5 could be produced in minutes instead of days.

Faster data compilation and analysis through RMIS allows more time for developing risk management recommendations. In addition, increased RMIS analytical capabilities (such as for loss forecasting, cost of risk allocation, cost/benefit analysis, and financial modeling) heighten the ability to perform sophisticated analyses and recognize opportunities for strengthening the risk management program. For example, suppose a risk management professional had to select a fire detection/suppression system. He or she could use computerized simulations and financial models to determine which fire protection alternative would provide the most effective fire loss reduction for a given cost or, alternatively, which system would provide a given level of fire protection at the least cost. A somewhat more sophisticated RMIS could also identify the tradeoffs between the cost and fire protection that each of these alternatives offers.

Reduced Costs

Senior management often finds that the savings that can be achieved through investing in an RMIS are attractive. These savings stem from fewer errors as manual operations are reduced, decreased personnel expenses (to perform now-computerized tasks), and prompter responses to risk management needs.

For example, through random inquiry of an RMIS database, the risk management professional for a hospital determined that 30 percent of all workers compensation claims originated at one particular nursing shift. Further investigation revealed that not enough nurses worked the shift; consequently, the overworked nurses suffered more back injuries. When the personnel department learned of this understaffing and subsequently increased the number of nurses on this shift, the incident rate of back injuries decreased markedly.

Improved Communication

Through computer networking and shared databases, properly computerized information is readily accessible simultaneously to many people both within and outside an organization. Moreover, computers can sort, manipulate, merge, summarize, and disseminate data with amazing speed. Therefore, an RMIS can be invaluable in presenting recommendations to departmental and senior management based on sound information and thorough analysis. The system can help present these recommendations concisely with visuals and clear calculations showing how the recommendations would affect the organization's cost of risk.

An RMIS can be, on the one hand, as detailed as necessary. For example, it can provide the details needed by the risk management department to discuss renewals with underwriters or to compare various retention options. On the other hand, the system can produce reports that present "the big picture" to senior and other managers. The timeliness of presenting this information is extremely important. A chief financial officer, for example, might ask the risk management professional for an historical trend for workers compensation losses over the past five years. Without an RMIS, this task would require perhaps days of manually searching through old files. Many RMIS could present this material within perhaps minutes, depending on the system. Because less time is consumed in gathering and processing data, more staff and managerial time is available for interpreting the information and pondering its implications.

Particularly when integrated with an overall MIS, an RMIS can increase the risk management professional's contributions to the organization's daily and strategic decisions. Through the MIS, departments can communicate quickly with, and receive prompt advice from, the risk management department regarding routine activities. On a more strategic level, money decisions—such as whether to merge with another organization—involve weighing risk management concerns. For example, how a merger would change the new organization's loss exposures may well be as important as the purely business risks that traditionally dominate merger negotiations. By using an RMIS that has proper information, a risk management professional can measure the effect that such a merger would have on the surviving organization's new cost of risk and can highlight for senior management the significance of such a change in the organization's overall costs.

Improved Credibility for Risk Management

Partly for psychological reasons, computer-generated output often gains more credibility than handwritten, or even typewritten, material. People tend to have more trust in computerized output. Unlike humans, computers cannot deviate from the programmed instructions and are thus unable to generate errors stemming from fatigue, ignorance, or emotion.

Computer-generated results can be wrong, however, because of human errors in programming or in providing the computer with incomplete or inaccurate data. For example, if a risk management department staff member has neglected to enter information about ten property losses, no computerized summary of total property losses to date will be meaningful. Similarly, if a clerical employee in a branch location has mistakenly coded four back injuries as leg injuries in a quarterly report to an organization's headquarters, the resulting computerized summary will underreport back injuries and overreport leg injuries.

Nonetheless, computers can greatly improve the credibility of risk management information by flagging logical errors in the underlying data. For example, an RMIS liability claim-tracking program can select for further human attention a claim report having a report date preceding an occurrence date, having a reserve for a claim that is already closed, having a new claim reported on a divested operation, or having the total of claims paid-to-date being less than the total claims paid last quarter. By being programmed to highlight specified types of errors, a computer can greatly enhance the integrity of an organization's underlying risk management data.

Higher Quality Information for Decisions

Because of their strength in organizing data and developing decision models from it, computers can derive great quantities of information from data, thus providing more and higher quality information for humans to use in making decisions. Well-organized data typically yield the high-quality information that statistical models need to support many risk management decisions.

Organized Data   The process of entering data into a computer requires that input be structured into files, spreadsheets, and other formats so that a risk management professional can quickly access and manipulate data, relying on the RMIS for both one-time queries and periodic reports. This data structuring also facilitates data analysis to reveal patterns in an organization's loss experience, claim management, risk financing costs, or other subjects of managerial concern. For example, computerized treatment of loss data permits calculations and comparisons of employee disability frequency and severity rates at different locations, under different operating conditions, or during different time periods. Such comparisons would not be cost-effective without a computer.

Models for Contingency Analysis   With a computer that has decision-support capabilities, a risk management professional can use various "What if . . . ?" techniques to test the validity, or build simplified models, of the real world based on certain assumptions. These models permit trying out some decision alternatives. For example, a computer can answer such questions as, "What if we had agreed to a $50,000 per-loss deductible for the last three years instead of a $25,000 per-loss deductible? How would our insurance premiums and our retained losses have been different (assuming we had the same actual loss experience over the past three years)?" Although computers cannot make decisions, they can facilitate analysis of specific decision alternatives.

Potential Limitations

Because computers can do no more than they have been programmed to do and have access to only the data that they have been given, no computerized RMIS can perform miracles. Specifically, every RMIS is limited because (1) it can only analyze, not decide; (2) it cannot guarantee any reduction in an organization's accidental losses or cost of risk; (3) its quality of outputs is limited by the quality of the information that it receives and the software that it employs; (4) it entails additional expenses; and (5) it ultimately depends on people and is subject to their weaknesses.

Only Analysis, Not Decisions

A computerized RMIS does not make decisions. It has no imagination or analytical insight and can only answer questions that people ask it on the basis of the data people provide. Most fundamentally, it cannot initiate an inquiry or any thought process leading to a decision. It cannot even recognize the need for a decision to be made. In short, computers are wonderful at giving answers to precise questions, but only people can create those questions and the data available to be processed for generating the answers.

No Necessary Loss/Cost Reduction

A computerized RMIS can reduce an organization's overall cost and risk in many ways such as cutting administrative costs and speeding the organization's response to changes in hazards and the resulting losses. However, an RMIS is a mere management information tool. It does not itself prevent accidental losses or make them less severe. In fact, as noted below, an RMIS creates or intensifies a number of exposures to accidental losses. Therefore, computerizing an already deficient risk management program does not significantly improve an organization's overall risk management effort.

Limited Quality of Inputs and Programs

When the data going into a computer are inaccurate, incomplete, or obsolete, no amount of computerized manipulation can generate reliable information or decision guidelines. Preventing "garbage in, garbage out" requires gathering accurate data on a timely basis, maintaining the integrity of the data as they are entered into and manipulated by the computer, and avoiding any attempts to infer from the data conclusions that the data cannot logically support.

RMIS Expenses

Although an RMIS improves the efficiency of an organization's overall risk management program and reduces its cost of risk, computerizing an existing manual RMIS entails additional costs. These include costs associated with purchasing or leasing the hardware or software, along with expenditures for various computer supplies such as paper and printer ribbons. Personnel need training to understand the hardware and to operate the software. Training requires both direct educational expenses and loss of employees' normal productive time during their training sessions. Overall, these costs can be significant, ranging into several thousand dollars annually for each regular RMIS user. Therefore, the decision to invest in a computerized RMIS can be analyzed using the same types of net cash flow analysis as any other major investment of the organization's financial, personnel, or other resources.

Human Error

The weakest link in most computerized RMIS systems involves the people who design and operate them. Most of the problems with these systems are not fundamentally technical but result from weaknesses in training operators and failing to give operators access to expert technical support. Even problems that at first seem principally technical, such as software that is not user-friendly or inappropriate system defaults, are ultimately "people problems." Those problems reflect poor decisions made by the people who designed or installed the RMIS.

Designing an RMIS[2]

> **What are the steps in designing an RMIS?**
>
> **What factors determine whether to purchase, make, or lease RMIS components?**

Securing the potential benefits and avoiding the potential disadvantages of an RMIS require that such a system be designed properly and tailored specifically to the organization's needs. This designing and tailoring entails the following four phases:

1. Analyzing the organization's particular RMIS requirements

2. Identifying the flows of information required to meet these needs

3. Determining the technological and financial feasibility of an RMIS to meet these needs

4. Deciding whether to build, buy, or lease the hardware and software components of such a system

Requirements Analysis[3]

The purpose of a requirements analysis is to identify all intended users of the RMIS, their respective information needs, and the organization's present resources that might meet these needs. The four steps in performing a requirements analysis are as follows:

1. Identify all intended users.

2. Conduct structured interviews of these users.

3. Analyze the findings from these interviews.

4. Assemble this analysis into a report or recommendations.

Identifying Users

Potential intended RMIS users should include not only the people who will rely on the RMIS to manage information or to reach decisions but also the people who will supply the data that the RMIS needs. Although most users of an RMIS will be personnel within the risk management department, a significant number of users will work in other departments within the organization, and a few will work outside the organization. Of those outside the risk management department, some will supply data to the department, while others will receive information from the department. Within this context, likely users to be interviewed might include representatives of the following departments or functions:

- Internal to the Organization
  - Employee Health and Safety
  - Compensation and Benefits
  - Management Information Systems (or Electronic Data Processing, EDP)
  - Risk Management
  - Legal
  - Accounting
  - Purchasing
  - Senior Management
  - Regional Management (or Department Heads)
  - Local Management (such as Plant Managers)
- External to the Organization
  - Insurance Brokers/Agents
  - Insurers
  - Risk Management Consultants
  - External Legal Counsel
  - External Claims Administrators/Adjusters
  - Trade Associations
  - Personnel of Captives, Pools
  - Officials of State and Local Government

Conducting Interviews

Questionnaires, tailored to each interviewee's functions, should be structured to guide each interview but not to exclude valuable insights that an interviewee may offer. The objective is to enable both the interviewer and the interviewee to understand, in a risk management context, one another's perceptions regarding the following:

- Data that are currently being collected and the procedures and reasons for their collection
- Additional data, or information from new or existing data, that are needed or desired
- Present data, or information derived from those data, that are not worth the cost and difficulty of gathering or analyzing them
- Gaps and bottlenecks in recurrent procedures for gathering data, analyzing them, or disseminating the resulting information

Each interview should emphasize the goal of designing the RMIS to enhance each interviewee's job performance and to fulfill individual objectives. In addition to being among the interviewees, representatives of the organization's MIS department should be directly involved in, or available for consultation on, the entire interviewing process. MIS personnel have special expertise on the standards and constraints with which the new RMIS must comply and the capabilities of the organization's current and (potentially new) hardware and software.

It is a good practice to send each interviewee a written summary of the key points of his or her interview for review and approval before assembling the interview information for the final report. This further participation by each interviewee not only ensures greater accuracy but also promotes each interviewee's acceptance of the interview/report recommendation process, thus easing the eventual implementation of a sound RMIS.

Analyzing the Interview Findings

Analyzing the "small pictures" provided by each interviewee's perspective should yield an integrated "big picture" of the organization's RMIS needs, resources, and opportunities for improving information flows and risk management decisions. Knowing both present and future possible information flows, discussed subsequently, is essential to this analysis because an important aim of RMIS is to eliminate cumbersome manual data-gathering and management procedures, automating them to improve the accuracy and timeliness of managerial decisions. Achieving this goal requires detailed knowledge of current information flows and decision procedures.

Making a Report or Recommendations

This analysis, supported by interview results and other pertinent information, should be assembled into the completed requirements analysis or recommenda-

Exhibit 13-4
Sample Format for an RMIS Report

I.   Identification of Users

II. Description of Current System Information Flows

III. Requirements Definition

    A. Objectives

    B. Required Reports

        (Note: "Reports" should be defined broadly to mean "information needs," including day-to-day ad hoc queries as well as regularly scheduled reports.)

    C. Required System Functions and Operations

    D. Performance Requirements

    E. Data Requirements

    F. Constraints

    G. Expected Benefits

IV. Description of Proposed System Information Flows

V.   Recommendations

    (Note: Recommendations can deal with manual procedural concerns as well as with computer-related matters.)

VI. Appendixes

    A. Interview Results

    B. Data Source Documents

        1. Manual Data Source Forms

        2. Automated Data Source Documentation (file layouts and coding schemes from existing computerized components)

        3. Data Sourcing Summary (summarizing sources and volumes of various categories of data over time)

    C. Required Report Samples

tions. With many possible adaptations for the particular customs or situations of any given organization, the report or recommendations often addresses the topics shown in Exhibit 13-4. Because information flows (current and proposed as well as computerized and manual) are essential to the design of a proper RMIS, identifying these flows deserves recognition as a design step. The design step, while related inexplicably to the others, merits a separate discussion.

Identification of Information Flows

Given the ideal tasks for the RMIS to perform, an expert in management information systems from within or specifically hired by the organization can detail

Exhibit 13-5

Possible Global RMIS Information Flows

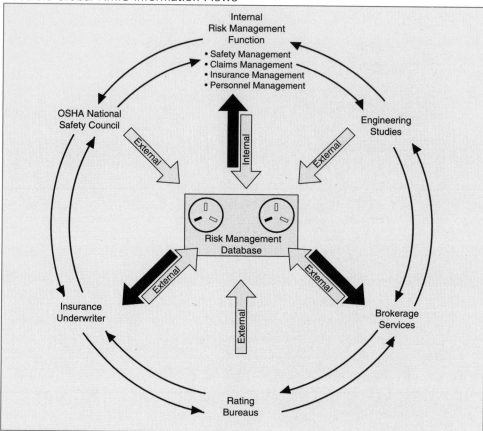

Reprinted with permission from Laurie Weiss, Kay Goodier, and Marvin Gwinn, "Identification of Data Flow," in James D. Blinn and Mitchell J.. Cole (eds.), *Pathways to RMIS* (New York, NY: Risk Management Society Publishing, Inc., 1985), p. 37.

the flows of risk management information, or **information flows** within the organization, into the organization from outside sources and from the organization to outside entities. Exhibit 13-5 suggests one possible global perspective on these information flows through which the risk management department interacts with other departments and with several outside entities. Exhibit 13-6 focuses on one portion of this global information flow, dealing with how the information in the report of an accident covered by insurance reaches the claim administrator, insurer, and the risk management department. (Neither of these exhibits is designed to prescribe an ideal information flow; they only suggest some frequent patterns.)

Information flows, both current and recommended, should be indicated by flowcharts and supporting narrative. A flowchart can simply show the information

Exhibit 13-6

Possible Information Flow (Regarding an Accident) to a Claims Administrator, an Insurer, and a Risk Management Department

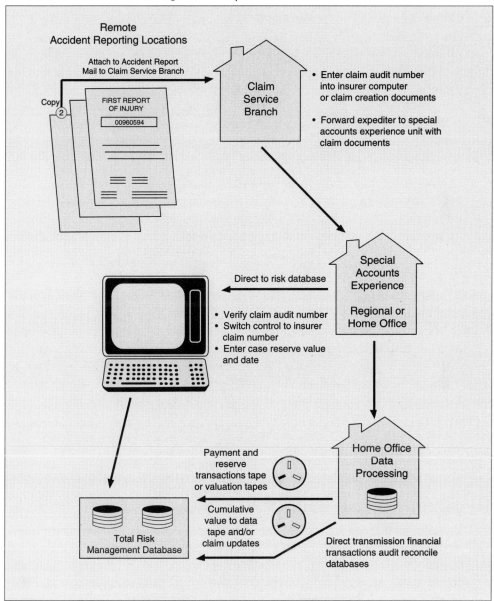

Reprinted with permission from Laurie Weiss, Kay Goodier, and Marvin Gwinn, "Identification of Data Flow," in James D. Blinn and Mitchell J. Cole (eds.), *Pathways to RMIS* (New York, NY: Risk Management Society Publishing, Inc., 1985), p. 41.

flows from department to department or entity to entity. These charts and narratives frequently reveal how the underlying data are gathered and how they are processed to generate desired information.

Out of the many detailed information flowcharts like the one in Exhibit 13-6 emerge the detailed specifications for the RMIS regarding (1) the content of information flows, (2) the RMIS hardware and software needed at various locations to process this information, and (3) the skills of persons needed at various locations to operate the hardware and software. These specifications can be analyzed to project the technological, financial, and human resource requirements of the ideal RMIS.

Determination of Feasibility

The resources that the ideal RMIS is likely to require can be detailed, probably by the risk management and information system professionals working together, into various cost components, such as those suggested in the upper portion of Exhibit 13-7. These costs should be projected for each of at least the first three years and totaled for the life of the system to recognize the importance of the time value of money to the organization.

Similarly, the benefits projected for this ideal RMIS can be estimated following the format suggested in the lower portion of Exhibit 13-7. The cost information is likely to be more detailed and concrete than that for benefits. However, forecast costs and benefits of the RMIS presented in this way can give senior financial and other executives the soundest possible information on which to evaluate the financial desirability of any particular RMIS to the organization.

To this point, the design decisions and financial analyses discussed in this chapter have focused on an ideal RMIS. Senior management might find such a system unacceptable because of a high cost/benefit ratio or low projected time-adjusted internal rate of return. Gaining senior management support might require that one or more system alternatives eliminate the need for some expensive hardware, software, or personnel. These alternatives might forego some less essential tasks and might be designed and presented as fallbacks. Rather than attempt to gain approval for an extensive, expensive system, the risk management professional could begin with a basic, economical system to be upgraded or expanded at a later date. Anticipating the possible need to present such basic alternatives, those conducting the initial RMIS requirements interviews could ask interviewees to categorize or rank the desirability of each of the tasks that they would like the ideal system to perform.

Exhibit 13-7
Cost/Benefit Analysis of an RMIS

COSTS				
Type of Cost	Cost in Year			Total
	1	2	3	
Design/Feasibility Study	——	——	——	——
Data Conversion (Existing Insurers or Claim Administrators)	——	——	——	——
Loading Historical Data	——	——	——	——
Particular Data Entry	——	——	——	——
Specialized Reporting	——	——	——	——
• OSHA	——	——	——	——
• Safety Monitor	——	——	——	——
• Cost of Risk	——	——	——	——
• Property Valuation System	——	——	——	——
• Policy Tracking	——	——	——	——
Training/Documentation	——	——	——	——
Administration/Quality Assurance	——	——	——	——
Travel	——	——	——	——
Out-of-Pocket	——	——	——	——
Subtotal	——	——	——	——
Equipment Lease or Rental	——	——	——	——
Computer Resources	——	——	——	——
Communications (Connected Time Charges)	——	——	——	——
Computer Storage	——	——	——	——
Printing	——	——	——	——
Microfiche	——	——	——	——
Graphics	——	——	——	——
Standard Reporting	——	——	——	——
Ad Hoc (One-Time Reporting)	——	——	——	——
Loss Forecasting	——	——	——	——
Reserve Analysis	——	——	——	——
Financial Planning	——	——	——	——
Graphic Displays	——	——	——	——
License Fee	——	——	——	——
People Resources	——	——	——	——
• Loading/Verifying Data Sources	——	——	——	——
• Assistance in Designing or Product Reports	——	——	——	——
• Maintenance of Software	——	——	——	——
Subtotal	——	——	——	——
TOTAL COSTS	——	——	——	——

Continued on next page.

	BENEFITS		
Type of Benefit	Savings in Year		Total
	1	2	3
Tangible			
1. Staff Reduction	____	____	____ ____
2. Claims Administration	____	____	____ ____
3. Financial	____	____	____ ____
Intangible			
1. Reduced Staff Time	____	____	____ ____
2. Improved Response to Special Requests	____	____	____ ____
3. Better Marketing by Control of Data	____	____	____ ____
4. Improved Morale in the Risk Management Department	____	____	____ ____
5. Opportunity To Do Some Valuable "Back-Burner" Projects	____	____	____ ____
TOTAL BENEFITS	____	____	____ ____

Buy/Lease/Build Decisions

Once senior management has approved a specific RMIS and its related software, hardware, and personnel, the next crucial design decisions are whether to buy existing software programs or to construct ("build") these programs and whether to buy or lease the RMIS hardware. These decisions lead, in turn, to a choice between developing RMIS capabilities within the organization's own personnel or, alternatively, relying on vendor support.

Software Decisions

Previously, the most important software decision was between generic types of software. For example, organizations would consider whether a mainframe program be selected that emphasized primarily numerical analysis or that emphasized word processing and report writing, thereby requiring more words than numbers. Such a choice is no longer necessary because currently available multipurpose programs generally provide a package of a diverse set of capabilities.

Instead, the most fundamental software decisions now typically involve a choice between buying some unified software package available from one vendor versus custom designing individual programs for specific tasks. If a unified standardized program is chosen, the next decision is to select a particular vendor. On the other hand, an organization that opts for a series of customized programs might be able to target software acquisitions for particular tasks, provided that these various programs are compatible in allowing communication and a transfer of data from one program to another.

All of those choices must be governed by the system's ability to meet the organization's requirements. Beyond that fundamental concern, other decision criteria include (1) budgetary constraints (both one-time and ongoing); (2) the time required to make software operational; and (3) the compatibility of the software with the organization's present, computerized MIS.

Many brokerage organizations, insurers, and independent software and hardware vendors are willing to provide prepackaged RMIS software that will perform most of the tasks required of an RMIS for most small and medium-sized organizations. This software, already tested and usually backed by the provider's warranty or service agreement, usually costs an organization less than developing its own software program.

Thus, the only organizations for which designing their own software is a cost-effective option tend to be those that meet the following three criteria: (1) having substantial MIS expertise on staff, (2) having a substantial volume of risk management data in computerized form that are not compatible with the computer language or programs that the brokers, insurers, or other vendors have used to develop their software, or (3) having some specialized RMIS needs that prepackaged software cannot address.

The risk management professional for an organization that meets the first of these three criteria should explore the costs and benefits of developing RMIS software internally to (1) use existing personnel, (2) ensure the compatibility of the RMIS with the overall MIS, and (3) establish and maintain good working relationships with the in-house information system staff. An organization that meets the second criterion could consider the relative merits of transforming its data to make them compatible with outside software or could ask the outside provider to transform its existing software, rather than developing new software within the organization. For an organization that meets the third criterion, the cost-effective option might be to purchase the outside software for most of its RMIS needs and to develop its own software only for those special tasks that the pre-packaged programs cannot easily perform.

When an organization chooses to rely on ready-made or customized, externally generated software, it should consider price and, more important, the following:

- The reliability of the software (based on the proven experience record of the particular programs or of the supplying firm)

- The adaptability of the software (both to potential new uses within the organization's RMIS and to technological advances through upgrades in the supplier's software)

- The supplier's ability to provide support, training, and service as new persons join the risk management staff, as the RMIS evolves, or as software problems might develop in the future

Although few rules are definite for making software decisions, the experience of many organizations suggests the following:

- Making software choices first because hardware commitments often limit software choices.

- Choosing widely used software over relatively obscure software because of the greater availability of trained personnel and more frequent software upgrades.

- Enlisting the cooperation of the organization's own computer personnel to gain their expertise and their support before choosing.

- Remembering the option to not computerize—to continue manual operations—if software/hardware or other RMIS options do not promise greatly increased efficiency.

Hardware Decisions

When computer hardware was much larger and more expensive than it now is, most organizations chose to lease rather than to buy their computer equipment to avoid large cash outlays for its purchase, to leave the risk of loss (principally through technological obsolescence) with the owner/vendor, and to ensure the vendor's continued servicing of the equipment. Those considerations still apply to large mainframes, which frequently are leased rather than purchased. However, as stand-alone micro- and minicomputers have dropped in price and size and have risen in popularity and reliability, more organizations now purchase this equipment.

For an RMIS, the lease/purchase decision is typically made on a basis consistent with the organization's choice for its overall MIS. Using the same (or at least compatible) hardware and software for both the RMIS and the MIS facilitates integrating the two systems and promotes exchanges of information throughout the organization's computer network and among all its users. Thus, while not feeling bound to the machinery of an existing MIS, a risk management professional contemplating a separate system for special risk management needs should be confident of, and be able to document fully, the advantages of the separate equipment for the RMIS.

An organization without an existing MIS should decide whether to lease or to purchase the hardware as in any other lease/purchase decision, considering the following factors:

- The difference in the expected net present value of the cash flows over the equipment's projected life

- The way that the organization's various loss exposures—including both physical damage and technological obsolescence—are affected by the choice between buying and leasing

- The flexibility that both the buy and the lease options give the organization to update its RMIS (or MIS) in the foreseeable future as the organization or computer technology changes

Personnel Decisions

The three fundamental options that any organization has for finding people to operate its RMIS are to rely on (1) the organization's own employees; (2) the personnel of an outside organization, such as an insurer, agency, brokerage, or consulting organization, or of a hardware/software vendor; or (3) some combination of the organization's own and other's personnel. The objective is to secure the expertise of specific individuals who can make the RMIS perform to meet risk management needs. Therefore, no textbook or risk management professional can generalize about the best sources of needed persons. Nonetheless, the following are the essential factors to consider in staffing the RMIS function:

- Management information expertise sufficient to operate the RMIS as desired

- Knowledge of the organization and of its RMIS needs

- Integrity and honesty in protecting any confidential aspects of the information in the RMIS or the aspects of the organization's operations

- Ability to respond promptly to any unplanned immediate needs for risk management information or to work with risk management personnel in modifying the RMIS to meet other special needs

- Personnel costs, including direct compensation and employee benefits, in both the long and short run

How an organization staffs its RMIS activities can be influenced greatly by its choice of hardware and software vendors and its lease purchase decisions. A supplier of particularly complex hardware or software, or one that only leases rather than sells its computers and related materials, might provide personnel to operate the system as part of its overall package. The choice of the system dictates the source of the RMIS personnel, but not necessarily the particular individuals who operate the system. Thus, the software, hardware, and personnel decisions often are not three independent choices but, instead, are closely linked.

Implementing an RMIS

What are the key steps in setting up an RMIS?

How do many organizations use their RMIS?

Implementing or installing an RMIS is analogous to the step in the risk management process of implementing chosen techniques of risk control or risk financing. The precise moment of implementation occurs when the current method of doing things is discarded and replaced by a new method.

In implementing either an RMIS or a new technique of risk management or risk financing, the successful risk manager must plan, organize, motivate, monitor, and communicate to do the following:

- Reduce initial resistance
- Effect a smooth transition
- Respond to the changes caused by implementation
- Overcome operating problems

In both kinds of implementation, the risk management professional must secure the necessary commitment from key management, colleagues, and staff by the time that the decision is officially made and responsibilities and schedules are announced. Going from the "decision to implement" to "completed implementation" requires much work.

Although much of the work will be done by others, the risk management professional will be reviewing the progress and the results of that work, ensuring that it meets the results standards and the activity standards that have been established. The risk management professional and the people who will be installing and operating the RMIS must continually communicate. New procedural instructions will be written, and necessary training will be conducted. Sometimes the new method will be tried by running the system (at test sites) parallel to the old method. Sometimes the new method, particularly if it is extensive or involves many people, will be gradually introduced instead of suddenly implemented corporate-wide. If the consequences of failure or delay are grave enough, the risk management professional also might formulate a contingency plan.

Reducing Initial Resistance

To reduce initial resistance to an RMIS, the risk management professional should follow a structured procedure for the requirements analysis and the feasibility study and include key personnel in the process so that they feel as if they are an integral part of the RMIS.

The risk management professional can also avoid initial resistance to the RMIS by doing the following:

- Explaining to each person how the RMIS will facilitate his or her achievement of personal objectives
- Clarifying each person's role, duties, and responsibilities
- Communicating frequently with operational staff about the progress of the implementation (including success stories about achieving intermediate target dates and milestones or changes to anticipated schedules)
- Designing and conducting training programs so that each person will feel comfortable with the new RMIS and the new procedures
- Assigning operational staff to review and revise procedural instructions (both new manual procedures and RMIS system documentation) for clarity and correctness
- Establishing a "help" facility (a person to see or a telephone number to call) as problems occur when the RMIS is installed

Effecting a Smooth Transition

To ensure timeliness, the risk management professional will have established an implementation schedule of essential tasks (most of which will be performed by others) and target dates for completing those tasks. To ensure that the new RMIS works as anticipated, the risk management professional will have to consider the correctness of both data and system operation.

One widely used test plan for correctness of data is to process data through the new RMIS as they were processed through the old methods. Another test plan for correctness of data is to feed already-processed data (last month's claims) through the new RMIS. In either test plan, the acceptance test criterion is that both sets of results are identical. A popular test plan to ensure correctness of processing is to feed a small number of carefully chosen test cases (with desired results for each case) through the RMIS to see that the RMIS processes and screens out errors as it should. A thoroughly tested RMIS will have gone through **alpha testing** (testing by the people who developed or supplied it) and **beta testing** (live testing in a real field situation). It will have gone through these procedures both in unit testing (meaning that each component has been alpha-tested and beta-tested) and in integrated testing (meaning that the entire RMIS, with all components interacting and sharing data, has been alpha-tested and beta-tested). The testers will have tried to make the RMIS work and, equally important, will have tried to make the RMIS fail under controlled conditions. Both parallel processing and gradual phase-in (common steps in any implementation, whether it be an RMIS or a new risk control or risk financing technique) can be used as methods to test the correctness of RMIS processing results and RMIS data results.

Responding to Changes

Implementing an RMIS will cause certain changes in many personnel roles, responsibilities, and reporting relationships. It will also change procedures and will potentially change the form or content of information that various indirect users will supply to or receive from the RMIS. The risk management professional can minimize or avoid adverse effects from these changes by using the methods to reduce initial resistance that were previously discussed in this chapter.

The risk management professional must also prepare to respond to changes that would adversely affect the smooth functioning of the RMIS. For example, trained staff might resign or be promoted. Any resulting adverse effect can be minimized if procedures are well documented and if training and support for replacement staff are readily available.

Overcoming Operating Problems

Even when an RMIS is in place and accepted, operating problems might arise. Potential operating problems can involve data, systems, hardware, software, or personnel.

Data Problems

Three potentially important problems in the data with which an organization's RMIS operates involve data integrity, data ownership, and insufficient data.

Data Integrity

Perhaps the biggest data problem is ensuring **data integrity**, that is, freedom from negligent, unrecognized, or malicious corruption or destruction of data. Proper collection, verification, and entry of accurate information for the RMIS are essential, as are adequate built-in editing routines in the software (to prevent such errors as entering a date such as February 32) and security procedures to protect against sabotage.

To preserve this integrity, the procedures for entering data into the RMIS should include the following:

- Personal verification by the risk management professional of major changes in the parameters (such as for establishing reserves for open claims) that the system uses to project risk management budgets and to develop reports of risk management results

- Restrictions on the numbers of persons authorized to enter data into the RMIS, to manipulate the data, or to access the system for output
- Periodic auditing of the loss records and other information in the system, such as by asking individual departments or geographic locations to confirm the accuracy of the data applicable to them, so that any erroneous data can be corrected or eliminated promptly

Data Ownership

When the underlying data in an RMIS are compiled from several sources (such as the organization, its insurer(s), and its agent/broker/consultant) questions can arise about who "owns" these data, that is, who can extract them from the system for any particular purpose and who is responsible for updating them or removing errors. The same questions can arise when an organization works with an outside software vendor whose personnel help to operate the RMIS. Here, an important additional concern can be separating ownership of the programs from ownership of the information generated by applying these programs to raw data or losses and other measures of risk management performance. All of those questions become more complex when an organization seeks to change insurers or vendors or when the organization itself becomes involved in a merger.

Generally, insurers and software vendors take the position that they own the data and the information that the RMIS produces from those data. This position is communicated through their sales and service agreements and in their day-to-day dealings with an organization's risk management department. In return, these insurers and vendors agree to maintain and correct the basic data. Some organizations want to control their own data or to extract from the insurer's or the vendor's systems particular information reports. Consequently, the risk management professional should pay special attention to contract provisions relating to various parties' rights and duties with respect to an insured's or a client's loss data. Those parties include the insured or client, insurers, brokers, vendors, and perhaps others. This special concern is appropriate for the following two reasons:

1. To assert the organization's **data ownership** (that is, the right to reproduce, alter, or sell data and to control others' access to it) and the insurer's/ vendor's custodial responsibilities

2. To establish procedures for removing the organization's data from the insurer's/vendor's systems and to establish appropriate fees that the organization will pay when the organization wants to terminate or continue (perhaps on some modified basis) its relationship with the insurer/vendor

Insufficient Data

For the many sophisticated RMIS now on the market to meaningfully use their analytical modules capable of predicting expected losses or plotting trends, these systems must contain sufficient data to produce statistically significant results. The amount of data required for statistical significance depends on the probability of error that management is willing to tolerate. Producing results that have only a 5 percent probability of being wrong by a given margin (that is, they are statistically significant at the 5 percent level) requires much more data than are needed for results that are significant at the 10 percent level. Gathering data imposes costs, and some data simply might not be available at any cost. Therefore, designing an RMIS requires the risk management professional to join with senior management in deciding what choices it wants to make among the tradeoffs between the costs of data and the costs of perhaps making a wrong decision because of insufficient data.

System Problems

Apart from data and hardware incompatibility problems, the hardware/software of an RMIS could fail to perform as expected because the system is not matched to the organization's needs, because the risk management professional or other managers overemphasize the system's gadgetry, or because the system generates an overkill of data/information.

System/Organization Mismatch

The organization's risk management requirements might not correspond with the capabilities of its RMIS, creating **system/organization mismatches**. If, for example, the risk management professional has underestimated these needs, a "prepackaged" RMIS might not have the analytical or database management capabilities to meet these needs and generate the detailed reports that senior and other managers expect.

Similar incompatibility results if an outside vendor hired to develop and operate an RMIS lacks the expertise or insight into the organization's philosophy or objectives needed to fulfill its expectations. Similar disappointment with an outside vendor could result if the vendor's contract has been so rigorously negotiated that the vendor's fee does not enable it to fulfill its contractual duties, especially when the contract covers a long term and makes no provision for inflation.

Finally, the RMIS might not be sufficiently expandable or adaptive to avoid technological obsolescence. It might lack the capacity to accept new modules, giving it additional analytical and reporting capabilities or enabling it to exchange data or programs with other internal or external computers. In such a situation, the risk management department could become dependent on an antiquated inefficient system that is more expensive to maintain than would be a newer, more expandable, and more comprehensive RMIS.

Overemphasis on Gadgetry

A computer hardware/software vendor understandably tries to emphasize the unique or unusual features of its products. This tendency can conflict with the responsibility of a risk management professional to select wisely in purchasing an RMIS, choosing only the features that the system needs and avoiding unnecessary gadgetry. Alternatively, an organization's risk management or other official could become so enthralled with a system's sophisticated capabilities that he or she fails to ensure that the benefits of these advanced capabilities are worth their costs. To avoid either of these difficulties and to ensure that RMIS selection and operation remain cost-effective, the procedures for determining and fulfilling the RMIS needs must be carefully drafted and conscientiously followed.

Data/Information Overkill

Having too much useless data or information results in **information overkill**. The capability of an RMIS to generate forty or fifty pages of data, or even five or six pages of information, does not mean that all these pages will contribute to a risk management program's effectiveness. A risk management or other executive seeking an answer to a particular question or wanting to know the status of some aspect of the risk management program often will not have time to read a lengthy report. An RMIS, or the persons who operate it, should be able to provide specific answers targeted to particular questions or to generate an "executive summary," which presents and interprets the highlights of the more detailed report. This ability to summarize information, and often to supplement it with graphs, enables the risk management professional to communicate quickly and effectively with senior management and other managers.

Hardware Problems

Two potentially important problems with RMIS hardware are mechanical failure and technological obsolescence.

Mechanical Failure

The mechanical failure of hardware can best be prevented and minimized by ensuring that competent in-house staff or external technical support personnel are readily available for system maintenance, servicing, and repair. As a safeguard against unpreventable breakdown, sound risk management requires contracting with appropriate vendors or other organizations with comparable equipment for the use of backup facilities during hardware downtime.

Obsolescence

Even though computer manufacturers constantly introduce new models, the resulting obsolescence does not always present immediate problems. As long as the organization's present hardware performs as needed and parts and service staff remain available, the age of the present equipment often does not matter. Obsolescence becomes a problem only when parts or services are difficult to obtain or when expansion or modification of an RMIS requires additional hardware.

Hardware advances very quickly. Much of what was state-of-the-art equipment five years ago has gone through several generations of improvement. Therefore, upward compatibility (the ability to transfer data and software from older to newer hardware) is vital to the decision of whether to acquire new equipment. Such compatibility through progressive models receives more emphasis from some hardware manufactures than from others, which can be an important factor in initially choosing among hardware vendors.

Software Problems

Software can fail or develop "bugs," become obsolete, or prove inappropriate for adapting to an organization's changing RMIS needs.

Failure and Obsolescence

Problems of software failure can best be handled by providing reliable, competent internal or external support staff to advise the organization's personnel in overcoming "bugs" or, if necessary, to reprogram the software to eliminate defects.

Software obsolescence, like hardware obsolescence, need not become a problem until technical support for the old software is unavailable or the organization loses cost-effective access to hardware that would run the software. Lack of upward compatibility in hardware can also render dependent software obsolete. Choosing software that is widely used tends to reduce problems of obsolescence.

Lack of Adaptability

Because an organization's risk control and risk financing requirements and products change, as does the general technological and economic environment in which many organizations operate, an organization's RMIS needs will also change. Consequently, software becomes less than ideal for meeting new challenges. Because some change is inevitable, and because change usually marks progress, an RMIS that is never adjusted for change is probably a less-than-optimal RMIS.

An organization's risk management professional should therefore periodically update the software that supports the RMIS. He or she should regard these required changes as opportunities to upgrade the entire system and to correct any RMIS weakness that experience with the system has revealed. The best way to meet these challenges and to seize these opportunities is to frequently repeat the phases of the RMIS design process previously described in this chapter.

Personnel Problems

Employee turnover can create personnel problems for an RMIS because new employees must be trained before they can use the system. Also, new or infrequently used software might require employee retraining. Carefully and clearly written operating manuals and software documentation provide consistency and efficient training. Another sound risk control measure is to cross-train several persons in the use of the same software, especially for infrequently performed tasks such as annual risk management cost allocations.

Frequent Applications of an RMIS[4]

To suggest the uses that an organization can make of an RMIS throughout the entire risk management decision process, the following discussion focuses on the uses of an RMIS in (1) identifying and analyzing exposures, (2) examining and selecting risk management techniques, (3) implementing the chosen techniques, and (4) monitoring the results of these choices.

Identifying and Analyzing Loss Exposures

For this part of the risk management process, many organizations rely on an RMIS for accident/claim/incident reports, for property valuation, and for loss forecasting.

Accident/Claim/Incident Reports

In gathering risk management data, risk management professionals usually differentiate among accidents, claims, and incidents. In this context, an accident can be defined as an event that causes substantial loss to the organization. A claim is a legal demand against the organization arising from some loss, usually accidental, suffered by another. An incident is an event that, although it results in no substantial loss, could result in an accident or claim against the organization. Accidents and claims are losses to the organization. Incidents, under somewhat varied circumstances, or with less good luck, could become losses. Incidents should be considered warnings of potential future accidents and claims.

Thorough, detailed data on accidents, claims, and incidents are at the heart of an RMIS because many of the software programs rely on these fundamental data. At the least, the system will report on all past accidents and claims and will show the current status of unresolved (open) claims against the organization. Historical data and audit trails for past accidents and closed claims are also included in many systems.

Rather than simply generating a chronological loss run, which is difficult for its readers to analyze and, hence, often goes unread, an RMIS usually structures loss and claims data into more organized reports, such as a "large loss" listing. Such a report displays every loss or claim whose total exceeds some threshold value (for example, $5,000) and sorts them in descending dollar value. The biggest accidents and claims (those that can be said to deserve the most attention because they cost the most) appear first.

These large accidents and claims might also identify the need for risk control action in certain locations or for certain activities. Similarly, reports bringing together data on certain types of losses or claims can alert the risk management professional to prime targets for loss prevention or loss reduction. Such losses or claims could include loss of hearing cases and back injuries that, while initially apparently minor, could become more severe.

In addition to focusing on severe losses, an RMIS can be a valuable tool in identifying highly frequent types of losses that often go unnoticed because they tend to be individually small or routine. Examples include inventory shortages, employee back strains, and minor vehicle collisions. These accumulations of losses often deserve as much attention as do single, dramatic large accidents. Because the aggregate dollar cost of the many small losses can total more than one large loss, risk control attention can be profitably focused on them. A well-designed RMIS highlighting frequent losses can create this focus and target cost-effective risk controls.

Incident reports can also flash an "alert" sign to the risk management department. Although not actually causing a loss, an incident clearly suggests how a substantial loss might happen. Traditionally, hospitals have given the most emphasis to incident reports, such as of a patient receiving the wrong medication but, by good luck, suffering no adverse effects. Other organizations are beginning to give equal attention to incident reports because, according to Heinrich's "domino theory," about 300 "near misses" occur for each reported industrial accident. If one of those 300 were recognized as clearly signaling the need for improved safety, the one real accident or claim might be avoided. Thus, an organization of any size that is deeply committed to risk control should consider implementing a thorough, responsive incident reporting system grounded in its RMIS.

Property Valuation

Most risk management decisions involving real or personal property should be based on the replacement, functional replacement, or reproduction value of that property. Therefore, the historical cost of properties, usually shown in accounting records that adhere to generally accepted accounting principles, often have little risk management use. To recognize and treat property exposures properly, an RMIS can be used to gather and update data on the replacement or reproduction values of property. Having a thorough inventory of property and the appropriate valuation standards for each item greatly facilitates the revision of this record by adding or deleting property or bringing values up-to-date. For example, a computerized record of property purchases and sales is helpful in adding or deleting properties from the organization's records. Through an RMIS, property values can be regularly changed by individually considering the value of each item or class of property or by several formula techniques that recognize the combined effects on property values of both price level changes and depreciation.

Loss Forecasting

A **loss-forecasting program** in a RMIS can forecast the frequency and severity of losses using probability analysis or regression analysis with great speed and with the ability to consider several probability distributions or regression relationships simultaneously. For example, it is quite beneficial for a loss-forecasting program in an RMIS to perform the following sequence of projections:

- Establish a statistical (regression) relationship between an organization's past levels of activity and its past frequencies of loss (such as workers compensation back claims).

- Project the organization's level of activity for each of the next three to five years (using statistical techniques or management estimates) and apply that regression equation to these projected activity levels to forecast the frequency of employee back injury claims for these three to five years.

- Project the total cost of these losses (aggregate back injury loss severity) by first projecting the cost of the average claim (based on historical costs adjusted for price level changes, technology, or other factors) and then multiplying this per-claim value by the projected number of employee back injuries or other losses.

- Project the organization's aggregate annual cash outflow for these claims, considering that each claim might take several years to settle, with only a portion of the total cost of each claim being paid in any one year. (The present value of these annual outlays for such claims or other accidents represents their true cost to the organization.)

Those computations will generate expected future costs of accidents or claims. Actual cash outlays could be significantly higher or lower. The RMIS can be programmed to account for past differences between projected and actual losses so that future projections can be refined, thus improving the accuracy of subsequent forecasts.

Examining and Selecting Risk Management Techniques

The next two steps in the risk management decision process entail (1) projecting the likely operational and financial consequences of various risk control or risk financing alternatives for dealing with a particular loss exposure and (2) formulating net present value cash flow or other decision criteria for selecting among these alternatives or choosing combinations of them. At this point in the risk management decision process, a computerized RMIS can be particularly useful in financial modeling, analysis of alternative retention levels, and safety analysis.

Financial Modeling

Computerized **financial modeling** involves developing a set of relationships among the assets, liabilities, equities, expenses, and revenues within an organization's financial structure. Based on the model's assumptions, the effects of given events on the organization's balance sheet, statement of profit and loss, and statement of sources and uses of funds are traced on a yearly or other periodic basis.

Such models can forecast the organization's overall financial condition under various risk management scenarios: the effects that particular property, liability, personnel, or net income losses could be expected to have on the organization's financial strength and how the organization's financial viability might be improved by using various risk management techniques. Such modeling is really a period-by-period simulation of the organization's financial health under given sets of assumptions. The modeling can be most helpful in drawing senior management attention to critical risk management decisions and in selecting risk management techniques that are particularly likely to generate desired results.

Analysis of Retention Levels

A frequent, special case of financial modeling focuses on deciding what dollar amount or portion of particular kinds of losses the organization should retain (that is, pay with internally generated funds). This decision involves selecting retention levels for various kinds of losses so that the organization controls its overall loss costs without subjecting itself to excessively high levels of uncertainty about what these costs will be.

For this purpose, the RMIS can be programmed to assume various levels of retention and limits of insurance, simulate various loss frequency and severity patterns, and then compute the total costs of retained losses and of insurance premiums. The RMIS can then generate both the expected total risk financing costs (retention plus insurance expenses) for a given period and a range of possible outcomes around this total. Each outcome within this range also can be assigned its own probability so that senior management can evaluate the varying degrees of uncertainty for the various possible outcomes that might result from the choice of a given retention level. Here, the RMIS can alert management to the consequences of its decisions and assist in refining these decisions.

Safety Analysis

One of the most straightforward and valuable uses of an RMIS is to analyze detailed information on the organization's losses and claims to discover patterns so that responsible personnel can take appropriate preventive or corrective actions. The foundation for such analysis is detailed information on the circumstances, causes, persons, and activities from which these accidents and claims arise. Such information is gathered and entered into the RMIS within a structured format so that RMIS can analyze the data in terms of any particular variable (for example, location, time of day, weather conditions, and employees involved) to extract from the data patterns useful for risk control.

Frequent RMIS safety analyses focus on the following:

- Causes of work injuries (or other frequent accidents or claims) so that preventive measures can be targeted on the most prevalent causes
- Accident or injury frequency by location so that managers responsible for these locations can be encouraged to enhance their safety efforts
- Accident frequency rates that can be compared with rates from one or two years ago to identify quickly any adverse trends in these rates and to take corrective actions

Illustrative Analyses of Options

To better understand how an RMIS is often used in evaluating and selecting between risk control and risk financing options, consider a supermarket chain that experiences a marked increase in general liability claims arising from customer slips and falls in its produce sections.

In a risk control context, the chain's risk management professional might consider such loss prevention options as installing carpets in the produce sections; bagging the lettuce, grapes, and similar produce rather than selling them loose; and other safety measures. If the chain experiences a sharply rising trend of workers compensation claims involving back injuries, the risk management professional might consider such loss control options as training employees in proper lifting techniques or repositioning stocks so that heavy items are not stored on high shelves. In either of these situations, an RMIS analysis of the causes of the past accidents that these loss control measures might prevent and of the costs of implementing these measures will be most helpful in determining whether the present value of the benefits of each of these measures would be likely to exceed the present value of their costs.

In a risk financing context, this chain's management might recognize that the company's automobile liability claims almost always have been less than $50,000 per occurrence and $1 million per year. Different insurers charge different premiums for different amounts of automobile liability coverage per occurrence and as annual aggregate. The chain's executives could use any of several financial modeling programs to select the combination of coverage limits and retention levels that could be expected to best control the chain's overall costs of both retained liability losses and liability insurance premiums.

Implementing Chosen Techniques

Once an organization has selected particular risk control and risk financing techniques, it can implement them through RMIS software programs that perform a number of repetitive tasks with large amounts of data, such as for insurance policy management and reporting claim administration and for the preparation of routine documents.

Insurance Policy Management and Reporting

Many aspects of purchasing insurance protection and receiving insurance payments for covered losses have been widely computerized: keeping records of insurance coverages, premium charges and payments, and the insurer's claim payments to or on behalf of the insured. Such basic record keeping can be done by the most elementary versions of a computerized RMIS. More sophisticated insurance policy management and reporting systems go further. For example, the systems compile data on an insurer's reserves, claims payments, and loss adjusting expenses on specified individual claims or types of coverages (such as workers compensation or products liability) that are likely to generate numerous losses.

An RMIS can readily generate pre-formatted reports on insurance premiums and loss payments organized by type of coverage or by organizational subsidiary or location. Such an insurance-focused RMIS system can also track an organization's assets and activities to ensure that the coverages that the organization buys keep pace with changes—either increases or decreases—in the organization's insurable property, liability, personnel, and net income exposures.

Claims Administration

Virtually all organizations of substantial size experience a number of property, liability, personnel, and net income losses each month, quarter, or year. The organization itself, an insurer, or some other indemnitor under a noninsurance transfer agreement for risk financing is obligated to pay money for such losses to, or on behalf of, the organization. Claim administration entails planning for, making, and controlling payments for these losses, which require either a single-lump sum payment or a series of periodic settlement payments that might extend for several years or decades. With some losses, particularly those that involve property damage, the timing and amount of payments might be certain. For others, especially those involving compensation for injuries to persons who might not recover their health, the total amounts of payments for medical care and loss of income can be very difficult to predict or to reduce to a present value of an appropriate loss reserve.

Any organization having at least ten or twenty such significant claims a year can improve the speed and efficiency as well as lower the ultimate cost of paying these claims. An organization can rely on an appropriate claim administration package to do the following:

- Assemble basic data on each claim
- Track payments to date and current reserve values of the claim
- Assemble the records pertinent to that claim
- Generate routine documents and correspondence
- Compile statistics on the cause, duration, and costs of each claim for summary reports to senior management and other interested parties

For claims that reach litigation, computerized data will also include information on the legal representatives of all parties involved, the jurisdiction, and the ultimate legal and financial consequences of any suits.

Although an RMIS will certainly distinguish among claims that are retained, those paid by insurers, and those paid by other parties, the system is likely to gather and process the same types of information for all types of claims regardless of the payor. In contrast to the claim-reporting function through which many RMIS assist in the exposure-recognition phase of risk management, the claim administration capabilities of many RMIS focus on forecasting, making, and monitoring actual claim payments by an organization or payments it receives for losses it has suffered.

Preparation of Routine Documents

Properly administering either the risk control or risk financing activities of a well-managed risk management program requires preparing many routine documents. These documents include incident reports; safety inspection forms; insurance certificates; and reports required by national, state, or local workplace safety or environmental protection regulations among many others. Each of these documents typically has its own format that requires inserting particular names; places; dollar or other quantitative measures; and perhaps brief, often standardized, explanations of events. Such reports lend themselves to ready computerization for easy preparation and quick and reliable dissemination. Before the RMIS, many of these documents and standardized reports were generated by hand or typewriter using preprinted forms. With computerization, the ability to program the production of both the form and the information it requires has greatly increased the efficiency of these otherwise burdensome routine documents.

Monitoring Results

In tracing the success and identifying the shortcomings of a risk management program, an RMIS has many uses. Two of them are producing management reports and allocating risk management costs among an organization's department or activities.

Production of Management Reports

Assessing the extent to which a risk management program is meeting its objectives requires comparing actual performance to activity or results standards. A computerized RMIS database is an excellent tool for gathering data on actual performance, compiling standards for desired performance, and performing the many calculations needed to properly compare actual with desired results. The RMIS also offers opportunities for consciously or automatically adjusting standards for changes in operating or economic conditions and for tracing performance over time. The resulting information must be reported to management for its evaluation and response. Being able to gather and analyze this management information significantly facilitates generating, and greatly improves the accuracy of, risk management reports.

Cost Allocation

A system for allocating costs of risk (retained losses + insurance costs + risk control costs + risk management administrative expenses) among an organization's departments can be a most powerful tool for motivating personnel within those departments to practice risk control. The underlying rationale for such a system is that, to the extent that a department's specific costs of risk can be identified, charging those costs against the budget of that department makes risk management a more meaningful responsibility of the department's manager.

An RMIS can be an indispensable aid in designing and implementing a cost allocation system in the following three ways:

1. Programming the RMIS to allocate costs among departments provides an ideal opportunity for examining the assumptions underlying such allocation and gaining managers' understanding and support of the allocation system.
2. The RMIS acts impartially—indeed, mechanically—in allocating particular costs to particular departments according to the fixed rules in the computer program.

3. The RMIS can compute and allocate costs rapidly, thus making the system particularly responsive to individual managers' risk control efforts.

The allocation of risk management costs is complex, involving numerous decisions and tradeoffs about the kinds and amounts of costs to be allocated and the formulas for their allocation. The essential point is that an RMIS makes many cost allocation options feasible.

Managing RMIS Loss Exposures

What exposures to accidental losses does an RMIS create or intensify?

How should possible losses from these exposures be controlled?

An organization's risk management professional and program can easily become dependent on a computerized RMIS for accomplishing necessary tasks that were once performed manually. That dependency creates its own loss exposures if access to the RMIS and its output is partially or fully interrupted. For example, an otherwise sound risk management program built on a computerized RMIS could be devastated by any of the following:

- The disappearance of a major hardware or software vendor
- The organization's intentional change of such a vendor
- Unauthorized access to RMIS data
- Computer viruses
- Other computer-related exposures
    - PC hard drive failure
    - User error
    - Damage to software
    - Damage to hardware

The material under this heading concludes this chapter by examining these loss exposures and how they can be managed, particularly through effective risk control measures.

Vendor Disappearance[5]

Any RMIS vendor could stop doing business or could discontinue an RMIS product or service on which an organization's risk management program depends Pre-loss prevention and reduction measures to cope with this exposure, particularly when selecting vendors or renegotiating contracts with them, include the following:

- Consideration of the vendor's financial stability

- Consideration of the present and probable future breadth of use (popularity) of the vendor's hardware, software, or other goods and services
- Service contract revisions that provide appropriate guarantees or procedural safeguards

Although the first two measures are prudent practices of good business judgment, they do not provide absolute protection against loss of RMIS capabilities. Like any company, an RMIS vendor can lose market share, be acquired by another firm under adverse conditions, or suffer other financial reversals that drive it out of business. Again, like any other organization, an RMIS vendor also can choose to discontinue a product or service, often primarily to improve its own overall financial position.

To safeguard against vendor disappearance, every RMIS should be structured according to the following recommendations:

- The original computer programming (the "source code") for the RMIS is available to the organization, held either by the organization or by an independent custodian.
- The software is written in a popular computer language.
- The RMIS operates on widely used hardware.
- The organization and the vendor cooperate daily.

These common-sense recommendations help maintain good relations with vendors, through procedures that vendors are increasingly willing to accept. These recommendations protect the client organization if the vendor fails or makes a business judgment contrary to the client organization's best interest. These measures also serve the vendor's best interest because if a vendor discontinues the product or service but remains in business, the favorable publicity resulting from a well-managed transition of the client's RMIS vendor/hardware/software can be a valuable business asset to the former vendor.

Intentional Change of Vendors

An organization may choose to change RMIS vendors for any number of financial, managerial, or technical reasons. However, when an organization's RMIS facilities are provided by insurers, brokers, or third-party administrators, an RMIS change is often inextricably linked with a change in an insurer, broker, or administrator. A decision to make one RMIS change often leads to making another change. Therefore, an important concern when changing insurers, brokers, or administrators is how best to maintain access to either one's present RMIS or a suitable substitute.

To ensure such access and control of the confidentiality of the sensitive information that might be stored on an RMIS, an organization should do the following:

- Be certain from the outset that any vendor-provided RMIS is offered on an "unbundled" basis, available independently of any other insurance coverages, brokerage services, or other commitments.

- Explain that the RMIS data—distinct from the vendor-provided RMIS software that typically remains the vendor's property—are owned by the client organization and that they will be supplied to the organization on request at a reasonable cost within a reasonable time on an industry-standard, computer-readable medium in a suitable format.

- Confirm that any new RMIS can accept data and software programs from the old system without significant manual re-entry of any input.

- Ensure continuation of the previous RMIS technical support service until the new system is fully implemented, including during any period of parallel operation of the two systems.

- If both the old and new RMIS providers are insurers, brokers, or administrators, clarify the details of how "runoff claims" (old claims that are still open, closed claims that might be reopened or require additional payments beyond present reserves, or claims arising out of past events that have not yet been reported) will be handled by the two vendors.

Those arrangements for an orderly transition are no different in principle than the arrangements that an organization would prudently make when it changes janitorial service firms, office supply providers, or other vendors. The above recommendations for a loss-free transition are only computer-specific applications of these same common-sense principles.

Unauthorized Access to Data

Because any person with access to computerized data or programs is potentially able to modify, copy, or delete this computerized material, either out of malice or ignorance, it is important that only qualified, loyal persons be able to enter the RMIS. Controlled access is often maintained through a series of physical barriers, passwords, and other identity checks and procedural controls. For example, access to a computerized RMIS typically is covered by a series of separate, individualized passwords for entry into the entire system, entry into particular parts of the database, and entry into the software. Furthermore, individuals may be given their own passwords that allow them access to only that information and those functions that are necessary for their particular responsibilities, but no more. For example, some users will be authorized to only read data or output, while others will be able to change data, and still others will be empowered to modify the procedures by which that data are manipulated to generate information.

Passwords are perhaps the most widely used safeguards of computer security. For a password to be effective, the following precautions should be taken:

- Each user should have an individual password, or series of passwords, that differ from the generic passwords with which much new software is provided.
- Each user should change passwords both on a regular basis and whenever an unusual incident could have compromised the security of a password.
- Each user should keep personal passwords secret and respect colleagues' secrecy regarding theirs.

Despite passwords and other physical and procedural safeguards, unauthorized access to data and software does occur. As computer security measures become more sophisticated, so do the methods of those who would violate that security. Therefore, appropriate security measures should cover all of an organization's essential computerized operations, including its RMIS. One of these procedures is to maintain backup copies of computerized risk management work on a regular basis, often daily. These backup copies should be safely stored away from the areas in which they are normally generated or used. For further protection, many software packages now provide "audit trails" of the identity of persons using the software and the tasks they perform so that unauthorized users can be traced and their future access prevented.

Computer Viruses

A **computer virus** is a set of computer instructions that are maliciously inserted into other computer programs to cause them to perform operations other than those that the programs were designed or represented to perform. A virus is usually inserted in a computer program so that computer programs or users are unaware of their existence and of their ability to clone themselves and to spread among all programs they contact.

The term "virus" is well chosen because a computer virus often changes the structure and function of a computer program much like a virus attacks a living cell, impairs its function, and destroys its health. A computer virus is not a computer "bug," and is often more difficult to detect and to purge than is a mere unintentional error. Some viruses are set to go off at predetermined dates and times, while others become active after the "infected" program has been used a predetermined number of times. Some viruses are mere bothersome pranks, but others can be devastatingly destructive.

An organization's RMIS, along with all of its other computerized operations, become vulnerable to viruses whenever they communicate or come in contact with other computers, especially those to which the public can gain access through computer bulletin boards and other networks and libraries. Significant, although not total, security against computer viruses can be gained by the following:

- Cautiously introducing untested software into an organization's computer system, such as software downloaded from a computer bulletin board or any other questionable source

- Installing antiviral programs into an organization's main computer facility to test other programs for known forms of viruses, especially for testing all new programs and for periodically testing the organization's entire computer before installing the new programs

Although computer viruses typically "live" in software, all elements of an RMIS or other computerized operation are vulnerable to virus infection. As yet, no foolproof set of safeguards against them is available. Every organization should therefore have a computer disaster recovery plan, including procedures for restoring pre-infection versions of files and backup copies of data files and software programs from original system disks and other documentation.

Other Computer-Related Exposures

Data stored on computers are vulnerable to destruction, theft, or scrambling from most of the hazards already described in this section. Beyond these general hazards, data are particularly subject to loss because of failure of personal computer hard drives and user error.

PC Hard Drive Failure

Many personal computers come with hard drives. Hard drives are physically inflexible storage media for data and programs that reside within the computer in contrast to floppy disks for data and program storage that are easily removed from or inserted into the personal computer through the disk drive.

For both floppies and hard drives, many experienced computer operators believe that the significant risk management questions are not about if the drive will fail but, instead, when it will fail. The principle precaution against such failure is to back up the work of a personal computer, that is, to faithfully copy the software that a personal computer is using and its most recent output for storage on a backup disk outside the personal computer. Then, when the personal computer fails, the resulting loss is limited to work done since the last backup was performed.

The backup schedule need not be daily, but it should be frequent and, more important, faithfully followed. Not every RMIS (or other computer operations) requires a daily backup, but every operation does have an appropriate backup interval. The more intensely an RMIS or other computer program is used, the more valuable and difficult it becomes to reproduce its output, and the more frequently should its product be backed up.

When a hard disk, floppy disk, personal computer, or another component of a computerized system fails, the failed component should not be used again until the defective element has been restored and the cause of the failure has been determined and eliminated. All data, but particularly RMIS data, are likely to be so valuable that they should not be entrusted to a disk or other equipment that has once failed. Another reason for not using a failed storage disk is that, even though the disk is faulty, experts might be able to recover much data and software from it, thus reducing the severity of the failure. However, once the failed disk has been overwritten through reuse, any information that it once contained is lost forever.

User Error

A mistake by a system user—often colloquially but quite accurately called the "Oops Syndrome"—is perhaps the most frequent cause of loss of data. Loss occurs whenever a user deletes a record, file, or program that should have been retained or mistakenly reformats a personal computer's hard drive instead of a floppy diskette (thereby erasing perhaps a month's work, which should be backed up in some other storage medium).

The keys to preventing data loss through user error include the following:

- Training all users
- Requiring each user to frequently back up his or her work
- Providing ready access to a "help desk," "hotline," or other source of informational help in case of any real emergency
- Installing software features to prevent or cancel errors, such as computerized requests for user confirmation before deleting material; on-line, context-responsive, computerized "help"; well-chosen defaults, such as saving information unless otherwise instructed instead of only saving information when instructed; and a "cancel-preceding" action or "undelete" option

Damage to Software

Software, which instructs a computer how to organize and manage data, is stored in files within a computer's memory or on removable floppy disks. Like data files, software files are vulnerable to loss or corruption and need to be backed up. Software can fail in two ways: (1) bugs can be discovered and (2) new errors can be introduced through modifications, enhancements, or attempts to fix existing bugs.

Many bugs can be prevented by thorough initial testing, but some can only be discovered through actual use. Any bug found must be reported and corrected. Many suppliers of standard software routinely send out upgraded versions of their software, which correct bugs discovered and reported by their entire client base.

When programs are modified or enhanced, either to meet changed or expanded needs or to fix a bug, new errors can be introduced. Software that once worked well and that has no apparent connection to the enhancement no longer functions properly.

Therefore, as a good practice, always back up software before replacing it with a new version (so that the old version can be restored just in case the new one is seriously defective). Similarly, always thoroughly test new software before putting it into the production mode.

Damage to Hardware

Hardware can fail through age. It can also be stolen or damaged by accident or vandalism. Pre-loss treatment methods include the following:

- For vandalism, using security measures (including locked doors, security guards, cardkeys or other devices that screen unauthorized entry, and locking devices on PCs) to prevent unauthorized access to hardware.

- For accident prevention, instituting proper location controls (locating hardware on a high floor to safeguard against floods or in an interior room to safeguard against wind damage) and proper environmental controls (sufficient air conditioning as required for large machines to prevent damage from overheating and appropriate fire detection and suppression systems to control damage from fire and natural perils).

- For system damage due to age or malfunction, employing a computer repair service for regularly scheduled preventive maintenance and repair visits. If shutting down the RMIS system for regular preventive maintenance presents a problem, the risk manager might arrange for the use of backup computer facilities.

Summary

An organization's risk management information system (RMIS) consists of data (usually computerized) and the procedures for manipulating and interpreting that data. The particular functions for which an organization relies on a computerized or manual RMIS may vary: some systems only perform repetitive tasks in processing transactions with insurers and claimants; other systems generate standard reports that the risk management department issues periodically to insurers, senior executives, and other managers throughout the organization; still more advanced systems give the risk management professional or other managers the ability to make "random access" inquiries to the RMIS database to answer particular questions or to generate reports on a virtually instantaneous (on-line) basis. Finally, the most advanced type of RMIS currently available contains in its software programs many of the decision criteria on which a particular organization's risk management choices are based.

Possessing both the appropriate data in suitable form and the relevant decision rules, these RMIS can make, or recommend, suitable choices on such matters as selecting retention levels or directing risk control efforts to the most significant hazards. Not all RMIS perform all of these functions—based on the organization's risk management needs and the costs and values of gathering and computerizing particular kinds of risk management information, an organization may wisely choose a less expensive and more basic system without incurring the expense of a more sophisticated one.

Regardless of their costs or their capabilities, all RMIS possess four common components: (1) the database (usually divided into loss, exposure, legal, financial, administrative, and risk control data), (2) software elements for organizing and manipulating this data, (3) hardware elements (computers, printers, and the like), and (4) personnel who operate the RMIS. An organization has a number of specific choices with respect to each of these components. Its selection from among these choices should enhance its ability to achieve the benefits that an RMIS can provide (increased efficiency, reduced costs, and improved communications throughout the organization) while minimizing the potential disadvantages of an RMIS (excessive cost, system inadequacy, incompatibility with an MIS, and adverse personnel effects).

Designing an RMIS for any particular organization involves a variety of considerations, including detailed analysis of its specific RMIS requirements, identification of the information flows required to fulfill those requirements, analysis of the costs and benefits of the feasible hardware/software alternatives that reliably can generate those information flows, and decisions on the most cost-effective sources of the software, hardware, and personnel to operate the RMIS.

Once the RMIS has been designed and is in place, managing the system entails securing the greatest potential benefits from the system while controlling the system's potential limitations throughout each of the steps in the risk management decision process. The benefits of an RMIS include increased efficiency, reduced costs, strengthened communication throughout the organization on risk management matters, improved credibility for risk management activities, and higher quality information on which to base better risk management decisions. The limitations of an RMIS frequently stem from human failures in not recognizing that a computer can only perform analysis; it cannot make decisions and cannot necessarily reduce the organization's actual losses or cost of risk. Successful reliance on an RMIS requires diligence in overcoming various problems that may arise from the underlying data of the hardware or software, personnel operating the system, or the entire system. Because an RMIS is exposed to the same potential accidental losses as any other computer facility, managing an RMIS requires appropriate risk management of the loss exposures that the RMIS creates or intensifies.

Chapter Notes

1. This discussion of information systems concepts is adapted from two main sources. The first is James D. Blinn and Mitchell J. Cole, *Pathways to RMIS* (New York: Risk Management Society Publishing, Inc., 1985), *passim*. The second is James Gatza, Alan J. Turner, and Norbert R. Stone, *Managing Information Resources*, 3d ed. (Malvern, PA: American Institute for CPCU, 1995), *passim*.

2. This section draws on David A. Tweedy, "Do Homework Before Choosing RMIS: Overlook Bells and Whistles, Focus on System Needs," *Business Insurance*, March 19, 1990, p. 24

3. Much current information on organizations' needs for computerized risk management information systems is now available on the Internet at the following website address: http://rmisweb.com. For information on this website, see Glenn Trutner, "RMIS Arrives On The Internet: RMIS-Web Home Page Inaugurated," *Marsh & McLennan, RISQ Newsletter*, June 1996, pp. 1-3. A good annual update of RMIS information on the Internet and from other sources is available in the issue of *Business Insurance* published early each December. This issue also includes a current directory of RMIS vendors.

4. Some of this material is adapted from Michael N. Singer, "RMIS," *Risk Management Manual* (Santa Monica, CA: The Merritt Company, 1986), pp. 167-188

5. This discussion is based on David A. Tweedy, "Planning Eases RMIS Vendor's Exit," *Business Insurance*, February 27, 1989, p. 21.

Index

S